the Age of Aquarius

What finally divides the men of today into two camps is not class but an attitude of mind—the spirit of movement. On the one hand there are those who simply wish to make the world a comfortable dwelling-place; on the other hand, those who can only conceive of it as a machine for progress—or better, an organism that is progressing.

Teilhard de Chardin,
The Future of Man

William Braden

the Age of Aquarius,

TECHNOLOGY
AND THE
CULTURAL
REVOLUTION

Chicago
**Quadrangle
Books**
1970

The Age of Aquarius. Copyright © 1970 by William Braden. All rights reserved, including the right to reproduce this book or portions thereof in any form. For information, address: Quadrangle Books, Inc., 12 East Delaware Place, Chicago 60611. Manufactured in the United States of America. Published simultaneously in Canada by Burns and Mac-Eachern Ltd.

Grateful acknowledgment is made to Holt, Rinehart and Winston for permission to quote from "Mending Wall" by Robert Frost; to the *New York Review of Books* for permission to quote from an essay by C. H. Waddington, copyright © 1969 by the *New York Review of Books;* and to the Macmillan Company for permission to quote from *The Empty Fortress* by Bruno Bettelheim.

Library of Congress Catalog Card Number: 70-101069

Designed by Joan Stoliar

to my flower children, Anne and Jennifer

Acknowledgments

For conversations and personal interviews that contributed significantly to the content of this book, I am grateful to Thomas J. J. Altizer, Bruno Bettelheim, Jarl E. Dyrud, Erik H. Erikson, Richard Flacks, Daniel X. Freedman, Andrew M. Greeley, William H. Grier, Edward T. Hall, Fred Hampton, Kenneth Keniston, Christopher Lasch, Timothy Leary, Martin E. Marty, Milton W. Monson, Jr., Daniel Offer, David Polish, John A. T. Robinson, Peter Rossi, Hugh J. Schonfield, Joseph J. Schwab, George Wald, and Gibson Winter.

Contents

the Age of Aquarius

the Technetronic Society

An expressway at rush hour. In the distance, the towers of a latter-day Zenith aspire above the morning smog.

In bumper-to-bumper chain gangs and blue clouds of monoxide, the suburban darkies are inching their way toward the nine-to-five plantations.

They drive past mills and factories and tall smokestacks that belch sulphurous coal fumes. They drive through slums and the burned-out ruins of last summer's riot area. They drive by many billboards. They listen to the radio news, and they listen to commercials. But they see no connection between the billboards, the commercials, and the nature of the news, although the nature of the news disturbs them; nor does it occur to them that the jobs they are headed for now might have something to do with the arson and looting, or the poisoned air, or the fact that they no longer dare or care to live in the city, as they did in the past. They

3

are well paid, and they consider themselves to be well off: indeed affluent. They also believe that they are free men.

Only in humor do they sometimes refer to their jobs as cotton-picking—that is just an expression—and they will tell you that they work not for a master but a boss, or management, or a management team. They are at liberty to quit whenever they wish; they can leave without notice and look for a job somewhere else. Of course they are less inclined to do so as their pension credits accumulate, as debts increase and obligations mount, and even now perhaps they are wondering if management is planning to sell them down the river again under the executive transfer system. But the final decision is their own, after all. They can always say no, if they care to. They can do what they please with their lives.

Or can they? Do they?

They can quit one job but must soon have another. And there is no need for sheriffs and hounds: they can be counted upon to appear and perform, to fear wrath and curry favor, to devote the greater part of their wakeful lives to the service of a man or a company. They are in fact indentured to their needs, or the supposed needs that require them to maintain a certain income. In the end, then, a man who sells his labor is less free than any slave—because a slave can escape.

This view of course is caricature. It derives in part from the philosopher Herbert Marcuse's analysis of technological man, and Marcuse is often denounced as a superficial critic. He was at first highly regarded by the political New Left but later seems to have lost favor personally (although his concepts remain in vogue). Precedent for the imagery suggested here is nevertheless provided by another (still popular) hero of radical youth. The quotation is from Henry David Thoreau's *Walden*:

I sometimes wonder that we can be so frivolous . . . as to attend to the gross but somewhat foreign form of servitude called Negro Slavery, there are so many keen and subtle masters that enslave both North and South. It is hard to have a Southern overseer; it is worse to have a Northern one; but worst of all when you are the slave-driver of yourself. Talk of a divinity in man! Look at the teamster on the highway, wending to market by day or night; does any divinity stir within him? His highest duty to fodder and water his horses! What is his destiny to him compared with the shipping interests? Does not he strive for Squire Make-a-stir? How godlike, how immortal, is he? . . . Public opinion is a weak tyrant compared with our own private opinion. What a man thinks of himself, that it is which determines, or rather indicates, his fate. Self-emancipation even in the West Indian provinces of the fancy and imagination—what Wilberforce is there to bring that about?

This too may be caricature. But many young people are convinced that it describes the essential character of our adult society—it reminds them of their parents, in other words—and, heeding the Zen master's advice, they have decided to ride their own horse. They have proclaimed their emancipation, in fancy if not in fact, and have joined the nebulous movement referred to as the "cultural revolution." In itself their commitment might be dismissed as adolescent romanticism, which to some extent it is; but it appears to represent merely one aspect of a much more fundamental phenomenon: namely, a humanistic revolt against technology, against the debatable form of affluence that technology has so far produced in this country, and indeed against the basic psychological, philosophical, and theological assumptions that underlie the technological impulse to manipulate the environment and thereby to dominate the universe. In a real sense, what is called into question is no less than the whole thrust of Western civilization since at least the Renaissance and Reformation.

Humanism in this context is defined very broadly as a concept of life that puts primary emphasis on the dignity and value and welfare of individual human beings—right now, today, at this moment, on this planet (a more precise definition will be attempted later). Humanists in this sense would, for example, rather feed the hungry than fly to Jupiter, or at least would feed the hungry before flying to Jupiter; they also would deny that man is some kind of genetic Erector Set for biologists to take apart and put together at their whim; humanists do not consider efficiency an end in itself and therefore will often seek the most satisfying line between two points, not necessarily the shortest; they do not feel challenged to do something simply to prove that the thing can be done, or to climb mountains because they are there; finally, they are not preoccupied with the abstractions of theoretical science ("What is life?") but are more inclined to ask themselves: "What is a good life?"

There has been opposition to technology from the beginning of the industrial era. In the Luddite revolt in the first years of the nineteenth century, textile workers in England burned factories and smashed labor-saving machines to protest the decline of handicrafts and the inferior quality of the goods produced by machine. Thoreau warned that we had become the tools of our tools. But the Luddites were put down by force of arms, Thoreau was ignored—as were other Cassandras—and as time passed man took a growing pride in his technological achievements, which he now saw as liberating; they had freed him from nature's blind determinism and would allow him at last to shape his own destiny. This naive optimism prevailed also in his assessment of social and political problems. Thus in the 1950's and early 1960's the sociologist Daniel Bell and others felt confident in declaring "the end of ideology." The fundamental problems of the industrial revolution had all been solved, and America had developed a stable political system. Marx's economic predictions had proved false; capitalism had been reformed to meet the needs of the overall society; production lines were delivering the goods; intellectuals were united in a common front against the Cold War enemy; there was general agreement on national goals, the functions of the welfare state, the dynamics of the economy. The conflicts of the past were over. All was well and would be better.

Then one day the nation woke from its American dream to find that its alabaster cities were in flames. Now in the streets and on the campuses was heard the sound of angry voices.

These were muted at first. They rose in pitch and volume. *"I am a human being. Do not fold, spindle or mutilate."*

That was the rallying cry during the Free Speech Movement in 1964 at Berkeley—a shout of protest against our apparent acceleration toward a wholly computerized, IBM civilization. Other issues were involved there of course, some of them still a bit obscure (to say the least); but the FSM did bring to the surface a deep undercurrent of emotional hostility to certain implications of modern technology. The British scientist C. P. Snow taught us a decade ago to think in terms of Two Cultures within the intellectual community: one oriented toward the sciences, and one oriented toward the humanities. It now appears that the conflict between these cultures has spread from the groves of academe to the wider society, including the suburb and the black ghetto. This development is much more complicated than it might at first seem, and it certainly goes far beyond a mere dainty aversion to the hum of machinery, or an innocent yen for some pastoral past; it may in some cases represent utter nonsense—and often enough it does—but it also can be pragmatic and realistic. Unless we are aware of it, however, and unless it is understood, no real sense can be made of the chaotic divisions that have occurred in America in recent years.

This book will argue that the Two Cultures conflict can be seen as a basic factor in the Black Power movement; in the protest of the New Left; in the supposed confusion of sexual roles; in the development of an LSD subculture; in the so-called Leap to the East by many drugstore disciples of Hinduism and Zen Buddhism; in the current faddish enthusiasm for astrology, witchcraft, and sensitivity training; in anti-scientism; in the newly emerging emphasis on ecology, environmental control, and the often mystical worship of nature; in the reassertion of ethnicity; in the now-defunct Death of God theology as well as the newer attraction referred to as the Theology of Hope. We also will argue that all of these phenomena are in one way or another related to the question of identity.

In adolescent psychology, it is common to speak of a psychosocial identity crisis that marks the passage from childhood to adulthood. This is said to be resolved when a young person achieves a firm sense of inner identity and then decides in addition what social role he intends to assume or prepare for. In this sense it might be said that America as a nation is now suffering an identity crisis. It is not simply a question of bewildered individuals who are wondering at what point they should enter the society; the social structure itself has been challenged—and many young people are saying that the structure must be radically changed before they will enter it. Many black people are saying that they no longer care to enter the society; they have found a better way, they believe. But other blacks are saying that they and the young white radicals together will create a new society, and that black culture in fact will provide the necessary antidote for our technological malaise. And so there arises the vision of a new American identity—a collective identity that will be blacker, more feminine, more oriental, more emotional, more intuitive, more exuberant—and, just possibly, better than the old one.

This vision also calls for a new ontology—or a new understanding of an individual's relationship to the Other: to his fellow men and the natural environment. We will see that American attitudes on this subject may, in the past, have been unconsciously influenced by the atomistic ontology of John Locke, who held that there is absolutely no bond or connection whatever between one man and another. Locke's ideas made a deep impression on Thomas Jefferson and thus found their way into the Declaration of Independence and the Constitution of the United States. They may also have found their way into the American soul: the national *Zeitgeist*. But there has perhaps been a sea change. This new generation has very often expressed an empathy for human suffering which somehow suggests a conviction that there is a bond between man and man; that there does exist some sort of universal identity; that in some strange sense we do each of us bleed when the other is cut. (We will discuss this later with the anthropologist Edward T. Hall.) In the ideas of the young there is also a suggestion that man and nature are not properly antagonists, and that a man could live in harmony with the world— if only he could call off his total campaign to subjugate it. This quasi-mystical view may in some cases have its origin in a psychedelic drug experience, as we shall see, but that does not explain it away. There is evidence that the radical-producing family is typically matriarchal in character, centered around a nurturant mother figure, and this raises the possibility that early home life may have contributed in part to a shift in emphasis from patriarchal to matriarchal standards of conduct and concern: to a more empathetic and egalitarian concept of the human condition. This point will be explored in some detail in connection with certain theories of Erich Fromm.

Some critics of the young neo-humanists have charged them with an irrational "retreat from complexity." They are anti-intellectual; they have no respect for logic or disciplined thought; they think with their glands; they are simplistic, impulsive, and overly emotional. The psychiatrist Daniel X. Freedman has said of them, and of their parents: "They mistake vividness, intensity, and urgency for cultured sensitivity and responsible morality. They don't know what they like, but whatever they or their emotions like must be art—or must be right, and certainly righteous."

This is true. And it stains their image. A humanism that denies reason denies its own tradition: the belief that man has the rational capacity to solve his problems and create a decent life for himself. Nor can humanism afford to turn up its precious nose at the whole of science—as the Nobel laureate George Wald will point out with impressive eloquence further on in these pages. But of course there is a reason for everything, including the refusal to use reason, and it might be better to understand than merely to condemn. Consider the judicial rule that nobody may shout fire in a crowded theater. To the young it must sometimes appear that a perversion of logic has twisted that to read: nobody may shout fire in a burning theater. The older generation would probably reply that "fire" is not the four-letter word the young people have been shouting, but that rather misses the point.

At the turn of the century Henry Adams stood in the Gallery of Machines at the Paris Exposition, in the great hall of dynamos, and pondered the shape of things to come. He saw science and technology as a force that was accelerating in the direct ratio of its squares, doubling or quadrupling its complexities every ten years. The mind so far had been able to keep pace, he wrote, and there was a chance at least that it would continue to do so in the future: "but it would need to jump." Now, just seven decades later, the acceleration is nearing warp speed, and even the most rational minds may find it difficult to maintain that pace. According to the political scientist Zbigniew Brzezinski, post-industrial America "is being shaped to an ever increasing degree by technology and electronics, and thus [is] becoming the first *technetronic society.*" In such a society power will gravitate into the hands of an intellectual and scientific elite: a "meritocratic few" who can understand the new electronic-computer language. Life will be so complicated that it may be necessary to pass a constitutional amendment requiring a President-elect "to spend at least a year getting himself educationally up-to-date." Already there has been a profound change in the intellectual community. "The largely humanist-oriented, occasionally ideologically-minded intellectual dissenter, who saw his role largely in terms of proffering social critiques, is rapidly being displaced either by experts and specialists, who become involved in special governmental undertakings, or by the generalists-integrators, who become in effect house-ideologues for those in power, providing overall intellectual integration for disparate actions." These are the so-called New Mandarins described by the linguistics scholar and social critic Noam Chomsky. Brzezinski seems to feel that the changes he has outlined "augur well for the future," and for the most part he approves of the technetronic society; but he recognizes that others do not, and thus he writes that its emergence "is at least in part the cause for much of the current tensions and violence."

What kind of science the new elite may choose to practice is also a matter for concern. Advances in biology in the next few decades are expected to match those in physics during the first part of the century, and the public so far is only dimly aware of the possible consequences. Organ transplants are just a beginning. The science journalist Gordon Rattray Taylor has proposed that the day may come when somebody will say to you, by way of introduction: "I want you to meet my uncle and niece. They were in a car smash, but fortunately the surgeon was able to get one complete body out of the undamaged bits." It is possible the brain itself will be transplanted, and human brains may even be placed in mechanical bodies—creating a new race of man-machine hybrids. It has been suggested that a human arm might be coupled to a computer, and that men could be provided with mechanical hands they could plug in for special tasks—such as webbed hands for swimming and asbestos hands for working with hot metals. Also, robots could be equipped with a simulacrum of human emotions. "In short," concludes Taylor, "a complex marriage seems to be taking place between man and machine. . . . One day it may become impossible to tell whether one is talking to a mechanized human being or a humanized machine. Or even which one is oneself."

Genetic engineering is another possibility. Babies could be bred in laboratories, their heredity predetermined by the microsurgical insertion or deletion of genes. There is talk of making men immortal, and also of creating life: first simple cells, then complex organisms, including people, and then perhaps life forms that have never existed. There is talk of cloning people or making "people from cuttings," a process comparable to the vegetative reproduction of plants. A human body has about fifty trillion cells. In cloning, a single cell would be removed and grown in a culture to reproduce the individual from which it was taken; the resulting organism would be called a clone and would exactly duplicate the cell donor. You could produce as many of these one-parent clones as desired, reduplicating the parent hundreds or thousands of times. This might be done with a prize-winning race horse (a Sea Biscuit) or an especially valuable human being (an Albert Einstein). Presumably, such decisions would be made by the meritocrats.

Biomedical researchers also have been working on memory transfer. Thus in one experiment flatworms were first conditioned to react to an electric shock; they were then chopped up and fed to other flatworms. The experimenters were able to condition these cannibal worms to the same shock in less time— suggesting they may in some manner have acquired the memories of the worms they ate. Learning time also was reduced when RNA from trained hamsters was injected into untrained rats, indicating that memory transfer might cross the species barrier and that men might ultimately acquire the memories of animals. There has been considerable criticism of the methodology employed in these experiments, and their validity is seriously in doubt. But science marches on, wherever it is off to, and the mind-benders already have predicted an educational revolution in which rote lessons will be eliminated: students will learn facts and dates by memory transfusion, allowing more time for creative thought. With the flatworms in mind, some clowns have proposed that students will obtain their educations by eating their professors. The students may do so in any case, if only to protest this Orwellian blueprint of their future.

It would be comforting to believe that such ideas came out of an opium pipe or a pulp magazine. On the contrary, they are endorsed and promoted with enthusiasm by distinguished men of science, including many Nobel Prize winners. There has in fact emerged a new breed of molecular biologists who feel that the time has come for man to take charge of his own evolution: a program the geneticist Joshua Lederberg has termed euphenics, or "the engineering of human development." This program moreover is supported by many behavioral psychologists who apparently believe that human happiness can best be accomplished with pills and electrodes, altering the psyche instead of the environment, and also by many future-oriented theologians and others who share the cosmic ambitions of the scientist-priest Teilhard de Chardin. Teilhard divided mankind into two camps: "On the one hand there are those who simply wish to make the world a comfortable dwelling place; on the other hand, those who can only conceive of it as a machine for progress—or better, an organism that is progressing." Teilhard put himself in the second camp. He rejoiced in the thought of an ever-increasing complexity he saw leading toward that New Jerusalem he called the Omega Point: a hypercentration of matter in a final state of super-organization and super-awareness, all life compressed to form one mind in one body, the Other dissolved in a monistic Whole. Some scientists find this concept attractive, and the physicist Gerald Feinberg has seriously suggested that mankind adopt it as a final goal: "the creation of a universal consciousness." This effort would be called the Prometheus Project.

This of course is a one-sided picture of science. Also, it would be naive to assume that all of these developments are bound to occur because they are technically possible—there must first be an operational investment, as we shall see, and society is by no means obliged to provide it. The New Biologists are opposed by eminent scientists, including George Wald in this country and Andrei D. Sakharov in Russia. The fact remains, however, that our technical culture too often displays the kind of tunnel vision that equates *can* with *should*. All things considered, there is perhaps some excuse for an emotionally charged reaction to a technological complexification that threatens to destroy the democratic decision-making process; or a science that undermines our already precarious definitions of human identity; or an educational system that is designed primarily to train Brzezinski's managers; or a futuristic philosophy of progress that ignores both the pain and the pleasure of the present moment.

If humanists are concerned about the future, as they are and must be, they are equally concerned about the present effects

of our obsession with technological and economic progress—
and especially our obsession to increase the Gross National
Product. They argue that poverty in America is a direct result
of American affluence, and that the only way to reduce poverty
is to reduce our production and consumption.

This is not the paradox it may seem.

Let us return for a moment to those commuters on the
expressway, and consider as well the workers and consumers
who still live within the city. Marcuse has asserted that their
"democratic unfreedom" is a consequence of "repressive needs"
that are generated by the production system. They want the
products that the system produces—because they are told that
they should want them—and therefore they work in order to
pay for these products. And the system delivers. If you are willing
to work, you can satisfy your supposed needs. The economy pros-
pers, and new needs are created. But that doesn't matter; if you
accept the system—and work a little harder—you can afford
them too. The result is a "paralysis of criticism" and an "integration of opposites," the collusion of business and labor to maintain the status quo. In an advanced industrial society, then, the
machine has become a political instrument; any qualitative
changes in the society are contained not by terror but technology. The citizen consumer cannot even conceive a way of life
that would offer him real autonomy: in short, "freedom from
the economy." His thought is one-dimensional and allows him
to consider only those limited alternatives that exist within the
economy. What is needed, therefore, is a redefinition of needs.
"Men must . . . find their way from false to true consciousness,
from their immediate to their real interest."

But this says no more than Thoreau said, and it supposes
morever that our immediate interest is served by the system.
Marcuse in fact does not go far enough. A man may consider
himself affluent because he has a comfortable home and two
cars. When he leaves that home, however, he steps into an
environment that is ugly and dangerous to life. He and his
neighbors together cannot afford to pay for fresh air and pure

water, pleasant parks and recreation areas, an efficient system of rapid mass transportation, or other essential services including even a decent public schooling for their children. They cannot afford to build metropolitan centers that are both safe and attractive. The suburban commuters are afraid to live in the inner cities where they are employed, and the working people who do still live there are dismayed to see their property investments imperiled as their neighborhoods decay and the ghetto encroaches.

We live in a national slum. Why?

One of the reasons for this public poverty has at last come to public attention—like one of those war-movie U-boats that are finally forced to the surface by depth charges. The first charge was dropped by Dwight D. Eisenhower in his farewell address when he warned the nation of the lurking menace he called the military-industrial complex: the collaboration of the Pentagon and American manufacturers to maintain a high level of defense spending—paid for with tax dollars that might have been allocated for other purposes. The military-industrial complex has now been put on the defensive, and this is no doubt all to the good. But some critics feel that attention to the military has actually obscured a more fundamental problem inherent in our capitalistic system—and they point again to our fascination with growth: the escalation of the GNP. As the historian Christopher Lasch expressed it in a conversation one night: "It isn't just people who make bombs and airplanes. It's people who make lipstick."

We will ask him later what he meant by that. The answer will explain in part why some people are convinced that it is not possible to work for change within the present system.

Even if our affluence today is a pseudo-affluence, however, some tea-leaf economists predict that technology will eventually produce a state of superabundance—and that this in turn will create problems (and opportunities) of an entirely new dimension. Cybernation will lead at last to a leisure society in which work for the vast majority of the population will all but disappear; we will face the prospect of "retirement at birth." Having overcome our puritanical fear of sex, we may soon find it necessary to overcome our puritanical fear of loafing. From this point of view, the hippie may come to be regarded as a welcome social mutation, an ideal citizen (or subject) in the workless world of the future. Marcuse indeed has contended that technology in this sense could ultimately transcend itself—could become in fact "the very base of all forms of human freedom." With the elimination of repressive labor, the individual would be free to develop his inner potential. With the pacification of existence, science itself would be liberated; no longer compelled to wage war on nature, it could turn its attention to trans-utilitarian ends, including perhaps "the translation of values into technical tasks."

Maybe. Somebody once remarked that the chastity belt was probably the last example of technological research designed to preserve values. Marcuse has also said that the good life he describes will never result from technical progress alone; there must also be "a political reversal." And many economists have asserted that a jobless America is pure fantasy (due in part to rising expectations in this country and due in part to our moral obligation to alleviate poverty in other areas of the world). But the abolition of labor is already occurring, in spite of these sound arguments, and the blacks and the students can be offered in evidence. They can talk about their rejection of society; it is more a case of society rejecting them. The unskilled worker has been automated out of the economy, forcing many of the blacks onto welfare. Students are held in ivy-covered detention camps, their entry into the job market postponed by an extension of the educational process. In the chapters to follow, expert testimony will be introduced to show that this latter development has had a profound effect on the life cycle. By denying students full status as psychosocial adults, the technological culture has created serious identity problems for some of the young people and may well have produced a new stage of life in America: what the psychologist Kenneth Keniston has called the stage of "youth." And this can be interpreted as being all very nice or altogether bad, depending upon the expert who is called as a witness.

Different verdicts also are delivered in the overall assessment of technology. Technology is evil (Jacques Ellul). Technology is wonderful (Marshall McLuhan and Eric Hoffer). Technology is whatever we decide to make it (Bertrand de Jouvenel). Among the humanists, some starry-eyed astrologers are very sanguine about the long-term prospects for man. They believe we have reached the end of the bitter and divisive Piscean Epoch and have entered the harmonious Aquarian Epoch. According to the *Dictionary of Mysticism*, this period began in March of 1948, when the sun entered the constellation Aquarius, and we are told it will last for two thousand years. The dawn of the age of Aquarius was celebrated in the Broadway musical *Hair*, which proclaimed it as a time when peace will guide the planets and love will steer the stars.

This is a very campy vision at the moment; if one searches for it, however, there also is ample cause for pessimism. Some advocates of Black Power appear to be stuck tight in the middle of a dialectic, confusing antithesis with synthesis. Some elements of the New Left have responded to the threat of technological elitism by espousing a revolutionary elitism that could be equally destructive of democratic values. Cultural revolutionaries often fail to recognize that their hedonistic life style could as easily enslave as liberate them: that a technetronic dictatorship would rely on bread *and* circuses to pacify the multitudes who were not plugged into the electronic power structure. The psychedelic drug movement has degenerated from a religious crusade to psychic masturbation. There is some danger that the Theology of Hope could result in a futuristic disregard for this world and this time; our domestic Buddhists, on the other hand, are in bondage to the present and would have us believe that Egypt is the Promised Land. There is a paucity of fresh ideas and a surfeit of imported ideologies: one must seriously doubt that all of the answers to the contemporary American crisis can be found in *The Book of Changes* or even *Quotations from Chairman Mao Tse-tung*. (As a Chicago newspaper editor once put it, we need some new clichés.) The need for drastic social reform is difficult to impress upon a public that seems more interested in the tactics of the protesters than the sources of discontent; the theologian Robert McAfee Brown has said that a man holding four aces is not likely to ask for a new deal, and no major political figure has so far dared to suggest that those affluent aces may actually be jokers—that perhaps we need today not a New Deal but a New Deck. Finally, there is a possibility that the technological Juggernaut already is out of control—rumbling down a mountain while the managers oil its wheels. Nobody really steering it. Nobody able to stop it. Not the Congress or the President or the merit-badge bureaucrats or anybody else.

Nobody in charge. That is more frightening to contemplate than a competent dictatorship, benevolent or otherwise.

But there also are grounds for optimism. If no solution has been offered, there is a growing awareness at least that a problem exists. There is a lot of shouting, and that keeps us awake. Many people have suddenly come to feel that they are *not* free, and many people have suddenly come to feel that they *are* free, and people who feel either way will usually try very hard to change their world. They will not accept what is given to them or what is done to them. They will fight for their lives. They will fight also for quality in their lives. And nowhere is it written that they shall fail. Armageddon is possible. So is Aquarius.

2

Green Apples

"If anything ail a man, so that he does not perform his functions, if he have a pain in his bowels even . . . he forthwith sets about reforming the world. . . . I believe that what so saddens the reformer is not the sympathy with his fellows in distress, but, though he be the holiest son of God, is his private ail. Let this be righted, let the spring come to him, the morning rise over his couch, and he will forsake his generous companions without apology."

The passage is from *Walden*. New Left scripture thus provides us with some precedent for psychologizing the motives of the humanist protesters. Nor can this be avoided, for some of the protesters obviously have been eating green apples—and, as Thoreau said, this often leads a person to believe that the world is a green apple. Let us consult the Freudian charts, then, and examine the reductionist analysis of contemporary dissent— beginning with the popular theory that young radicals are the product of parental permissiveness, and that this in turn is primarily the fault of a sinister baby doctor, one Benjamin Spock.

Freud said the human personality consists of three major systems: *id, ego,* and *superego.*

The first of these, the id, is the seat of man's primitive drives and passions. It operates on the pleasure principle, which seeks to discharge tension, and if tension occurs—hunger, for example—the id demands immediate relief. It is irrational and has no contact with reality: with the outer world that represents the Other. A newborn baby has only an id, a wholly inner life, an oceanic consciousness that knows no boundaries. This is sometimes called the unity stage, or the primary stage of undifferentiation. The baby cannot think: "I end *here,* and the rest of the world begins *there.*" He is all in all. If he is hungry or wet, he screams and howls until somebody comes to feed or change him; but there is no recognition that the one who comes is in any way external to him. The psychoanalyst Bruno Bettelheim has referred to this period of early infancy as the source of the myth of a golden age or a paradise lost "when nothing was asked of us and all that we wanted was given," when "a merciful deity stood ready to satisfy our every desire." It also accounts for "our eternal wish for a union that will put an end to our separateness again." But as Bettelheim has added, ". . . the same myth tells that man could not stand being less than himself, however briefly. That no sooner was he given everything, without the need to do anything on his own, than he defied the Giver of all things. Man wished to act on his own even if it cost him apartness." And so the child must leave his Eden.

Gradually he develops an ego, which Freud defined as that part of the id which has been modified by the direct influence of the external world. This is not to be confused with the sense of self or the idea of excessive pride. The Freudian ego is the executive of the personality, and it operates on the reality principle. It does not replace the id, but in a healthy personality it controls the id. In its relation to the id, said Freud, the ego "is like a man on horseback, who has to hold in check the superior strength of the horse." If an older child is hungry, therefore, his ego may tell his id: "Wait. Lunch is at noon." Or it may say: "There is nobody home. You had better go look in the refrigerator." The ego, then, is constantly *testing reality;* it is the ego's job to "face up to the facts." But the ego is not always in charge. It sleeps at night, while the id impulses are allowed to express themselves symbolically in dreams. Psychosis can be defined as a loss of ego control. Even a normal person will sometimes lose control in an extreme situation; the horse will bolt, and the id will temporarily take charge of the personality. Whenever somebody acts impulsively—flies into a rage, for example, or kicks some object he has tripped over—that is his id acting up.

The child also develops a superego. This has been called the judicial branch of the personality, and it is based on moral standards expressed by the parents either consciously or unconsciously (although the parents themselves may not live by those standards). It consists of (1) an *ego ideal,* which represents the child's idea of what is morally good, and (2) a *conscience,* which represents the child's idea of what is morally bad. The child in effect internalizes his parents and carries them around in his head for the rest of his life. The superego, then, becomes an inner judge of one's personal conduct. But it is a hanging judge, severe in its verdicts: like the id, it is not subject to reason and has no contact with outer reality; its province is not the real but the ideal. If the ego says to wait, the superego says: "No, mustn't touch." You can disobey it, but you will be punished in some way if you do. Found guilty, you will carry out the penalty yourself. You may lose your wallet or forget an appointment, have a bad headache or bang your hand in a car door. You'll come up with something. And what is more, since it cannot distinguish between thought and action, the superego will demand that you be punished just for *thinking* something evil, whether you do it or not. In summary, wrote Freud, "it may be said of the id that it is totally non-moral, of the ego that it strives to be moral, and of the superego that it can be hyper-moral and then becomes as ruthless as only the id can be." The ego is seen "as a poor creature owing service to three masters and consequently menaced by three different dangers: from the external world, from the libido of the id, and from the severity of the superego."

So much for the moment for Freud. Let us go back now to 1946, when Dr. Spock wrote a book called *Baby and Child Care*. Following the fashion in pediatrics, most parents until then had been feeding their children on a strict schedule by the clock; but Dr. Spock suggested instead that babies should be fed on demand —whenever they screamed for the bottle. So parents became what is now called "permissive." Baby was picked up whenever he cried; he was fed, changed, and loved on demand. It was not necessary for him to do much reality testing; his id was instantly gratified whenever he squawked. Dr. Spock (who doesn't look very sinister) said in a recent interview that parental permissiveness reached a point where baby was not even put to bed until he practically asked to be put to bed. Revising his book in 1957, the doctor "put a lot of emphasis on the need that the child has for firm leadership from parents." But it was too late. And permissiveness in the meantime had been extended also to education— to the point where one pupil finally asked, in a now-famous plea: "Teacher, *must* we do today what we *want* to do?"

And so—the theory goes—the picked-up generation has gone out of control. It cannot tolerate authority; it cannot tolerate frustration; it continues to demand immediate satisfaction. According to the sociologist Lewis S. Feuer, Columbia University during the uprising in the spring of 1968 became "an enclave for the rule of the id." Discussing student unrest, Bettelheim has stated that Freud's patients all suffered from an overpowering superego and an inhibited id. "But today," said Bettelheim, "we suffer from an underdeveloped superego and an underdeveloped ego and a virtually unrestricted id." He suggests that the educational system "should direct itself toward developing more solid egos and superegos."

A typical criticism of permissiveness can be found in the work of Carl Frankenstein, a Jungian analyst at Hebrew University in Jerusalem. Frankenstein writes that a child who is over-protected by an overanxious or guilt-ridden mother "is not grow-ing up sufficiently prepared for the unavoidable encounter with frustration." Such a child may become "defective in his ability to differentiate." He may "come to see the non-ego [the environ-ment] as a kind of ego extension, so that he will later expect the non-ego to behave as though it were not an independent reality." In short("the child whose culture fails to supply him with suffi-cient opportunities to experience the environment as limiting and frustrating will grow up to continue a life pattern of primitive externality of behavior and thinking.")

A case in point might be Helen Keller, left blind and deaf by a childhood disease. The Kellers were extremely permissive with their afflicted daughter, as might be expected, and Helen was little more than a wild animal—until her teacher Anne Sulli-van arrived one day in 1887. Miss Sullivan wrote shortly after-ward: "I have told Captain and Mrs. Keller that they must not interfere with me in any way. I have done my best to make them see the terrible injustice to Helen of allowing her to have her way in everything." Those explosive scenes in the play *The Miracle Worker* were all literally adapted from letters that were written by Miss Sullivan:

I had a battle royal with Helen this morning. . . . Helen was lying on the floor, kicking and screaming and trying to pull my chair from under me. She kept this up for half an hour, then she got up to see what I was doing. I let her see that I was eating, but did not let her put her hand in the plate. She pinched me, and I slapped her every time she did it. . . . I gave her a spoon, which she threw on the floor. I forced her out of the chair and made her pick it up. Finally I succeeded in getting her back in her chair again, and held the spoon in her hand, compelling her to take up the food with it and put it in her mouth. . . . Then we had another tussle over folding her napkin. When she had finished, she threw it on the floor and ran toward the door. Finding it locked, she began to kick and scream all over again. It was another hour before I succeeded in getting her napkin folded. Then I let her out in the warm sunshine and went up to my room and threw myself on the bed exhausted. . . . I saw clearly that it was useless to try to teach her language or anything else until she learned to obey me. I have thought about it a great deal, and the more I think, the more certain I am that obedience is the gateway through which knowledge, yes, and love, too, enter the mind of a child. . . . I insisted that she must go to bed. We had a terrific tussle, I can tell you. The struggle lasted for nearly two hours. I never saw such strength and endurance in a child. But fortunately for us both, I am a little stronger. . . . You will be glad to hear that my experiment is working out finely. I have not had any trouble with Helen, either yesterday or today. . . . A miracle has happened! The light of understanding has shone upon my little pupil's mind, and behold, all things are changed!

On her arrival Miss Sullivan had written of Helen: "Her face is hard to describe. It is intelligent, but lacks mobility, or soul, or something." Four months later she wrote: "She has been unusually affectionate . . . and it seems to me there is a sweetness —a soul beauty in her face which I have not seen before." Years later the grateful pupil looked back on that time before Miss Sullivan broke through to her. "Before that supreme event," said Helen Keller, "there was nothing in me except the instinct to eat and drink and sleep. My days were a blank without past, present, or future, without hope or anticipation, without interest or joy. . . . Then, suddenly, I knew not how or where or when, my brain felt the impact of another mind, and I awoke to language, to knowledge, to love. . . . Thus I came up out of Egypt and stood before Sinai, and a power divine touched my spirit and gave it sight, so that I beheld many wonders."

It might be said that Anne Sullivan in this case represented the reality principle. She was the Other asserting its existence, compelling a narcissistic id to recognize an external reality that runs by its own rules and demands certain compromises. That analogy was suggested to Bettelheim during an interview one day and he thought it was valid. He applied it to some of the more violent student protesters and said: "I'm afraid they will grow up into Helen Kellers without Anne Sullivans."

Herbert Marcuse has provided a variation on this theme, which supports his theory of technological dictatorship. Technology tends to pacify the external environment. As a result, Marcuse says, "the tension between that which is desired and that which is permitted seems considerably lowered, and the Reality Principle no longer seems to require a sweeping and painful transformation of instinctual needs. The individual must adapt himself to a world which does not seem to demand the denial of his innermost needs—a world which is not essentially hostile. The organism is thus being preconditioned for the spontaneous acceptance of what is offered." This interpretation raises some rather disturbing questions about the leisure society that affluence may ultimately create. It may also serve to emphasize the possible dangers inherent in the hedonism of the cultural revolution. While the revolutionaries exult in their freedom— sucking on their warm bottles—the permissive elite can go about their business of managing, mismanaging, or nonmanaging the country.

Another variation is offered by Feuer, who suggests that student movements are based on generational conflict: an Oedipal revolt of Freud's primal sons against their fathers. Generational conflict always exists, Feuer writes; it will not manifest itself in the form of a student movement unless there has first occurred a "moral de-authoritization" of the older generation—unless the young people feel that the older generation "has discredited itself and lost its moral standing." It would certainly be possible to apply this formula without dragging in the Oedipus complex, however, and the dissenters of course are saying quite clearly that the older generation in their eyes *has* discredited itself. In mining this vein, Feuer might have stopped somewhere to ask just why de-authoritization seems to have taken place at this particular point in America's history. Since he did not, it is hard to take him seriously.

Still another approach would trace dissent to the argument developed by the social philosopher Eric Hoffer in his well-known book *The True Believer*. Hoffer wrote: "Discontent is likely to be highest when misery is bearable; when conditions have so improved that an ideal state seems almost within reach. A grievance is most poignant when almost redressed." And the extension of liberty also creates another set of psychological problems; in fact, the "burden" of freedom becomes the root of the new discontent. "Freedom aggravates at least as much as it alleviates frustration. Freedom of choice places the whole blame of failure on the shoulders of the individual." One is left with the "fears and hopelessness of an untenable individual existence." So one joins a mass movement. One does this, according to Hoffer, because "a mass movement, particularly in its active, revivalist phase, appeals not to those intent on bolstering a cherished self, but to those who crave to be rid of an unwanted self." It appeals in particular to "the failures, misfits, outcasts, criminals, and all those who have lost their footing, or never had one, in the ranks of respectable humanity."

The True Believer is a remarkable book. It appears to have been constructed by the repetition, paragraph upon paragraph, of two powerful themes borrowed from Alexis de Tocqueville (the idea that revolutions occur with the lifting of oppression, when prospects begin to improve) and from Fyodor Dostoyevsky (the idea that men fear their freedom). The first of these provides the philosophical base for the so-called revolution of rising expectations; if it applies at all, it probably applies to the Black Power movement—and this will be considered in another chapter. The second theme relates more directly to the students perhaps, and it deserves our attention.

The flight-from-freedom is the classic thesis of the Grand Inquisitor scene in Dostoyevsky's novel *The Brothers Karamazov*. It also is essential to the existential philosophy of Jean-Paul Sartre and others, while Erich Fromm in particular has had a good deal to say on the subject. Fromm's socio-analytic viewpoint is derived in part from Otto Rank and Karl Marx. Rank asserted that all neurosis and anxiety in life have their origin in the birth trauma—the separation from the mother—which can lead either to *life fear* or to *death fear*. In the first case a person fears that any expression of creativity may cut him off from the crowd, may isolate him from his fellow men. In the second case he fears that his individuality will be lost *in* the crowd. Most men choose to lose themselves in the comforting anonymity of social conformity, and a few will express themselves to the limits of their creative capacities; neurotics on the other hand will waver between the two alternatives—wanting their freedom but also afraid of it. Fromm went further to propose that mankind as a whole has evolved historically in the direction of increased individualism and increased alienation. There was first of all the alienation that occurred when man divorced himself from nature and the natural order, and after that his alienation from the social order. In the Middle Ages men still felt themselves to be very much a part of their society, if not of nature, and in fact the individual as such did not exist at that time: men did not really think of themselves as separate persons but rather as parts of an organic whole, and even the most humble were secure in their stations, their social roles assured them. But then came the Reformation and the rise of capitalism (a cause-and-effect sequence, according to the sociologist Max Weber), and with them the birth of the individual—ever freer and ever more estranged. This is not to say that individualism is bad—quite the contrary. But man must pay a price for it, and he suffers the pangs of separation anxiety. He stands alone before God and alone in the marketplace. He faces a plethora of choices. And this is the core of Sartre's existentialism: the idea of choice, and the necessity to choose. Man does not evolve according to some predetermined plan; his existence precedes his essence, and he must decide what his essence shall be: he is free to choose his own destiny— and more than that, he is obliged to do so. But this freedom is terrifying. Obliged to choose, Sartre wants to vomit. He experiences fear, trembling, and nausea. And so it is with all men.

There is a constant temptation to surrender one's freedom to the crowd, or a noble cause, or some other authority: perhaps to a mass movement.

This surrender also has been attributed to permissiveness.

Bettelheim, as noted, believes that permissiveness tends to produce underdeveloped egos and underdeveloped superegos. But some of his colleagues express just the opposite viewpoint. "I don't think these kids grow up with weak egos," said the psychiatrist Jarl E. Dyrud. "I think they grow up with punishing superegos. Everybody talks about this new youth—so free, so happy. Well, these permissively raised kids have had to develop their own internal constraints on their behavior—and these are a great deal more rigid and punishing than the average good parent would have given them, if he had taken the trouble to set limits." These vague, cheerful parents fail to provide a reasonable standard of morality which the child can incorporate as a kind of internal guidance system to control his impulses. The child is required to set his own limits; it can be a hellish sort of freedom. An interesting if extreme example of this is sometimes seen in the psychedelic drug experience, which very often will create an impression at least that the superego has somehow been suspended. In many cases this sensation has resulted in a "bad trip." As one subject reported: "I had the feeling I might do almost anything—something crazy or awful. I might even kill somebody. It wasn't that I wanted to, because I didn't, and there was no reason I should. But there was no reason I *shouldn't* either. Not really, I mean. And that's what frightened me, I remember. It's hard to explain. But there weren't any laws or rules you had to follow—no good or bad, no right or wrong. You couldn't trust yourself, and you couldn't be sure that you weren't going to do something really wild. Finally, I locked myself in my room, so I wouldn't be near anybody and couldn't hurt anything, and I didn't come out of there for days."

A study conducted by the psychiatrist Daniel Offer indicates that teen-agers worry considerably about the control of their "antisocial tendencies," and they cite this as one of their most serious problems. Offer concludes: "The subjects who were concerned with stopping world conflicts were often those who were most concerned with controls for themselves." Any number of studies show that teen-agers as a group tend to resent parents who allow them too much freedom. They interpret this as an indication of parental disinterest. More than 90 per cent of Offer's subjects attributed juvenile delinquency to "too much freedom associated with too little love." The typical adolescent prefers a strong father. "This gives the adolescent not only a worthy adversary but one who can set limits to his strengths. The strict father enables the boy to take responsibility for his own rebellion when he does rebel." In this connection, extreme acting-out behavior may sometimes be seen as a plea for limits: "Please stop me. How far must I go?"

"The good parent sets limits," said Dyrud. "He helps the child define reality. This means that the child is provided with a problem-solving range, between these limits, that is appropriate to his skills. If this happens he moves from success to success with a growing sense of well-being and personal competence, and he is never placed in a disastrous situation where the problems are beyond his capacity of solution. In Spain, for example, they have the duenna system. When a girl goes out on a date, she takes an older woman with her as a chaperon. So the girl then is free to develop her feelings of attractiveness. She's free to enjoy her growing erotic feelings, because there are limits within which she is safe. But we take young people even twelve or fourteen years old and put them in situations which demand extreme self-restraint, so they can't afford to feel and develop seductive behavior. And this is constricting. Take the Pill. By giving adolescents the Pill we are very often depriving them of the chance to develop emotional depth and real texture in their lives. We're saying in effect to go ahead and act on this, at a time when you might appropriately be setting limits."

"But most teen-agers don't experiment with sexuality," said Offer. "They set very strict limits on themselves." Most of the high school boys he studied were reluctant to engage in sexual intercourse, suggesting an awareness of their immaturity. "They said they were afraid of getting the girls pregnant," said Offer. "Which is interesting to me, because after all they know all about contraceptives. So I pressed them on that issue, and that was the only time in my years of experience they became very anxious and kind of angry. Because it was obviously a rationalization. If it wasn't pregnancy it would be venereal disease, and if these two were taken out it would be, you know, because someone up there doesn't like it."

Referring again to the concept of a punishing superego, Daniel X. Freedman said: "These untempered attitudes you see today come from a lack of authentic autonomy tested out by a sequence of developmental experiences, whereby your inner vision of what you are and what others are is modified. The most authoritarian people are those who either see the world as a conspiracy in which they are helpless or are ready themselves to impose upon the world a bunch of super-strict behaviors. We're talking about aberrant developments of the superego, and you see this now in these kids who won't listen. Because they *know* they're right. They say to you, 'Look, talk to us about anything, but don't talk to us about whether we're right. We know morally we're right.' What they're really engaged in, however, is moral masochism—and moral sadism."

Radicalism also may lend itself to a comparison with the religious conversion process. People often will say they were "radicalized" on a certain day, at a certain hour, in the same way that others speak of their conversion to the Faith. Suddenly their eyes were opened, and for the first time they saw it: "I believe! I believe in the military-industrial conspiracy!" Suddenly they *knew.*

The best analysis of conversion is still to be found in *The Varieties of Religious Experience*, where the psychologist William James refers to "the hot place in a man's consciousness, the group of ideas to which he devotes himself, and from which he works." James called this "the habitual center of personal energy." To say that a man is converted means in essence that "religious ideas, previously peripheral in his consciousness, now take a central place, and that religious aims form the habitual center of his energy." This change in focus may occur quite abruptly, as it did on the road to Damascus: "a complete division is established in the twinkling of an eye between the old life and the new." The religious convert experiences a sense of perceiving truths not known before, a sense of newness, and an ecstasy of happiness: he discovers to his joy that everything is All Right. The radical convert, on the other hand, discovers that everything is All Wrong. But he too perceives a new set of truths; he experiences the world from a wholly new perspective, and the shock of discovery produces an ecstasy of righteous anger. At last a pattern has emerged from the chaos of complexity. Psychic energies are integrated, and the convert in a real sense is born again to a different life—a new mode of perception, a new style of reaction. His divided self is healed and made whole.

In his comments on conversion, James referred to E. D. Starbuck's statistical studies in the field of religious psychology. These showed, he wrote, "how closely parallel in its manifestations the ordinary 'conversion' which occurs in young people brought up in evangelical circles is to that growth into a larger spiritual life which is a normal phase of adolescence in every class of human beings." James added:

The age is the same, falling usually between fourteen and seventeen. The symptoms are the same—sense of incompleteness and imperfection; brooding, depression, morbid introspection, and sense of sin; anxiety about the hereafter; distress over doubts, and the like. And the result is the same—a happy relief and objectivity, as the confidence in self gets greater through the adjustment of the faculties to the wider outlook. In spontaneous religious awakening, apart from revivalistic examples, and in the ordinary storm and stress moulting-time of adolescence, we also may meet with mystical experiences, astonishing the subjects by their suddenness, just as in revivalistic conversion. The analogy, in fact, is complete; and Starbuck's conclusion as to these ordi-

nary youthful conversions would seem to be the only sound one: Conversion is in its essence a normal adolescent phenomenon, incidental to the passage from the child's small universe to the wider intellectual and spiritual life of maturity.

"Theology," says Dr. Starbuck, "takes the adolescent tendencies and builds upon them; it sees that the essential thing in adolescent growth is bringing the person out of childhood into the new life of maturity and personal insight. It accordingly brings those means to bear which will intensify the normal tendencies. It shortens up the period of duration of storm and stress." The conversion phenomena of *"conviction of sin"* last, by this investigator's statistics, about one-fifth as long as the periods of adolescent storm and stress phenomena of which he also got statistics, *but they are very much more intense. Bodily accompaniments, loss of sleep and appetite, for example, are much more frequent in them.* "The essential distinction appears to be that conversion intensifies but shortens the period by bringing the person to a definite crisis."

The conversions which Dr. Starbuck here has in mind are of course mainly those of very commonplace persons, kept true to a pre-appointed type by instruction, appeal, and example. The particular form which they affect is the result of suggestion and imitation. *If they went through their growth-crisis in other faiths and other countries, although the essence of the change would be the same (since it is one in the main so inevitable), its accidents would be different* [roman ours].

The following chapter will contest the assumption that adolescence is a universal phenomenon, and also the idea that storm and stress are a necessary aspect of the adolescent period in our own society. James's conclusions are nevertheless of interest. The duration of the adolescent period in America is now much longer than it used to be, as we shall see, and radical conversion in some cases may represent a youthful effort to resolve a psychosocial identity crisis that has been protracted beyond all endurance. Since radicals tend to come from liberal families, as we also shall see, the "accident" of their political conversion would appear to be obvious. James perhaps offers us another clue in his observation that there will usually be two things in the mind of a candidate for conversion: "first, the present incompleteness or wrongness, the 'sin' which he is eager to escape from; and, second, the positive ideal which he longs to compass." James also agreed with Starbuck's assertion that conversion, in a majority of cases, is *a process of struggling away from sin rather than of striving towards righteousness.*" Substitute the word affluence for the word sin, and this statement may well apply to some of the upper middle-class young people who rebel against the luxury and comfort of their home environment. (Does the preacher in *Rain* come to mind?) Also worth noting is the emphasis James places on the element of self-surrender in the conversion process.

Discussing the viability of cultures, Dyrud said: "Most people you know probably need or want about 85 per cent of their decisions made for them, and the other 15 per cent they'd like to make themselves. Regardless of its complexity, a society is viable so long as it provides sufficient ambiguity in those areas in which people wish to choose—and provides sufficient clarity in those areas in which they wish to be relieved of choice. Now, unfortunately, we've had a phase shift. And that's our trouble. Our society no longer answers the questions, automatically, that need to be answered. And it leaves ambiguous the areas that a young person can most profitably explore in. Therefore, he is uncomfortable. And that brings us to this business of a conversion experience of being radicalized. I think this happens to a person who's looking for a place where he fits. And all of a sudden he finds something where his character structure snaps into place in a group, and he feels comfortable again. It doesn't matter much what the content is. And that's the alarming part of it."

What alarms Dyrud perhaps is the abruptness of "the snap." We are naturally suspicious of an instant commitment made in some moment of passion, without deliberation; the basis of the commitment must be irrational, it would seem, or purely psychological. But this is not necessarily the case. James for example quotes an interesting example of counter-conversion, reported by Tolstoy, that involved a young man identified only as S. "He was 26 years old when one day on a hunting expedition, the time for sleep having come, he set himself to pray according to the custom he had held from childhood. His brother, who was hunting with him, lay upon the hay and looked at him. When S. had finished his prayer and was turning to sleep, the brother said, 'Do you still keep up that thing?' Nothing more was said. But since that day, now more than thirty years ago, S. has never prayed again; he never takes communion, and does not go to church." Apparently, said Tolstoy, the brother's comment was "like the light push of a finger against a leaning wall already about to tumble by its own weight." Or as James put it, like "that touch of a needle which makes the salt in a supersaturated fluid suddenly begin to crystallize out." James suggested that instantaneous conversions are preceded by "subconscious cerebration" and "subconsciously maturing processes eventuating in results of which we suddenly grow conscious." He spoke of the subconscious ripening of one affection and the exhaustion of another, resulting in a change of equilibrium: "the movement of new psychic energies towards the personal center and the recession of old ones towards the margin." At last, "the higher condition, having reached the due degree of energy, bursts through all barriers and sweeps in like a sudden flood." A conversion, then, may result from a subliminal weighing of the evidence—it may, that is, represent a rational conclusion. James himself recognized many different kinds of conversion. "For example, the new birth may be away from religion into incredulity; or it may be from moral scrupulosity into freedom and license; or it may be produced by the irruption into the individual's life of some new stimulus or passion, such as love, ambition, cupidity, revenge, or patriotic devotion. In all these instances we have precisely the same psychological form of event—a firmness, stability, and equilibrium succeeding a period of storm and stress and inconsistency. In these non-religious cases the new man may also be born either gradually or suddenly."

It is necessary to understand the "firmness and stability" of this new birth to appreciate the reason why so many radicals and nonradicals find it impossible to communicate. It is probably a waste of breath when they argue a specific issue; their point of view on any subject is colored or even predetermined by their *Weltansicht,* or their basic apprehension of reality as a whole. We have suggested that radical conversion produces a *Weltansicht* in which the social reality is viewed as fundamentally All Wrong. Most nonradicals see much that is wrong in the society, and much that is hateful, but the social foundations for them are still viable and therefore fundamentally All Right. The All Wrong people and the All Right people will seldom agree on anything, and seldom understand each other, because their perceptual patterns are so antithetical. They can't talk to each other. It is not simply that they speak different languages; they *think* differently. The linguistics scholar Benjamin Lee Whorf has shown that man's perception of the world is programmed by his language, and that men from different cultures live in different sensory worlds. Thus the language of the Hopi Indians does not provide for abstract or imaginary space, and the Hopi therefore cannot visualize a place or an object they do not see before them with their own eyes. But we too inhabit different "thought worlds." In our case, however, it is the pattern of social perception that programs our political language: for example, the way we react to various slogans and aphorisms ("justice," "democracy," "freedom"). The All Right people not only do not see the society in the same way that the All Wrong people see it; they *cannot* see it that way—unless they too are converted and almost literally change their minds. The same limitation applies to the radicals as well.

If an effort is made, however, there are times when it is possible to experience just for a moment the thought world of another person—while listening to a powerful speaker, for example, or reading an especially provocative passage in a book such as *Soul on Ice*. There are times, as James put it, when we "see masses of truth together, and often get glimpses of relations which we divine rather than see, for they shoot beyond the [mental] field into still remoter regions of objectivity, regions which we seem rather to be about to perceive than to perceive actually." And the effort is worth making for men of all persuasions. The perception that everything is wrong may or may not be valid in any given case, but it serves us well if it accentuates what really is wrong and creates a sense of urgency; it does not serve us well in so far as it distorts reality and creates a sense of frustration, or leads to mindless action. The truth is always elusive, and the white heat of a conversion experience may blind a person to some of it, at least temporarily. Starbuck believed that conversion merely marks the passage to a richer life of the mind and spirit. He concluded that the overall effect of religious conversion is "a changed attitude towards life, which is fairly constant and permanent, although the feelings fluctuate. . . . In other words, the persons who have passed through conversion, having once taken a stand for the religious life, tend to feel themselves identified with it, no matter how much their religious enthusiasm declines." And so it should be perhaps in the case of radical conversion—a passing through that leads ultimately to a more mature perspective. Most humanists hopefully are trying to attain that perspective. They seek the possible as well as the profound.

As for the permissiveness theory, there is probably some truth to it. The popular version of course is simplistic diaperology; it ignores among other things the importance of developmental stages and the fact that personality development is a continuous process that ends only at death; it also is blatantly reductionist. Even to a sympathetic observer, however, it must be painfully obvious that some of the young dissenters are psychopathic, that some of them indeed are stony-hearted Rasputins rather than pure-hearted Parsifals, and that some of them are either id-dominated, as Freud would have it, or simply spoiled brats. The conduct of their crusade often brings to mind those coin-collection cans that are sold in novelty shops: "Give to Mental Health or I'll Kill You." There is a lot of free-floating anxiety in the atmosphere these days, and this is always easier to handle if you can focus it on some discrete object in the environment. One recalls the deep sense of loss one felt when Senator Joseph R. McCarthy died in 1957, and the first thought that occurred when the news bulletin was flashed: "My God, who am I going to hate?" Or consider the case of the naval officer from the spy ship *Pueblo* who later told of his hatred for his North Korean captors. "At that time," he said, "the only thing that I wished . . . what I wanted to do was take my life. I couldn't do it." So he turned his attention to a plant his captors had put in his room. "I urinated on it," he said. "I had an extreme hatred for everything there, and when they gave me this damn plant it took me four months but I finally killed it." A knowledge of psychoanalysis is hardly necessary to appreciate that people often act rather oddly and vent their aggression in strange ways. There is something to be said for the argument that the post-Sputnik downgrading of sports has denied college students a traditional outlet for their aggressive impulses, and Offer has in fact found that most of his "normal" high school students still turn to competitive sports to sublimate their aggression *and* their genital sexuality. Feuer reminds us that an official of the Intercollegiate Socialist Society complained back in 1925 that football had been one of "the chief obstacles to interesting college students in labor conditions."

Finally, humanists in general are open to the charge that they pay too much attention to the evil that exists in man's institutions and too little attention to the evil that exists in man himself. They tend to externalize their devils and refuse to acknowledge, as the poet Archibald MacLeish did, that in the last analysis "the trouble is man." Stuck somewhere between ape and angel, as a zoologist once described him, man is somehow flawed. This may be the real meaning of sin, which is a collective phenomenon, an imperfection of the species. The self-righteous humanist rants at the conventional Satan who rose from the nether regions to plague Marlowe's Faust and does not recognize the inner

Tempter that Goethe's Faust heard whispering in his own divided soul; he denies the hidden self Jung called "the shadow," the Mr. Hyde who lurks in all of us, and he shuts his ears to the poet Marianne Moore's determined pledge: "I must fight till I have conquered in myself what causes war." Or so it may have seemed in the past, at any rate. But the external Satan has become increasingly difficult to identify of late—unless he is Complexity itself (as Henry Adams implied), or else that spectral Mafia the Establishment—and this lends some substance to the concern that nobody is really in charge. If nobody is in charge, there is nobody to blame. This in turn may account (in part) for the fact that the contemporary revolt is more cultural than political, emphasizing life styles more than ideologies. This is not a comforting thought.

All of the put-down theories described in this chapter are popular with the members of the Geritol set, whose tired blood is boiling. It might also be said that all of them are valid, to a point; that is, some of them no doubt explain in part the motivation of some dissenters, and some of them to some degree no doubt apply to the whole of humanity. But let us take another look at them now.

We must first apologize to Dr. Spock. The doctor once remarked he would be pleased indeed to take credit for today's younger generation, if that were possible, but unfortunately he did not deserve such a compliment. Obviously he does not. As the sociologist Richard Flacks put it one day: "Dr. Spock wrote his book to reflect changing social practice, not to create social practice. That's one point people should be very clear on. If Dr. Spock hadn't written that book, ten other people would have, and did." There also is another side to the permissiveness theory as such, and this can be found of all places in the work of Bruno Bettelheim. In his classic study of autistic children, *The Empty Fortress*, the analyst warned parents that a child's view of himself and the world "will depend on the failure or success of his efforts. Consistent nonreward for being active may even lead to his giving up trying to shape his interactions and yield to passivity." A possible outcome is infantile autism, a schizophrenic rejection of reality. Especially in the nursing experience, an infant needs to develop that initial sense of trust that comes with "having acted on one's own within a context of mutuality, of having known what it is to be fully active, of having shaped the experience in spite of one's otherwise dependent state." When the infant's actions evoke no response, "he becomes flooded with impotent rage, a helpless victim of inner tensions." Bettelheim states that "artificial feeding times, arranged according to the clock, can dehumanize the infant." Time-clock feeding "prevents the infant from feeling that *his* actions (crying, smiling) have a significant effect on this important life experience of being fed." Bettelheim adds:

What humanizes the infant is not being fed, changed, or picked up when he feels the need for it, though they add greatly to his comfort and feeling of well-being. Nor does irregular care necessarily dehumanize, though it will tend to make him dissatisfied with life or may cause poor development or sickness. It is rather the experience that his crying for food brings about his satiation by others according to his timing that makes it a socializing and humanizing experience. It is that his smile, or facial grimacing, evokes a parallel or otherwise appropriate response in the mother. Conversely, the experience that his own actions (cry or smile) make no difference is what stops him from becoming a human being, for it discourages him from interacting with others and hence from forming a personality through which to deal with the environment. . . . The joke that fails to amuse, the loving gesture that goes unanswered, are some of the most painful experiences. And if we consistently and from an early age fail to meet the appropriate response to our expression of emotions, we stop communicating with others and eventually lose interest in the world. . . . I believe it to be a distinctly human experience to feel with conviction: I did it, and my doing made a difference.

We have said it is the id that demands satisfaction and the ego that learns to live with frustration. Bettelheim indicates, however, that some satisfaction is essential to ego development.

... the infant has repeatedly experienced that his needs are not always or immediately met. And the manageable frustration that follows is what makes him aware that an outer world even exists. The emphasis here is on the manageable. Because otherwise the child is so flooded by unpleasant emotions that nothing else seems to exist. Blotted out is the barely emerging awareness of a world that responds. Thus the child's expectation that something outside of him will satisfy his needs is what powerfully increases his interest in the world and his impulse to learn more about it. In a next and crucial step he fathoms that he, through his own efforts, through signals or the giving of signs, has been able to influence the external world—and this is the point at which he begins to become a social being. If his efforts keep succeeding, then eventually he wants to make the advantage a permanent one by coming to terms with this something outside him that has the power to satisfy or frustrate. . . . But things may go terribly wrong if the world is experienced as basically frustrating too soon; before the conviction of its satisfying nature has been established in an Anlage that will reappear once the child can do things on his own. . . . I can now be more specific about what essentially the autistic Anlage consists of: it is the conviction that one's own efforts have no power to influence the world, because of the earlier conviction that the world is insensitive to one's reactions. . . . I am not in favor of having the child, at an early age, shift for himself. This would mean he is overpowered and will end up defeated. There is a great tendency in our society to want children to be independent at an early age and to push them to "do things," particularly those things the parents want them to do. I believe this is most destructive to the development of autonomy. . . . Autonomy is neither dependent on nor helped by an absolute control of our feelings. That would only lead to a compulsively depleted personality. Our emotions, like our bowels, *must be free to assert their right to satisfaction and discharge.*

Bettelheim strikes a similar note in his book *The Children of the Dream.* "In order to build our society of affluence it became necessary to replace the pleasure principle by the reality principle in more and more areas of life. More important here, it became possible to arrange the life of the very young in ways that require them to give up the pleasure principle sooner and sooner in life. . . . A great deal of modern drug and sex behavior has its roots in the desperate effort to set things aright—to give the pleasure principle a belated chance to assert itself, after denying it too early." Affluence now makes it possible for us to decide for ourselves at what age the pleasure principle should yield to the reality principle, and the affluent society "can well afford to let the infant enjoy living for pleasure over a considerable span, so that when the time comes, he can easily relinquish it, step by step, for more exacting demands." It would appear from this, then, that the id is not unrestricted after all: it is undernourished.

Bettelheim no doubt can reconcile these views, but that is not the point. Freudian concepts are like those colored chips inside a kaleidoscope: just shake the tube and a different pattern is produced, depending perhaps on whether your subject of interest at the moment is autistic children or student protesters. And what is the purpose? The interpretation in the end is acceptable only on faith; there is no way to demonstrate that a particular analysis offers a valid explanation of mass behavior. Psychological theories may often explain or illuminate an individual's behavior, and that is our main defense for injecting them here: they can sometimes help us understand ourselves a little better, and it never hurts a person to examine his own motives. But psychology alone is not very helpful when it comes to social criticism. Everybody is psychologically motivated, after all, and it might make more sense to forget about the humanists for a while and to ask instead what motivates a man who wants to be President of the United States (anybody who seeks that office perhaps should be automatically disqualified). And if some humanists are secretly afraid of their own freedom, for example, the same might be said of some technological meritocrats (Fromm makes a case that the computer has replaced God as a "guarantor of certainty," and that managers now turn to the computerized solution to relieve the burden of personal choice). Or go back to James for a moment. Applying his pragmatic philosophy to the conversion phenomenon, he argued "against the notion that the worth of a thing can be decided by its origin." He explained: "Our spiritual judgment . . . our opinion of the significance and value of a human event or condition, must be decided on empirical grounds exclusively. If the *fruits for life* of the state of conversion are good, we ought to idealize and venerate it, even though it be a piece of natural psychology; if not, we ought to make short work of it, no matter what supernatural being may have infused it." The same test might be applied to social dissent. As it is, our penchant for psychologizing might tempt us to reject the number four while we explore the psyche of somebody who was prompted for some reason to add two and two. Whatever made him do that: a counting compulsion? Or suppose that somebody were to tell us that our house was on fire, and seemed rather insistent on the point; should we consider the possibility of a pyrophobic obsession—or should we look first for smoke?

There is another reason to doubt that classical psychology is much of a star to steer by these days. Psychoanalysis itself has moved away from Freud's biological determinism and the sweeping theories about "human nature" that were based on his observation of some hysterical Portnoys who lived in Victorian Austria. The neo-Freudian school has weighed the evidence that was introduced later by the anthropologists and the cultural historians, and the conclusion is inescapable: man is not just a collection of biological demands; he is a product also of his culture and society. We must leave Freud's stuffy office behind, then, if we are to understand the nature of the humanist complaint.

So. Now we may perhaps to begin. Yes?

Technology and Adolescence

In his foreword to Margaret Mead's study, *Coming of Age in Samoa*, the anthropologist Franz Boas wrote in 1928: "In our own civilization the individual is beset with difficulties which we are likely to ascribe to fundamental human traits. When we speak of the difficulties of childhood and adolescence, we are thinking of them as unavoidable periods of adjustment through which everyone has to pass. The whole psychoanalytic approach is largely based on this supposition. The anthropologist doubts the correctness of these views. . . . Much of what we ascribe to human nature is no more than a reaction to the restraints put upon us by our civilization."

The anthropologists had made an important discovery. Adolescence is not a biological stage of life that occurs between childhood and adulthood; in some societies there is no such thing as an adolescent, no such thing as a "teen-ager." The implications of this insight were slow to dawn upon us, and only recently has their full impact been felt in the form of a cultural shock wave: the youth rebellion. To understand this development, however, it is necessary to look first at another important discovery.

In our own Western society, there once were no children. There was no such thing as childhood, let alone adolescence.

The evidence for this claim is documented in the study *Centuries of Childhood* (1962), by the French cultural historian Philippe Ariès. In the art of the Middle Ages, for example, children are depicted as tiny adults: as Lilliputian figures with adult expressions and adult musculature. Only their size is reduced. Thus an Ottonian miniature of the twelfth century shows us the Gospel scene in which Jesus has asked that little children should come unto him. Ariès writes: "The Latin text is clear: *parvuli*. Yet the miniaturist has grouped around Jesus what are obviously eight men, without any of the characteristics of childhood; they have simply been depicted on a smaller scale." In the Bible of St. Louis, "Isaac is shown sitting between his two wives, surrounded by some fifteen little men who come up to the level of the grown-ups' waists: these are their children." Birthdays were not recorded with any precision; in a time when nobody ever knew a date for certain, "it was an uncommon and difficult thing to remember one's age exactly." As late as the sixteenth century, even in the educated classes, a curious custom prevailed that made it bad manners for a child openly to reveal his age. Ariès concludes that there was no place for children in the medieval world, and that the concept of childhood did not fully evolve until the seventeenth century. Before that children were not only painted as adults, they were dressed as adults and treated as adults.

As soon as children were removed from their swaddling clothes they were dressed in the same costumes worn by the adults in their class. As soon as they no longer needed the constant attention of their mother or nurse—around the age of seven—they were introduced at once into adult society. Before that they simply did not count; infant mortality was very high, and parents could not afford a great deal of emotional attachment.

But after infancy, children "immediately went straight into the great community of men, sharing in the work and play of their companions, old and young alike." Children and adults sang the same songs, danced the same dances, listened to the same fairy stories, and played the same games on an equal footing: children played cards and dice for money; adults played with hoops and joined the children in snowball fights. Young boys visited taverns and brothels. Adults told dirty stories in front of the children and took physical liberties with younger children that would strike us today as "bordering on sexual perversion." Children were believed to be indifferent to sex until puberty, and in any case there was no concern that exposure to sexual matters would soil their childish innocence, because "nobody thought that this innocence really existed." The child was considered "the natural companion of the adult." All of this changed very slowly, beginning in the upper classes; in the lower classes and in rural areas the old ways survived in some cases almost to the present day.

Bettelheim discusses Ariès' findings in his study of the Israeli kibbutzim, *The Children of the Dream,* and concludes that much of the alienation of Western man in the last two centuries has been caused by "the growing distance between child and adult." Bettelheim writes that life activities were far less specialized by age group in the period described by Ariès, and children therefore "did not infringe on the life of their parents nor the other way round." He attributes the development of childhood to increased specialization. It is not that children have become more childish but rather that adults have become much less so: "the life of adults has become so complex, so little accessible to the child, that despite our best efforts to bridge the abyss it continues to grow." This may be correct, but it is by no means the conclusion that Ariès intends to suggest.

Ariès in fact links childhood to the emergence in the seventeenth century of the modern family structure, and this in turn he attributes in part to the growing influence of Christianity: to pressure from moralists and humanist pedagogues who lectured parents on the holy sanctity of childhood. The moral aspect of religion was gradually taking precedence over the sacred or eschatological aspect, and the reformers waged verbal war on the supposed anarchy of medieval society. "Henceforth it was recognized that the child was not ready for life, and that he had to be subjected to a special treatment, a sort of quarantine, before he was allowed to join the adults." He had to be protected—and educated. Thus the two great events of the seventeenth century were the revival of education and the evolution of the family. "Family and school together removed the child from adult society." The new concept of family life also satisfied a craving for privacy and did away with the open society of the past; "it reinforced private life at the expense of neighborly relationships, friendships, and traditional contacts." It also gave rise to a class-consciousness that had not existed before. Life had been public and collective. Now the middle class in effect seceded from the lower class: "it withdrew from the vast polymorphous society to organize itself separately, in a homogeneous environment, among its families, in homes designed for privacy, in new districts kept free from all lower-class contamination." This transition was quickly forgotten, however, and it is common now to think that the family has always been the very foundation of our society— that it began to decay in the eighteenth century as a result of liberal individualism, and that it has continued its decline in the modern era. On the contrary, Ariès has decided, the family more likely has never been stronger; it was only in the recent past that the family came into being, freeing itself from biology and law to become "a value, a theme of expression, an occasion of emotion." And what is more, this new family was structured at first around the equally new concept of the child. It was not an abyss that was created but a pedestal. Every period in history appears to have had its privileged age, Ariès says. In the seventeenth century it was youth or the young man; in the eighteenth and nineteenth centuries it became the child; in the twentieth century it is the adolescent. Ariès adds his opinion:

The first typical adolescent of modern times was Wagner's [1869]

Siegfried: *the music of* Siegfried *expressed for the first time that combination of (provisional) purity, physical strength, naturism, spontaneity and joie de vivre which was to make the adolescent the hero of our twentieth century, the century of adolescence. What made its appearance in Wagnerian Germany was to enter France at a later date, in the years around 1900. The "youth" which at this time was adolescence soon became a literary theme and a subject of concern for moralists and politicians. People began wondering seriously what youth was thinking, and inquiries were made by such writers as Massis and Henriot. Youth gave the impression of secretly possessing new values capable of reviving an aged and sclerosed society. A like interest had been evidenced in the Romantic period, but not with such specific reference to a single age group, and moreover it had been limited to literature and the readers of that literature. Awareness of youth became a general phenomenon, however, after the end of the First World War, in which the troops at the front were solidly opposed to the older generation in the rear. The awareness of youth began by a feeling common to ex-servicemen, and this feeling was to be found in all the belligerent countries, even in the America of Dos Passos. From that point, adolescence expanded: it encroached upon childhood in one direction, maturity in the other. . . . Thus our society has passed from a period which was ignorant of adolescence to a period in which adolescence is the favorite age. We now want to come to it early and linger in it as long as possible.*

Adolescence of course could not emerge until childhood had, and it is, as indicated, a very recent phenomenon: a specific period of life that comes after childhood but before full adulthood. It has been produced in part by an extension of schooling, as was childhood before it, and also in part by military conscription (as Ariès has noted, age groups in our society tend to be organized around institutions: in this case the high school, the college, and the armed forces). And just as the origin of childhood was forgotten, so too was the origin of adolescence. The adolescent period was confused with puberty, which is a biological stage of development. It was assumed that adolescence is a restless and romantic condition of life that all young people must inevitably experience: a time of rebellion against authority, of philosophical perplexities, of flowering idealism, of conflict and struggle. It was precisely this point of view that sent the anthropologist Margaret Mead to Samoa in the 1920's. Her question: "Were these difficulties due to being adolescent or to being adolescent in America?"

Miss Mead studied the Samoan girls in particular and found that they passed painlessly from childhood to womanhood. She concluded: "The Samoan background which makes growing up so easy, so simple a matter, is the general casualness of the whole society. For Samoa is a place where no one plays for very high stakes. . . . No one is hurried along in life or punished harshly for slowness of development. Instead the gifted, the precocious, are held back, until the slowest among them have caught the pace. . . . Samoa is kind to those who have learned the lesson of not caring, and hard upon those few individuals who have failed to learn it." The Samoans had conventionalized the lack of deep feeling and made it the framework of all their attitudes toward life. Thus the inference: "where no one feels very strongly, the adolescent will not be tortured by poignant situations." There also was no sharp sense of difference between the concerns of children and adults in Samoa, and children at the age of four or five were required to perform definite tasks—running errands, carrying water—that were "functionally related to the world of adult activity." Nor was there any distinction in play activity. Children's play was like adults' play—dancing, singing, games—and children never translated adult activity into play: they did not play house or sail toy boats. A young boy "would climb into a real outrigger canoe and practice paddling it within the safety of the lagoon." By the time he was seventeen a boy could take a canoe over the reef safely; he could manage the stern paddle in a bonito boat, and had learned the rudiments of fishing; he could "plant taro or transplant cocoanut, husk cocoanuts on a stake and cut the meat out with one deft turn of the knife." And he was ready to join the *Aumaga*, the society of young men and older men without titles—the group that was called, and was in fact, "the strength of the village." Finally, as in medieval Europe, there was no institution comparable to the modern Western family. The Samoans avoided "the evils inherent in the too intimate family organization," and children from the first months of their life were "handed carelessly from one woman's hands to another's." A typical household consisted of a half-dozen adult women and a half-dozen adult males who shared all authority, and children did not sharply distinguish their actual parents. If nothing else, Miss Mead thought, this ruled out development of the Oedipus and Electra complexes.

In his classic study of magic and religion, *The Golden Bough*, the Scottish anthropologist Sir James George Frazer has left us a rich record of the puberty rites conducted by many primitive tribes. The primitive youth knew nothing of adolescence or the adolescent identity crisis; at puberty he was initiated at once into adulthood in a terrifying ceremony: a kind of tom-tom bar mitzvah. The most common of these rites simulated death and resurrection—a symbolic killing of the youth and bringing him to life again. In Australia and Northern New Guinea, for example, pubescent young men were swallowed and disgorged by a mock-up of a mythical monster whose voice was heard in the sound of a bull-roarer—a piece of wood that was swung round on a string to produce a loud humming noise.

For this purpose a hut about a hundred feet long is erected either in the village or in a lonely part of the forest. It is modelled in the shape of the mythical monster . . . and to complete the resemblance the butt end of the building is adorned by a native artist with a pair of goggle eyes and a gaping mouth. When after a tearful parting from their mothers and women folk, who believe or pretend to believe in the monster that swallows their dear ones, the awe-struck novices are brought face to face with this imposing structure, the huge creature emits a sullen growl, which is in

fact no other than the humming note of bull-roarers swung by
men concealed in the monster's belly.

Inside, the novices perhaps would pass under a scaffold on which a man would stand gulping water in a swallowing gesture. The gift of a pig would finally induce the monster to disgorge his victims, and the man on the scaffold would spit out the water onto the head of each novice. This signified that the young man had been released from the monster's stomach.

However, he has now to undergo the more painful and dangerous operation of circumcision. It follows immediately, and the cut made by the knife of the operator is explained to be a bite or scratch which the monster inflicted on the novice in spewing him out of his capacious maw. . . . When, as sometimes happens, a lad dies from the effect of the operation, he is buried secretly in the forest. . . . After they have been circumcised the lads must remain for some months in seclusion, shunning all contact with women and even the sight of them. They live in the long hut which represents the monster's belly. When at last the lads, now ranking as initiated men, are brought back with great pomp and ceremony to the village, they are received with sobs and tears of joy by the women, as if the grave had given up its dead. At first the young men keep their eyes rigidly closed or even sealed with a plaster of chalk, and they appear not to understand the words of command which are given them by an elder. Gradually, however, they come to themselves as if awakening from a stupor, and next day they bathe and wash off the crust of white chalk with which their bodies had been coated.

With the coming of the industrial era, children in America and in Europe were initiated into adulthood even before puberty —in some cases as early as nine or ten. They entered not a jungle hut, however, but the gaping doors of a mill. The boys who worked in the sweatshops were neither children nor adolescents; they were little men. Child labor, according to Ariès, "retained this characteristic of medieval society: the precocity of the entry into adult life." We tend to look back on this period now as if it were an aspect of ancient history, but living men remember it well—among them Ralph Frost, a veteran Chicago newspaper photographer who was born and reared in England. Frost worked in the coal mines, sailed as a merchant seaman, and finally worked his way to America.

"I grew up in South Shields," he says. "That was in Durham, up in the north country. The British system of free education ended then on your fourteenth birthday, whether you'd reached top grade or not—and that's when you graduated, so to speak. I left Stanhope Road School on September 11, 1919. That was a Thursday, and my fourteenth birthday. My parents gave me a pair of long pants, which meant I wasn't a boy any more—and nobody had better call me a boy. I was a man, that's what I was. Then on Monday I went to work on the belts at Bolden Colliery for one pound ten shillings a week. After two weeks on the belts I volunteered to go into the pit. I reported to the lamp cabin at 3:30 A.M., and they gave me my own personal Davy Safety Lamp, Number 1929, and I went down in the pit for two pounds one shilling a week. Hey! I was a man earning a man's paycheck!"

The young Frost had no opportunity to ask himself today's popular question, "Who am I?" He knew who he was. "I was a miner—a little miner, but a miner just the same." He was a workingman and, as such, a member of the laboring class; the paycheck was his passport to adulthood, and it established his identity. In today's semi-affluent and highly technical society, however, most young people wait much longer for that first paycheck—and for all that it implies. "The length of preparation for adulthood is increasing very steadily," says the psychologist Kenneth Keniston. "I'd guess about a year a decade, if you use education as the criterion." The economy can no longer absorb large numbers of unskilled workers; technical specialists require more preparation—and many parents in any case can now afford to subsidize a period of protracted adolescence (or intellectual

Technology and Adolescence

51

featherbedding, as it may be in some instances). Adolescence (like smog) can therefore be viewed as a by-product of the technological economy, in a real sense the creation of machines. In our modern culture it has come to mean a time of grace in which a young person is allowed to define himself psychologically and, after that, to find for himself what the analyst Erik H. Erikson has referred to as "a niche in some section of his society." Erikson is probably the most respected authority on adolescence and identity formation. He has described adolescence as a *psychosocial moratorium,* or a sanctioned delay of adult functioning. "It is a period that is characterized by a selective permissiveness on the part of society and [by] provocative playfulness on the part of youth, and yet it also often leads to deep, if often transitory, commitment on the part of youth, and ends in a more or less ceremonial confirmation of commitment on the part of society." Extrapolating from this, we can picture the older generation offering to strike a bargain with the younger generation, saying in effect: "Look, let's play a little game. You'll be something called teen-agers, and we'll be disapproving parents. You keep going to school, as long as you can, and while you're there you can put on funny clothes and listen to funny music; you can invent your own language, which we won't understand. We'll pretend to be shocked and dismayed. Just stay out of jail if you can, and don't get pregnant. And then when we're ready for you, we'll let you know."

Erikson writes:

Each society and each culture institutionalizes a certain moratorium for the majority of its young people. For the most part, these moratoria coincide with apprenticeships and adventures that are in line with the society's values. The moratorium may be a time for horse stealing and vision-quests, a time for Wanderschaft *or work "out West" or "down under," a time for "lost youth" or academic life, a time for self-sacrifice or for pranks — and today, often a time for patienthood or delinquency.*

One aspect of the moratorium is the *identity crisis*—a term that Erikson dimly recalls having minted during World War II in connection with "shellshocked" patients who had "lost a sense of personal sameness and historical continuity." The same central disturbance was later recognized "in severely conflicted young people whose sense of confusion is due, rather, to a war within themselves, and in confused rebels and destructive delinquents who war on their society." On the other hand, the typical adolescent crisis is by no means permanent or pathological; it is just a part of growing up, and crisis in this context denotes not an impending catastrophe but a "crucial moment" or a "necessary turning point" where an individual in his development must decide whether to move in one direction or another. The more severe disturbances are understood now to represent "a pathological aggravation, an undue prolongation of, or a regression to, a normative crisis 'belonging' to a particular stage of individual development. Thus, we have learned to ascribe a normative 'identity crisis' to the age of adolescence and young adulthood." Or as Erikson puts it elsewhere: "adolescence is not an affliction, but a *normative crisis*, i.e., a normal phase of increased conflict characterized by a seeming fluctuation in ego strength, and yet also by a high growth potential." The crisis in fact may be "contributive to the process of identity formation."

We will ask a bit later whether this crisis is really a normal phase after all. But first, using Erikson's conceptual framework, let us see how a young person today might attempt to resolve the crisis or otherwise react to it. A young American now poised on the brink of adulthood might be said to have at least five options open to him:

1. He can choose some social niche, satisfying or not, and make it his own. And possibly in so doing he will *foreclose* his identity by adopting a role with which he will permanently and exclusively identify himself—for example, an occupational role. This foreclosure can also be partial rather than complete, and it is possible to retain a receptive attitude toward the present and

future; it is possible always to grow. But such a decision usually implies some sort of lasting commitment, for better or worse.

2. He can bumble about in utter confusion. He can drop out of school, join a gang, or simply drift and kill time: read a lot of books, see a lot of movies, hang out at the pool hall or the library. He can grow up to be a helpless dilettante, dabbling in this and that, never really certain who or what he is. This is called *identity diffusion*, as opposed to *identity foreclosure*. It consists of a "marked avoidance of choices" and also "an excessive awareness of as well as abhorrence of competitiveness." And it recalls the predicament of Buridan's ass. That unfortunate animal found himself standing between two identical bales of hay, each of which looked equally delicious; unable to choose one or the other, he starved to death. In this connection, Margaret Mead attributed much of the adolescent neurosis in this country to the fact that American culture is "so charged with choice," which she called "the forerunner of conflict." Turning the same coin over: "Samoa's lack of difficult situations, of conflicting choice . . . will probably account for a large part of the absence of psychological maladjustment."

3. Our young American can adopt what Erikson has called a *negative identity*. This is "an identity perversely based on all those identifications and roles which, at critical stages of development, had been presented to the individual as most undesirable or dangerous and yet also the most real." What makes it attractive? "The history of such a choice reveals a set of conditions in which it is easier for the patient to derive a sense of identity out of a total identification with that which he is least supposed to be than to struggle for a feeling of reality in acceptable roles which are unattainable with his inner means." Thus a delinquent may fail to achieve a positive identity due to environmental pressures or constitutional factors, or both; but he feels the need for some kind of an identity, and society is quick to affirm the negative one when it slaps the youth into reform school and says, in effect: "Yes, punk, that's the real you, all right." What a relief to hear that. Perhaps this is why it is so difficult to

moralize with a delinquent about his conduct and attitude; if he agrees with you his whole existence seems threatened. According to Erikson, the lack of a positive identity might also express itself, for example, in a "general dislike for everything American and an irrational overestimation of everything foreign." In this case life and strength "seem to exist only where one is not." Or again, a negative identity may be dictated "by the necessity of finding and defending a niche of one's own against the excessive ideals either demanded by morbidly ambitious parents or indeed actualized by superior ones." This pattern of identity formation might be traced back to the fear-of-freedom syndrome, and it might explain in part the behavior of some gamblers, heroin addicts, and minor criminals. According to one theory, the compulsive gambler doubts his own ability to succeed in a competitive society; he therefore stakes his fortune on the turn of a card, or the speed of a horse, and this relieves him of any personal responsibility for making a wrong choice: the result can be blamed on a fickle Lady Luck. Similarly, it is argued that addicts and petty criminals are motivated to fail. One seldom sees a middle-aged heroin addict, and at least one study (at Cook County Jail in Chicago) indicates that misdemeanants generally turn honest when they reach middle age. Many addicts of course are simply killed off before middle age arrives, dead from overdoses and disease. But others do stop using drugs around the age of forty, and you will find them settled down, living in cheap hotels and holding some menial job: running an elevator perhaps, or doing custodial work. And the same is true of reformed criminals. They have their own explanation for this dropout phenomenon. As one morose addict put it one night, shortly before he was sentenced to a ten-year prison term that will doubtless end his drug career: "It just gets to be too much. All that Mickey Mouse with the police. All that hell and sweat to make a score and pay for that fix. Besides which the price keeps going up, and the quality of the stuff keeps going down. But mostly you're getting old, and you're getting tired, and you just can't hack it any more. It's easier to go straight." This seems plausible of course, but there also is another explanation. The dropout has achieved his ulterior purpose: he has smashed his life beyond all hope of repair, and nobody can expect him now to accomplish anything. He can run his elevator in peace. Other possible examples of this: the drunkard with his bottle (the supposed "cause" of his failure), and in some cases perhaps the radical with his manifesto. As Christopher Lasch said in one of his gloomy moments: "American leftists have to fail. They have a particular flair for it."

4. He can engage the society in open combat and make a strenuous effort to change it, declining meanwhile to enter it on its own terms. He can join the New Left.

5. He can reject the society as beyond all hope. He can drop out of the mainstream altogether and become a hippie or acidhead, seeking personal salvation in the supposed insights offered by psychedelic drugs. He may reject not only American society but Western civilization itself, turning instead to the religious and philosophical traditions of the East, perhaps to Hinduism or Zen Buddhism.

Most young people undoubtedly choose the first option—to find a niche in society—and hopefully a substantial number are able to do so without wholly foreclosing themselves. This has been the customary route to adulthood and the resolution of the adolescent identity crisis. According to Erikson and others, as we have seen, such a crisis is now considered a normal aspect of the adolescent years (usually thought of as the period from fourteen to eighteen). In adolescence proper, the crisis is considered abnormal only if there is an "undue prolongation."

As we also have seen, there has been a prolongation.

For many young people today the identity crisis extends well into their twenties. Some of these people no doubt are simply confused, and they might be assigned to the second of our five categories; others are serving long educational apprenticeships for specialized professions; still others have extended their educations simply to avoid the draft. But in many cases the prolongation of adolescence appears to be a matter of preference and an end in itself; in increasing numbers, young men and women are refusing to commit themselves to a well-defined psychosocial identity. In part this may reflect merely a desire to remain tentative, to explore the alternatives, to leave the doors of the personality wide open as long as possible. It may also in part reflect an angry reaction to the competitive pressures that have been exerted upon young people in recent years by their parents, the educational system, and society in general—pressures designed to rush them into the conformity of adulthood as quickly as possible, so they won't miss out when the technological goodies are distributed. But it also represents, in many cases, a basic rejection of the social structure as such; that is to say, the fourth option.

Whatever the reasons, the question remains: Is this prolongation "undue"?

One school of thought holds otherwise, and Kenneth Keniston has emerged as one of its principal spokesmen. He has argued in fact that we are witnessing the creation of a new psychosocial dimension in America: the introduction of a new stage of life that occurs between adolescence and adulthood. This idea is presented in his book *Young Radicals: Notes on Committed Youth,* in which Keniston examines the attitudes of some New Left activists who took part in the 1967 Vietnam Summer protest. Keniston concludes that these young people had already resolved what is normally thought of as the adolescent crisis. They had a sense of inner identity; they knew who they were and what they were good at; they had demonstrated an ability to succeed and excel in conventional fields, including academic work; they had come to terms with their sexuality, and they were capable of meaningful relationships with other people. By all criteria, they were indeed *psychological adults.*

And yet, they were *sociological adolescents.*

They rarely had spouses or children. They could work, and work hard, but they avoided all occupational commitments. They remained "deliberately uninvolved with the institutions, guilds, and organizations of their society." They had settled most of the basic questions that preoccupy the adolescent, but they had "not made the further commitment to occupation or to a lasting relationship with one other person that is said to be characteristic of adulthood." In short, they occupied "an uncharted stage of life" that has been "made possible by the affluence of the post-modern world, and made necessary by the ambivalence that world inspires in the most talented, thoughtful, principled, sensitive, or disturbed of those who have an adolescence." Keniston suggests that this new period might be called *"the stage of youth."*

As Keniston defines it, youth is "a further stage of development" after adolescence and before adulthood. It often lasts for almost a decade, spanning perhaps the ages eighteen to twenty-six. Keniston notes: "Upper-middle-class families in particular do not consider it alarming for their children to remain unemployed and unmarried until the age of thirty—as long as they are in school." Like adolescence, however, "youth is an option that society can only make possible: it is up to individuals whether they accept or refuse this option." Study in a graduate or professional school is only one way a youth may choose to defer his entry into sociological adulthood; he may become a "developmental dropout" and seek to "find himself" outside an institutional context; he may engage in independent study; he may join the Peace Corps or a protest organization; he may decide to be a hippie for a few years. In any case, job and marriage commitments are postponed while the young people ponder the conflicting claims of self and society; the fundamental question becomes their ultimate relationship to the established society: "deciding how, where, and whether they will enter it." Because youth must end someday. It is hardly possible, for example, to become a professional protester—not in a subculture where even a five-year age difference creates a generation gap. Besides which, the demands of full-time protesting virtually rule out a successful marriage and family life. And so at last youth comes to a close when the individual "moves into a more enduring social role." Some will find an obscure niche that suits them; maybe others will create a new niche in which they can in some way preserve their youthful commitments; some will feel they have "sold out." But Keniston seems to feel that most of them will benefit from their period of youth (or social moratorium), and if nothing else he thinks that none of them in their adulthood will ever become "blind loyalists to the status quo." He concludes:

These young men and women seek new forms of adulthood *in which the principled dedication of youth to the betterment of society can be continued in adult work. . . . They seek a new* orientation to the future, *one that avoids the fixed tasks and defined lifeworks of the past in favor of an openness and acceptance of flux and uncertainty. In their openness, they stress not ends but means, not goals but style, not programs but process, not the attainment of utopia but a* way *of doing things. . . . They seek new* values for living, *values that will fill the spiritual emptiness created by material affluence. . . . The new radicals are at least confronting the central issues of our time, and confronting them more directly than most of us can afford to. They are asking the basic questions, making the mistakes, and perhaps moving toward some of the answers we all desperately need. For this reason we should wish these young radicals success in their search. And more important, we should ourselves join in this search. For on its outcome rests not only the future quality of human life, but our very survival.*

Of course it also is possible to view these young people simply as Peter Pans who are reluctant to grow up—and Lewis Feuer in fact speaks of the radical student movement as "the last cry of the children, in despair at leaving the child's world, beholding in horror the competitive world of the adult." Talking about the youth idea, Bettelheim said: "That's very good. I wonder how Professor Keniston is going to feel if these youths break into his office and go into his private files." (To which Keniston replied, when told of the remark: "I would be furious if someone broke into my files, but no one has. Has anyone broken into Dr. Bettelheim's?")

Bettelheim added: "You know, this is all very nice in theory. But I think if you look back to your own adolescence—and I don't know if you can be objective; some people can and some people cannot—but looking backward it looks like a glorious time. When you're in it it's the most miserable time of life there can be. You are eaten up by tremendous insecurities, and typically you blame your own insecurity on society, on the father figures." In the same vein, the educator Joseph J. Schwab said of Keniston's youth period: "What in hell is so great about it? It seems to me that Keniston is caught up in the same thing that Erikson is; both of them trail along after Freud without taking a hard look at the frame, and they end up in the attempt to make what *is* the standard of what *ought* to be. The very phrase 'search for identity' is absurd, because identities are not found lurking in some odd corner you haven't looked in yet. They're made. And identity consists of what Erikson claims this youth group has, but which his own data seem to suggest they don't have. Identity is made when you have located and developed the competencies—the potential competencies you've got—and have made something of them, and have found a place in the environment where they make a difference."

On this same point, just for the record, I asked Erikson if *he* thought it was possible to be a psychological adult and a sociological adolescent. Keniston after all had told me that many of his ideas came from Erikson and that his youth theory was in part an "elaboration" of Erikson's work. "Erikson talks about the need to distinguish between early and late adolescence," said Keniston, "and one way of looking at what I'm trying to do at this point is to say, all right, you can even give them different names and talk about what Erikson calls late adolescence as a stage in its own right, rather than try to stretch adolescence from the age of twelve to thirty." Erikson responded: "I don't think you can in fact separate the sociological and the psychological. Since my concept is psychosocial, obviously you can't separate the two."

Bettelheim's statement in particular suggests a possible approach to the question of a separate stage of youth. Bettelheim is saying in effect, how can youth be any good when adolescence is so rotten? Or to rework the question in a neutral framework: if youth is an extension of adolescence, how healthy a stage is adolescence itself? Even in our own culture, is adolescent trauma really normal? Is the identity crisis worth having—does it enhance development—or is it simply a noxious excrescence of technological affluence?

Adolescence has its critics—prominent among them, Peter Blos and Carl Frankenstein. The latter in fact has diagnosed adolescence as a kind of cultural disease, not a stage of development but indeed "an interruption of developmental continuity" and a "retreat from maturity." Frankenstein in his study *The Roots of the Ego* is especially critical of the adolescent tendency "to live with principles." On every level, he writes, the adolescent "seeks to replace the concrete with the abstract, the friend with friendship, fair behavior with justice, the way towards realization of a task with anticipation of the goal. . . . The future is regarded as a perpetuation of a consummate present; it is experienced as already known, hence also as capable of being anticipated: principles are eternal, are beyond the dimensions of time. It is this unrealistic time concept that makes of adolescence a period of *staticness*. The adolescent himself, it is true, tends to indulge in exactly the opposite illusion: that his 'life with principles' is an essentially dynamic existence which is contradicted by the adults as the guardians of traditional values and demands." Thus the central symptom of adolescence is "the illusion of finality," which includes "the abandonment of reality in favor of principles."

The life with principles is not only "absurdly impracticable," it also is most unsatisfactory from a developmental viewpoint. "Abstraction as an exclusive mode of orientation isolates man not only from his environment but also from himself, from [his] own ego." The ego, after all, grows by testing reality, not by denying it. Adolescent abstractness and the unrealistic life of principles can result only in existential despair, and from this there are only three ways out: "suicide, psychotic withdrawal from reality, or giving up the abstract mode of orientation." The third solution is the rule. "But it is not easy to return to a reality which the adolescent has been neglecting or even treating with contempt for a number of years. His integrity is likely to suffer damage in the process." His vitality sapped by the adolescent period, he is in danger now of sinking into adult triviality—he may become what he had hated, his adult life guided by the cold ideals of objectivity and compromise. Health is balance, and normalcy does not arise merely from organizational ego strength. "Normalcy manifests itself in creativeness, in the courage to face new and changing conditions, in empathy and love, and in the ability to evaluate reality objectively, though the thus evaluated reality may be found to deserve negation and transformation." Frankenstein emphasizes that his criticisms of adolescence apply only to Western middle-class society, and he adds: "In the majority of human careers, however, that is, in most lower-class and in most rural families, the beginning of adulthood is almost undefinable in terms of age, and the slowness and gradualness of transition finds its expression in the absence of adolescent interruption of continuity and in immediate utilization of childhood achievements for adult adjustment."

Bettelheim found this to be true in the kibbutzim, where children are largely separated from their parents and reared in communal peer groups. If nothing else, the kibbutz experiment has demonstrated the inadequacy of Freud's biological orientation. By environmental control, the Israelis have created a radically new personality type in a single generation. Kibbutz children work hard, but their ultimate social role is assured them (the labor committee will decide the matter). They have almost no privacy and therefore almost no inner life, to the point that their egos and superegos appear to be collective rather than personal; there is so little individuation—the young people are so completely other-directed—that it is difficult to tell where one person ends and another begins. There is no solitude, no loneliness—and no identity crisis. Identity is defined by the community, and the kibbutz-born individual "is essentially himself when among others." Bettelheim certainly does not mention any tendency to live a life with principles, which may support Frankenstein's assumption that this tendency arises from intimacy ties with parents. Frankenstein writes that a life with principles and a moratory existence are possible only in a personalistic family climate. This in turn might seem to support Ariès' view that the modern concepts of childhood and adolescence have their origin in the evolution of the family.

But let us look at our own society. Margaret Mead suggested that adolescent turmoil resulted from being an adolescent in America, and she found no evidence of such turmoil in Samoa. But other researchers have since gone on to ask if turmoil is necessarily a typical aspect even of American adolescence. The idea that turmoil is inevitable seems to have been introduced early in this century by the American psychologist Granville Stanley Hall, who was the first to describe adolescence as a period of *Sturm und Drang* (storm and stress). Disruptive factors also were emphasized later by Anna Freud and others, who characterized adolescence as a time when the ego is weakened and the id forces reassert themselves. More recently, however, the psychoanalytic school has been criticized for basing its conclusions on clinical examples—studying disturbed adolescents and then projecting the results to describe teen-agers in general: making the abnormal the standard of normalcy. In a study referred to earlier, for example, Daniel Offer observed a number of teen-age boys over the four-year period they were in high school (the Modal Adolescent Project) and concluded that significant turmoil is by no means inevitable—or even common. Identity conflicts in the vast majority of the subjects ranged from mild to moderate, and in fact only a few subjects displayed even "the Eriksonian type" of normative identity crisis.

The subjects were from middle-class homes in two Chicago suburbs, Evanston and Park Forest, and almost 90 per cent of them planned to attend college. For the most part they shared their parents' middle-class values, and they seldom rebelled against parental authority—except for minor bickering that occurred mostly in early adolescence. Twelve and thirteen were the most difficult years, and most of the subjects had cooled off by the time they entered high school. They were not given to violent mood swings; they moved through their adolescence slowly but surely, without volcanic eruptions, edging toward independence and adulthood in almost microscopic steps, only gradually detaching themselves from their parents. Offer, in explaining this, referred back to the theory of a German psychiatrist, E. Spranger, who held that there are actually three routes from adolescence to adulthood: the route of turmoil described by Hall, growth in spurts, and a pattern of gradual development. Offer's group took the third route, and Offer suggested that "the antecedent of a nonturmoil path through adolescence is a nonstressful childhood." Offer found nothing to support the idea of an adolescent subculture that breeds its own value system. "The teen-agers we have studied were by and large an integral part of the culture within which they lived. They were proud of their schools, their communities, and the achievements of their parents." And vice versa. "It is our impression that, for better or for worse, the sample investigated by us is growing up to become very much a part of the culture into which they were born." They were not an idealistic group: "they were not going out of their way to work for a cause." Offer reported his findings in the book *The Psychological World of the Teen-ager: A Study of Normal Adolescent Boys* (1969). In discussing the group later, Offer estimated that they represent "about a third to 40 per cent of suburban teen-agers who are middle class." A follow-up study was conducted during the college years. "Although the subjects are shifting their object relationships," Offer found, "they are not discarding their parents' basic value system. Our subjects are not in open rebellion against the traditional values of the American society. The vast majority are not visible in the social field; they do not demonstrate, take drugs, or engage in delinquent activities. Though they might object to the war in Vietnam, all will go if drafted."

Proving what?

Keniston for one never claimed that his youth group represents a majority of young Americans. On the contrary, he has rather unfortunately referred to them as "clearly an elite." They are "psychologically, socially, and economically privileged, and often possessed of unusual talent and vitality." Keniston acknowledges that most young people move directly from adolescence to adulthood, if they have an adolescence at all. He grants that most of them are not radicals, dissenters, hippies, dropouts, protesters, or activists. He is perfectly willing to concede that Offer's young people are alive and well in Evanston and Park Forest. In fact, if Offer's subjects are not in rebellion against the values of their parents, neither are the radicals. A number of studies have clearly established that the radicals tend to come from liberal middle-class homes; they are attempting "to fulfill and renew the political traditions of their families." And the parents for the most part are likely to applaud their activist offspring—endorsing their motives if not always their tactics.

Again, proving what?

Indeed, as Daniel Freedman keeps asking: *What is the question?*

We will try to locate the central question of the youth moratorium. In the meanwhile, we have set the stage now for a debate that may help to clarify the answer, if there is one.

Two worthy opponents are waiting to be heard.

In one corner, Richard Flacks.

In the other, Bruno Bettelheim.

Rashomon: Bettelheim and Flacks

Among the many buildings seized by students in 1969 was the Administration Building at the University of Chicago. Several hundred students occupied the building and held it for fifteen days. The immediate source of their discontent was the University's refusal to renew the contract of Marlene Dixon, an assistant professor of sociology and human development, who was described by the *Chicago Tribune* as "an ultra-leftist radical." The University denied that her dismissal and her political views were in any way connected. The student body in general appeared to have little interest in the Dixon dispute; most students favored amnesty for the rebels, however, and most of them hoped the University would not call on the police to clear the captured building. Inside the building the invaders held liberation classes and press conferences, played phonograph records, and waited for the administration to make a move that might radicalize the campus. It was a boring business, as these affairs usually are.

During the course of it, however, one of the Chicago newspapers printed a brief but interesting item headlined: PROF CALLS SIT-IN 'MASS PARANOIA.'

The Prof was Bruno Bettelheim, the University's Stella M. Rowley professor of education, professor of psychology, professor of psychiatry, and director of the Sonia Shankman Orthogenic School. He was quoted as remarking that some protesters were acting very much like stormtroopers. The story also carried a one-sentence rebuttal from one of the few faculty members who supported the sit-in, Richard Flacks, assistant professor of sociology and director of the Youth and Social Change Project. Flacks had been one of the founding members of the Students for a Democratic Society. According to the newspaper, his reply to Bettelheim was: "That's a bunch of bull." I asked the two men if they would care to expand the debate—in separate interviews —and they said they would.

Bettelheim was sitting behind his desk at the Shankman School, on the University Midway, his feet propped up on the windowsill, peering out at the dusk. The office was clean and functional, the desk clear of papers. The lights had been turned on. Bettelheim looked tired. He sent for a pot of coffee, some tea, and a tray of cookies. His tea arrived in a steaming mug inscribed *Doctor B*. As he sipped at it he continued to stare out the window in the direction of the Administration Building, on the other side of the Midway; it is possible his thoughts had gone for a moment to the year he spent in Dachau.

Q. Dr. Bettelheim, you described some of the sit-in demonstrators as paranoiacs and said some of them act like stormtroopers. A number of people, including Richard Flacks, have accused you of psychologizing a social or political issue.

A. First, I would agree with Mr. Flacks that this to a considerable degree is a political movement. It is a movement where some of the leaders have decided that at this moment the university is a fulcrum, or whatever you want to call it—a lever—that can be used in a revolutionary way to radically change existing society. And I think this is one element that cannot be overlooked.

I got in response to what was written in the newspaper a long letter from a student in another university, in the East. He writes me a long letter from which I will only quote: "I hope you will admit that some student dissenters are not just acting out but, having understood rationally how American society in its present form is destructive of humanity, they have become revolution-aries—(underlined)—in the noble line which extends from Spartacus to Patrick Henry to José Martí to Lenin to Che Guevara and onward—all dedicated to the single vision of establishing a society which will visibly be worth living in." Unquote.

Well, let's look at the society which Lenin established. I think nobody can doubt Lenin's idealism. But I think if I would now say that Stalin was a paranoiac I'd be believed when I said that. When he came to power I was much maligned by the left. I think that everybody's concern with this movement—including my own, and Professor Flacks'—is conditioned by his own up-bringing, his own childhood, and his own life experiences and what he made of them. Now, I lived through the Nazi time in Austria and Germany. And don't forget for a moment that many of the Nazis, particularly among the students who were the earliest followers, were motivated by what they considered idealistic motives. They felt that the Germany of then was—as this young man puts it—destructive of humanity.

Q. The young man left out a few revolutionaries?

A. That's right. Hitler, or Napoleon—or I should rather say St. Just, because these students are much more like St. Just of the French Revolution. They tried too to establish a new religion of rationality—and they killed millions in its image. I said Hitler was a paranoiac, I said many of his followers were paranoiacs. I was then criticized for psychologizing politics. And I see here the same thing happen.

I think it's much too early to say whether this will blow over, whether we'll all be very happy, whether this will lead to a fascism of the left, like Lenin and Stalin, or a fascism of the right, like Hitler. Because in the early days, before the Nazis took over the universities, the Communists tried to take them over. For a time it was hit or miss who would win—the fascists of the left or the fascists of the right.

Q. Psychologically the same animal?

A. Very much so. And that's why so many Nazis now can have high positions in the East German government.

Let's face it. In every society created by man a lot of things are wrong. It is very easy to see what's wrong, and it's the privilege of the young person to see only what's wrong. It's the responsibility of the mature person to ask what can we put in its place that we are reasonably sure is better.

I do not wish to talk about the group which at this moment is sitting in the Administration Building. I don't even know who they are. But I have as a psychoanalyst worked with several, a small group of these extreme student activists. I've studied them intimately for several years, so therefore I know what motivates them. So I had taken this stand—the psychologizing stand—long before what happened here.

Q. What is the psychology of the activist?

A. Well, firstly, they hate themselves so much. And they are so unable to make a go in this world that they feel the only way they can make a go in this world is by destroying it, so the cares in the external world will be comparable with the cares in the inner world.

Q. Negative identity?

A. That's right. So you see to me, as a psychoanalyst, their behavior is an extreme defensive maneuver to avoid a total, a complete break with reality. If I cannot manage reality as it is, either I can change myself—that's hard work—or I can try to change reality in my image. Which is exactly what a paranoiac is trying to do, whether he's called Hitler or by any other name.

Q. Then you'd agree essentially with Eric Hoffer, that the true believer is an insecure person trying to lose himself in a mass movement?

A. That's right. I think this is as good a formulation as any. It depends on whether you look from the inside out or the outside in. But now I'll say something—I'll have to be careful.

But some of my colleagues have called adolescence a state of temporary insanity, and there is just a little bit of truth to it. I wouldn't call it that. But at various moments in our life we undergo certain developments which threaten our identities, threaten our grip on reality and make us extremely susceptible to the influence of paranoiac ideas. These temptations are tremendously attractive, because they're always very easy solutions, they're always black and white solutions. And you know at certain moments we just have to feel we're on the side of the angels, and it's very comfortable to think you're on the side of the angels. But let me take a little broader perspective.

These are what—maybe 200 or 250 out of 8,400 students? So I don't think we should overestimate them. What scares me is that adult society takes what they say seriously. That boys will be boys and sow their wild oats, I think this we should be able to take with equanimity. But we should not permit them to make irremediable damage; we should not permit them to prevent serious ongoing work. Otherwise, let boys be boys.

I think if a considerable majority of students say this University, while it meets some of their needs, is very uncomfortable for them, I think they are right. If they say higher education is in need of radical reformation, I think they are right. I think it is unnatural to keep a young person for some twenty years in dependency. Or in school. I think this is unnatural. I think this might be a way of life for a small elite which always in the past went to universities. There were those who could go to school for twenty years. But they were never more than a small percentage of the population. Now we have the tremendous push that everybody should go to college. It has brought an incredibly large number of kids into the university who do *not* find their self-realization through study, or the intellectual adventure.

Q. Therefore they try to change the nature of the university?

A. Therefore they think they need to find their early manhood, if I may use this term. They try to change the university to something where they can find their early manhood. Only that is no longer an institution dedicated to the intellectual virtues, to the frontiers of knowledge. It becomes a therapeutic institution which really is asked to do an impossible task: namely, to meet the needs of an adolescent age group in ways that they cannot be met.

Q. There didn't use to be adolescence, did there?

A. That's right. There was puberty. Puberty is a physiological process, the growing of the sex glands, the beginning of sex secretion and all that, the development of the body. Puberty exists in all societies. Adolescence exists only when a fully pubertal human being is kept in dependency—and somebody else foots the bill. And I'll tell you, if you ask, why we didn't have student revolts before. Because those students who had to put themselves through school, by the very fact that they could *do* that, of their own strengths, could prove their early manhood—at least to some degree. Now we pay them to go to school. Which makes them dependent when they should be, psychologically speaking, independent. And this is a very hard thing to take. Therefore they try to prove their manhood in totally irrational ways.

Q. Studies indicate that student radicals tend to come from educated, middle-class families in which the parents are very liberal politically. According to one theory, the students are simply trying to fulfill and renew their liberal traditions—or in some cases they may try to establish a separate identity by out-radicalizing their liberal parents.

A. That's right. Again I will be accused of psychologizing. But I think many of these kids and followers and sympathizers of all ages have never solved what we call the Oedipal conflict. They are still having to beat down father to show they are a big boy.

Somebody asked me once, if I think these young people have to assert their masculinity and independence, well, isn't that good what they do? I asked him if he had a son. I said, look, your son needs to become independent of you. He needs to assert his independence from you. Would you therefore suggest that a suitable way for him to do so is to beat up you, his father? That's nuts. And I think a father who enjoys his son beating him up, because this gives him a feeling of independence, such a father is nuts—to use the vernacular.

I think many of these radical students are essentially guilt-ridden individuals. They feel terribly guilty about all the advantages they've had. And there's also the guilt of their exemption from the draft, which is a serious guilt. Only again, they cannot bear to live with their guilt. They try to destroy society or certain institutions rather than deal with their own inner guilt, because they've had it so good. And so, out of their guilt, and out of their *identification* with their parents, they try both to please the parents and to beat them down at the same time. They please them by following the parents' kind of teaching—and they beat them down by carrying it to extreme lengths.

But let me tell you, exactly the same situation was true for the students who followed Hitler in the early days. They came from conservative, nationalistic, upper middle-class parents, in the vast majority. And they too took their parents' ideal—German nationalism—and carried it to extremes that destroyed society.

Q. A mirror image of the New Left?

A. That's right. That's right. As a matter of fact, I was just reading up these days to refresh my memory on the days of the Weimar Republic. And you know here that one of the demands is that special professorships—chairs, divisions—should be appointed to study this particular, that particular minority group. Well, I think we are studying minority groups already. But one of the first demands that were made by the Nazi students where the university was caved in was for chairs for the science of the race. Now, nobody talked more about the soul—the German soul, you understand, which will cure all the evils of the world because it's such a superior soul. Then it was the German soul. Now we have just added "soul," in quotation marks. This is the *mirror* image of what happened in Germany—with of course those variations that it's forty years later, you know, and it's the United States, and so on.

Q. Studies of the radical-producing homes also tend to show a very warm identification of the son with a strong, nurturant mother who often is the dominant personality in the family. The father in many cases may be professionally successful, but—

A. But real weak in the home. Exactly. And I think one of the characteristics of those I studied was tremendous anxiety about their masculinity—and therefore through violence, and violent aggression to parental authority, they try to demonstrate to themselves and to their colleagues that contrary to their anxieties they're really strong he-men.

Q. Does this kind of family also tend to produce homosexuals in some cases?

A. Yes. But you know, Freud has remarked that all very strongly organized boys, or adolescent society—it has a very strong homosexual element. But as you know, as a matter of fact the girls are much more radical than the boys in these movements. And in many ways, that has to do with the pressure to go to college, to go and compete and to strive. This is a little bit even more against the nature of the woman than it is against the nature of the man. My concern is, are we going to permit them out of their adolescent turmoil to destroy the society, as they were permitted to do in Germany?

Q. What about the permissiveness theory? Demand feeding and all that. This is the generation that was picked up whenever they cried, and now they continue to demand instant gratification. Do you buy it?

A. There is a lot of truth to that. You don't have to convince me that these kids are the result of what their parents made out of them. But the interesting thing is, if you look at some of them anyway, who their ideals are—it's Mao, or it's Ho Chi Minh. They chant Ho Ho Ho Chi Minh, as you know—it's like a football rally of the past. But the most strict dictators are their ideals—those who do not permit dissension, who do not permit discussion. Because these are the strong fathers they really wanted to have, they never had, and they want to have sometime in their lives.

Q. I assume then that you would agree with the theory that young people who challenge authority are really asking for authority—that they fear their freedom and are, in a sense, actually pleading for limits?

A. That's right. Absolutely. They ask for the limits. I'm running a treatment institution. I've been running it for a quarter of a century. And I know that what all young people need is certainly understanding, certainly gentle handling—but within firm limits. Because, as one of my delinquents said after we had cured him, he said: "You can't grow up if there are no walls to push against." And then, after a thought, he said: "But you can't grow up either if the walls give way when you push against them." Everything I know I learned from these children.

But in this culture— You know Neill at Summerhill, this school in England? It advocated, supposedly you know, a tremendous amount of freedom. And there was a Summerhill movement in this country. And when Neill was asked about it, he said: "All my life I have preached freedom, and what my American followers make out of it is chaos."

Another thing we have done. We have taken away all those institutions in the colleges where adolescents typically could be adolescents: the fraternities, the drunken party on a weekend, the visit to the red-light district. Do I have to go on? The football rally. All those things that are very important for boys to be boys, we have taken away. I think that was very unfair to them. I think what is needed is a ritualization and a reorganization of the adolescent life on the campuses. But not to let them take over the universities.

Q. You went along with the permissive idea, but—

A. Well, it's not quite as simple as that. The point is much more complicated. These parents took out of psychoanalysis what fit their own emotional needs, or shall we say their own neurosis. And it's true they picked him up each time the kid cried. On the other hand, they were more demanding than any Victorian parent possibly could have been. I'm talking about these families I know very well, because I've had their children here. These were not the families that beat down their children. But it only looks on the surface that they indulged their children. Actually they indulged them where it was convenient for the parents, where it met their own neurosis.

The point is the following. "I indulge you now. But for that you have to be the brightest kid in school. Haven't I let you have the bottle? Now you go and be a whiz in school." That is why these kids are so torn to pieces.

Let me give you an example. Toilet training. You have children? All right. You know toilet training is a problem. You remember? Okay. Now, I was brought up in the Victorian sense. I recall that because I recalled it in my analysis. I checked it with my parents. What was the typical situation there? The parents didn't like the mess—very few parents love the mess. After a certain age, you know. So at a certain time my parents made up their minds that it's time I became toilet trained. You know what I mean? There were no buts and ifs and whens. I was toilet trained, and I was toilet trained in about two weeks. Because there was no back and forth about it; it was *it,* and it was pretty tough on me. But in two weeks it was *all over.*

The modern parents kind of let their kid decide whether or not he wants to toilet train. They say: "Do what you want. But by golly, you know, it's time that you do it." They say: "Oh, it's all right, you know, to make in your pants." But then they are *disgusted.* So the poor kid now has to deal with this problem for six months or a year. And what does he get out of it? He gets out of it the following: "My parents are nice parents. But I am a disgusting individual." So that isn't lenient training. It's neurotic training. And this is what, as adolescents, tears these kids apart.

I've always said when I see some of these hippies, unkempt and unwashed: I know this was a kid who as an infant was scrubbed nearly out of existence. While we in our time were not expected to make big messes, neither did our parents think that cleanliness is next to godliness. They knew that kids are dirty. But these modern parents say: "Oh, it's perfectly all right just to mess in the mud." But then they dump the kid right away in the tub. And these contradictions are what ail our youth. This is why so many of these troublesome young people come from educated, enlightened, upper middle-class families.

Q. What about your analogy to the German family? Wasn't the Nazi-to-be reared in a nonpermissive home dominated by a strict father?

A. Not quite. Father had to fight in World War I, you know. The Hitler movement cannot be understood without understanding that these young people who spearheaded the movement grew up with their fathers away during the crucial years of their upbringing. Many of these fathers were killed, and many were in Russian prisons—gone for six or seven years.

Q. And mama was ruling the roost?

A. And mama was ruling the roost, yes.

Q. How would you sum up your reaction to the sit-in?

A. Radical adolescents act like radical adolescents have acted since time immemorial. There were societies that fell in with it, and these societies were destroyed. Nobody is more deeply committed to freedom than I. But freedom to me means that nobody—unless a legally constituted authority—has a right to force his will on me. And I have no right to force my will on others. I think students should make their opinions heard, I think they should be carefully listened to, I think anything they say should be taken into most careful consideration. But I don't think they should be permitted to coerce anybody.

Let me end by saying I have sympathy with the students. I have much greater sympathy and respect for those who do the hard work of getting an education. I even have sympathy for the students who took over the Administration Building. My impatience is with those adults who do not recognize youthful immaturity and extreme stances for what they are and think: this is the wave of the future, or higher maturity, or higher knowledge. And most of all I have absolutely no *respect* for adults who let young and immature people trample the most valuable institutions of our society in the dirt.

The office of Richard Flacks was located high in one of the Gothic towers of Harper Library on the University of Chicago campus. Wet snowflakes drifted down, sticking to the window-pane. A slushy, dismal afternoon. The gloomy little room was cluttered with books and papers, the walls plastered with revolutionary poster art. Flacks sat in the half-light, talking softly: a youngish man of mild if not meek appearance, no tie and his collar open. He looked tired and unhappy. He opened a fresh pack of cigarettes and lit one.

Q. Dr. Bettelheim has compared the sit-in here with the effort of German students to take over the universities during the Hitler movement. How do you react to that?

A. He's isolating from his own experience. We've had student movements everywhere in the world, not just in Nazi Germany. Some of them were precursors to social disaster, but many were precursors to all kinds of social renovation. Virtually every Third World country one can think of—countries in Latin America and Asia and Africa—have had strong student movements that have had renovative effects on society. Practically every major social transformation in the industrial era has been accompanied by student uprisings that included disruption of the universities. I think it would be hard to claim that the inevitable outcome of student uprisings is some kind of dictatorship. What Bettelheim seems to be afraid of more broadly is the willingness of people to take strong and coercive action on behalf of their beliefs. I think he has a responsibility to state to the students what would be an alternative that would provide them with some hope of accomplishing change within both the university and the larger society. On the whole, the kind of action the students have taken here usually comes after long efforts to accomplish change by more conventional means. If Dr. Bettelheim wants to claim there are other alternatives for the students, I wish he'd say what they are.

Q. What is your own view of the situation here?

A. Well, I think psychology is hardly relevant. I think the

root of society's difficulties has to do on the one hand with America's international role and on the other hand with the problem of racism within the society. And the university's a *part*, then, of that kind of society—a society with imperialist inclinations and racist institutions. And then you have a student body that has become increasingly disaffected from both of those aspects of American life—deeply concerned about inequality and deeply concerned about war. And they demand of the university critical independence. They demand of it that it be a place in which they can work out their relationship to the society—where they're not programmed to go into the existing society but can work out a way to be independent and autonomous and perhaps dissident within the larger society. Those are the kinds of *expectations* they have of the university. And they have them because the university *claims* to be that kind of place. It claims to be independent; it claims to be a place where men can think through the meaning of their lives and work out a life for themselves. What the students discover, however, is largely the reverse. They discover that to a great extent they're being programmed, and they're being programmed to play roles of domination in the society when they don't want to be people of domination. That is, they don't want to be controlling a society which they regard as in many ways immoral, or moving toward a state of decay.

Q. A one-dimensional society?

A. Yeah. And it's interesting why so many young people should have these kinds of impulses—that is, to break away from a society they define as corrupt. I think it does have to do with certain aspects of family life, but not the kinds of things that people like Dr. Bettelheim are pointing to. It has to do with the fact that many American middle-class families preach the idea of equality, the idea of being of service to other people, the idea of living a life based on reason and intelligence and humanism. And then their children find no coherent way to implement those values in either the university or the larger society. Now that to me is the heart of the difficulty, the heart of the crisis: this clash between the aspirations of youth for the university and what the university actually is, in a society which is morally dubious, to say the least.

Q. I believe you and Dr. Bettelheim would agree essentially on the socioeconomic structure of the radical-producing family. But I assume, for example, that you would not agree with his views on parental permissiveness.

A. It isn't that people have been instantly gratified, in my view, that is important in this situation. It's that they've been treated, and have developed expectations about treatment, in an autonomous fashion. The parents were not simply gratifying them. Many of these parents were providing them with the opportunity to work out certain solutions for themselves, with the opportunity to speak their minds freely. I say generally we've created this kind of a family structure in America. Within their own families, then, these young people have been led to expect that authority generally will be based on egalitarian principles, that it will be respectful of persons, that there will not be harsh or rigid hierarchical structures. That's what I see as the relationship between family upbringing and the current unrest among this generation. They've been bred with certain expectations about how the world ought to be. And those expectations are, I believe, democratic ones. And yet the young people find outside the family that the institutions they become involved with—schools, work bureaucracies, the army—are not those kinds of institutions at all, and that is the source of the unrest. And then that gets coupled with deep worries about the future of his society, indeed the world, due to the problems of nuclear war, the problems of war generally, and the problem of race. So the social crisis reinforces this unrest about the nature of authority.

Also, these parents were not people who demanded nothing of their kids. They demanded a great deal. They demanded a great deal of intellectual output; they demanded a great deal of social responsibility.

Q. Dr. Bettelheim made that same point—but reached a

different conclusion. He suggested the parents push the kids too hard, for neurotic reasons, and the kids can't stand the pressure when they arrive at the university.

A. Well, how would Dr. Bettelheim explain the young man who came to see me yesterday, who said he felt he had to drop out of school in order to learn philosophy? And that since he dropped out he'd had the opportunity to read Wittgenstein and other philosophers that were not being taught in his philosophy classes?

I might add one comment about Dr. Bettelheim. Is he acting in a professional and responsible way by making these kinds of allegations and interpretations of student behavior without to my knowledge ever having close up witnessed or observed the actual nature of the student movement, without to my knowledge actually doing extensive interviews or studies of the students or their families? I mean, on what grounds does he have the right to make psychological accusations against these people? I am sure if *I* leaped to psychological or other conclusions about these students without having studied them the roof would come down on my head. I feel I can make these kinds of statements because I'm backed by the authority of systematic research—and direct observation. I don't know what authority he has, other than a title.

Q. He said he was speaking generally about activists and their families he has worked with as a psychoanalyst. Would you—

A. Those are the people who went to see him because they needed therapy. He's getting pathological people—people who need therapy. And that's a very important fact. He has a biased view of the situation due to the people he's been talking to.

Q. Dr. Bettelheim suggested that the drive for universal education has filled the universities with young people who are not able to affirm their early manhood through academic study— so they protest.

A. Well, I think that's very superficial. First of all, what we have found repeatedly—and perhaps Dr. Bettelheim would be shocked by this—is that when you look at those who sit in and protest you find that a very large porportion of them are the very students who have decided to take academic careers. That is, they're not the people who are peripheral to academic life; they're the very people who are interested in staying within the university. So if this hypothesis were correct, you'd expect the future college professors, the kids who are oriented toward that, to be least active in this sort of situation. Actually they're the most active. And in the crisis here, one of the most active portions of the University have been the graduate student bodies, the people who are already involved in preparing themselves for future academic work. And I claim it is not that they are dissatisfied with academic life because they don't belong there. They're dissatisfied with the tradition that Dr. Bettelheim wants to uphold—a tradition which is essentially indifferent to the moral and social crises in the society, if not actually contributing to the moral and social crises.

You take a young man who wants to be a sociologist. He's committed to that because he wants to engage in criticism of the existing society and wants to work on behalf of racial equality and so forth. He discovers he's being programmed for a career in which he's aiding the managers. In which he's supporting the social order rather than trying to criticize it. That is the heart of the problem at a university like Chicago, not the problem of kids who don't belong here. Now, I agree there should be many other opportunities for self-fulfillment and self-development than simply a college education. But that would not necessarily solve the problem of the university in terms of its student body.

Q. Dr. Bettelheim describes radicals as, in many cases, guilt-ridden individuals. Do you think that's valid?

A. Well, I'm not sure what's referred to by guilt. What the race question has done to the most sensitive people in the society is to make them aware that their own privilege is based on the degradation of other human beings. Once you assimilate that fact—and I believe it is a fact, not just a feeling—then you are compelled to figure out some way of resolving that crisis; it becomes a personal crisis for you. And I suppose guilt would be expressed through charity, through some way of trying to ameliorate the condition of the poor while preserving your own situation. I would say that is not characteristic of the political activist. What's characteristic of him is the desire to abolish the whole situation in which one group is privileged and one group is degraded. And I wouldn't say that guilt is the primary motivation there. It's more a sense that one is caught in an intolerable position morally—and if you want to call that guilt, fine. But I think guilt implies expiation, which means giving money or other kinds of support.

Q. Something to make your conscience feel good, as opposed to a rational moral judgment?

A. I think that's a good way of putting it.

Q. There's also the implication that the radical in a sense is externalizing his inner devils. He really hates himself, but he turns that hate on targets in the external world.

A. Well, any social movement—whether it's against alcohol or for racial equality—any cause-oriented group is likely to have a considerable amount of self-righteousness, at least in its public presentation. But I believe—and this may mark me then as one of Dr. Bettelheim's paranoiacs—I believe there are actual men who make actual decisions that are dangerous and destructive to many human beings. Of course these men are caught in social systems which may limit their freedom of action. But certainly unless there is resistance to them and to the institutions they represent their actions will go on.

If I define the Pentagon as an enemy of mankind and of the American people, I don't think that's especially paranoid. And if I stop defining it that way the Pentagon will be permitted, I think, to undertake much more destructive activity than it undertakes even now. So there is a certain very important social function in knowing who the enemies of one's values and aspirations are, and in resisting and fighting against them.

On the other hand, one is struck by the fact, when you talk to a typical New Left activist, they have a sense of humanity with respect even to their opponents. Many of them of course do not. But I think in general they have a sense of their own moral limitations. The young people of this generation have learned an awful lot from the twentieth century. They may be ignorant of a lot of history, but they've learned an awful lot. There is no mass enthusiasm for heroes, and there is no mass hatred in this generation. There is a deep pessimism, I think, about the future—and a desire to resist that future—but not this overweening sense of right against absolutely hated objects.

Q. Dr. Bettelheim said some radicals admire certain revolutionary dictator types because they're shopping psychologically for a stern, authoritarian father figure. Any truth to that?

A. It's a myth to say that these people have adopted some set of heroes that they are in absolute adoration of. There are groups within the New Left that believe, say, as between the Soviet Union and Red China, as far as social revolution goes, it's better to opt for the Chinese. And they are rather orthodox Marxists, quite rigid in their ideological formulation. But they are a distinct minority of the people who are involved in the New Left, and even they as far as I can tell do not adulate anybody. Now, of course there is a certain idealization of Che Guevara. But what is that based on? Not that he was a commanding authority figure but the reverse—one of the few men in history who had a position of power, abandoned it, went into the mountains and fought for his beliefs—risked, and in fact gave his life in that way—a very striking figure for young people to be enamored of; not a person who had charismatic mass characteristics but a person who put his ideals above his own power. I should think Dr. Bettelheim would be proud of that kind of person.

Q. And I suppose you'd say that Mao and Ho are admired for their resistance to colonial authority, as opposed to the kinds of governments they run or their own authority?

A. I think that more than anything, yes.

Q. Another theory. The kids really are afraid of their freedom; they're hoping that authority will crack down and give them limits.

A. That kind of statement is certainly a plausible picture. But it doesn't seem to fit my sense—which is a very intimate sense, I think—of what's going on, you know, in the minds of the students. What exhilarates them is the sense that they can finally speak as equals with adults who previously had so much power over them. What exhilarates them is the opportunity finally to structure and determine a situation for themselves. It's exhilarating to be able to organize that building so that food can regularly be brought in, so that activities can go on, so that serious decisions can be made. It's exhilarating to organize a student radio station to broadcast all these complicated events. It's exhilarating to sit down in meetings and actually believe that one is actually having an effect on a powerful institution, that one is making decisions that will have a real effect. *That*, I think, is a much more powerful psychological motivation than the kind of thing you're suggesting.

Q. Yes. But even Sartre, who preached man's absolute freedom, said that freedom is frightening. At the limits of freedom, faced with the necessity to determine his own essence, Sartre wants to throw up.

A. Well, notice that the students are not asking for total freedom. They are asking for a share in the development of structures within which they can work. Not no classes, no discipline, no order, but classes that they find relevant to themselves, order that they have a chance to participate in creating, discipline that they compose as well as the faculty composing. I think to see them as totally anarchic, as seeking some total release from responsibility, is just the opposite of what my sense is of their motivation. And it's very important for people to understand the difference between a desire for release—which I'm sure is present in many in this generation, as well as in other generations—from a desire for a responsibility and a sense of power that so far has been denied them.

That's one of the major reasons why I support the sit-in, or a similar action. I think it has been highly creative. It's the first time—and I've been here five years—the first time that I have seen a genuine dialogue going on within the University about its purposes. It's the first time that I've seen students treat faculty as human beings instead of some sort of demigods, as it's the first time I've seen students fully able to articulate what's on their minds. Why? Because they have a sense of their own power, at last, to affect the institution. This has served to redress what was a *terribly* unequal relationship between students and faculty, to create a new relationship of forces between those two groups. And I think some sort of action in which the students actually used pressure on the institution was necessary in order to bring this about.

Q. What about that pressure? I'm thinking of an essay Camus wrote in 1946, "Neither Victims Nor Executioners." He said we have to end the legitimizing of murder—not murder itself, he wasn't that optimistic, but the idea that murder is ever legitimate. In the same sense, isn't there a danger that your endorsement of coercion will further legitimize that concept for all sides to use? Doesn't it legitimize the use of police to clear the Administration Building?

A. I can't believe that Camus would have opposed this action. I can't believe he would have opposed the workers when they went on strike and used coercion against their bosses. I can't believe that he could have opposed guerrilla resistance to the Germans during World War II, since he in fact was part of that. What we have here is the use of students' available power to try to bring about a relationship of equality between themselves and those who control their lives at the University. None of the advocates of nonviolent revolutionary change—whether it was Gandhi or King or Thoreau—none of them said you cannot be coercive. I mean, there is a coercive element in any use of one's body to stop an existing injustice. And that's what's going on.

Now, included in this is a preparation to take the consequences of one's actions. I think it should be clear that despite the fact that students are demanding amnesty—by which they mean an admission that their protest was legitimate—they also are psychologically prepared for rather severe consequences—the

Rashomon: Bettelheim and Flacks
85

possible damage to their careers, the possibility of jail, the possibility of being injured by the police, and so forth. So they are coerced. I'm amused when the University says the students have a gun at their heads. *They* have the guns—the actual, real, metal guns at their disposal. They can call out the police at any time. The students have no guns, no intention to use guns, but they do have an intention to put their bodies where they can disrupt the routine processes of the place, so that movement toward change will be made possible. I don't know what moral judgments mean if that is defined as a violent action.

Now, I want to add one thing. I am not a pacifist, nor are most Americans pacifists, and I will refuse to accept criticism of powerless people who use actual force from people who do not put themselves in direct opposition to the use of violence by the state. Whenever somebody criticizes black people for using violence or students for using violence, I want to know whether he is actually doing anything to stop the violence of the authorities. If he is not, then he is hypocritical; his criticisms make no sense in moral terms.

Finally, there's one point I want to make to Dr. Bettelheim —and I wish I could say this personally to him. He has as you know written a good deal about Nazism. And one of the key points that I at least read in his work is that Nazism was possible because people did not learn how to resist it—because people were passive in the face of it. People have read that kind of work Dr. Bettelheim and others have done on the concentration camps and other aspects of Nazism. They say: "What if you believe that American society contains a totalitarian potential, due to the overcommitment of the society to militarism, due to the over-involvement of the society in war, due to racism, due to super-technology?" And what if they say: "We don't intend to be good Germans passively accepting these trends—we intend to learn how to resist these trends?" Then I think you would turn the situation around entirely and not see the students as pre-Nazis but see them as people who are trying to *prevent* totalitarianism, to prevent the closing down of society—in fact taking the advice that Bettelheim and others have given them about resistance to totalitarianism. They're conscious of the very things he's written about—but seemingly come out with a totally different interpretation than he does. He wants them to accept the fundamental social trends; they try to resist those trends, take strong action, and then he condemns them for being totalitarian or something. It's a very curious fact.

q. All these high-flown theories aside, would you perhaps agree that this really is the nub of the quarrel between you two gentlemen—that he accepts the basic framework and thrust of American society, sees it as a viable democracy, while you do not?

A. Yes.

After talking to Flacks, a visit to the Administration Building.

The entrance was guarded by a security force of bearded young men equipped with walkie-talkie radios, but a press pass gained admittance to the main lobby. The lobby was crowded with students dressed for the most part in jeans and ponchos, long opera cloaks and ragged army-surplus coats. The floor was littered with orange peels and crusted over with puddles of spilled chili; on a table a partially snuffed cigarette smoldered in a half-consumed jar of raspberry jam. The walls were papered with Scotch-taped messages, bulletins, and anti-Bettelheim slogans · (many of them in verse). The reporters and photographers from the Chicago press were keeping grim vigil together in a secluded corner, waiting without much hope for the police to show up. Nothing had been happening, they said, and they wished their offices would either call them in or send them elsewhere. The decibel level in the lobby was painfully high. The students had imported a stereo record player, and the Beatles were performing at full volume.

Hey, Bungalow Bill!
What did you kill
Bungalow Bill?

There was in the air the smell of anarchy, and Mary Jane. A few of the students were plainly stoned, snapping their fingers and swaying to the music, laughing at private jokes. A glassy-eyed security guard pulled a nickel bag from a pocket of his surplus battle jacket and rolled his own with a cigarette machine and Bull Durham paper. A squad of Chicken-Shitters came in wearing orange armbands, armed with water pistols and toy rocket guns; they had been breaking in on classes to stage guerrilla theater skits, trying to stimulate some action from the administration. But no luck. The students were very friendly and happy to talk, but not about the sit-in. Consensus politics had been declared, and nobody wanted to be a spokesman for the group. You had to talk to a press representative to set up a group interview, and there weren't any press representatives around at the moment, but there would probably be one around in a few minutes.

There was a good deal of forced hilarity, but it failed to conceal the prevailing sense of boredom and frustration. Some of the people occupying the building looked suspiciously young, and they confessed they were actually pupils from nearby high schools, although they planned eventually to attend the University. They wished the police would come, they said. They wished something would happen. They were sick of this dirty dump, and they wanted to take a bath.

Three hours and no press representative. But consensus politics has its limits, and George Baral started to talk about the sit-in, more or less thinking out loud. He had long black hair and a gentle smile, and he said he was bothered about the sit-in. "It bothers me personally," he said. "It doesn't bother a lot of people in this building. But it does bother me, and I regret we had to do it. I mean, I regret it was necessary. We're working for changes that'll make it unnecessary. Personally I'm a nonviolent person. I'm a very firm believer in the love ethic. Whenever I catch myself not reacting to somebody with love, when I catch myself reacting emotionally and not giving him a chance—like my mother reacts to long hair and beards—I try to stop myself, and I say: 'Wait a minute, why do I hate that guy? I don't hate him.'

And after you do that a lot you sort of lay out a line of thought, and then you always react that way. But there are times when you have to deal with this sort of conflict. There's the necessity— I won't use the word struggle—but there's the necessity to work for change in an institution: a change which seems to be widely desired and which you are persuaded is good, and I guess that's about all you can ask, that you are rationally persuaded it's good and it's not based on emotional arguments or any of the other things that sway people so easily. I try to be reasonable and rational and not impassioned. On the other hand, there's the problem that there's no other way to do it. So I'm not hung up on it, you know. It's the sort of thing you don't like to do, and you hope you don't have to do it again. Some of us are putting our careers in serious jeopardy by this action. I don't think it's some- thing we take lightly."

He was twenty-three years old, he said, and a third-year graduate chemistry student. He thought that some of the things Bettelheim said were probably true as far as some of the people in the building were concerned, and some of the things Flacks said were true. "But I don't really like analyses of this sort. You know, 'You did this because your mother did that.' One way or the other. The kind of family you come from. So I really object to a lot of this work in sociology and psychology. It's all very good in the sense that it makes a point which is to be taken in connection with a whole lot of other points. But the way it's set up, you see, is not as a point. It's set up as *the* point, the explanation. And there is no *the* explanation for anything. It's not just in the fam- ily, although that probably does account for it to some extent. It's also in the society you're raised in, and the exposure to different ideas a person has, and his own thought process. A whole lot of things."

You might be in a book, George. Anything you'd like to say?

"Well, I think possibly one thing a lot of people don't understand is the love that a lot of us—and again, this isn't all of us—but a lot of us have for America in general. And things like this sit-in are a good example of the misunderstanding. They just don't comprehend why we do it. They think: 'They'll learn. They'll grow up. They'll be assimilated into the society and brainwashed so they're not interested in changing things.' Well, that's not true. Or they think we're subversive, and I understand the red squad [of the Chicago police] is in here looking for Communists. That really burns me up. They may find some, but a lot of innocent people are going to get tagged with this label. The thing is, we're not doing this out of hate for America. That's not the case in most of these youth demonstrations that have been going on the last several years. Now it's true there are these individuals who do hate, who don't know how to do anything else, and some of the people in the building are like that. Some of them are pushing the proposals to extremes which are in a sense ridiculous. I think it's probably true that some of them are really asking to be put down. I should point out that I'm one of the moderates in the building—one of the Realists, as we call ourselves. And then in between there are a lot of people who are just confused, you know, or who go along with it for the fun. But I'd like to say there's a very strong feeling—I don't know if it's the majority, but I do feel I'm not alone in my view that this is done out of real love for America. We've been brought up in this country, and we owe it a great debt. It's given us a lot of things that are very good for us. It's given us a lot of things that are very bad for us too. It's taught us to hate. It's made us hate. It's given many of us, many of our brothers, a very bad deal. But I really do love this country. I guess that's all I really meant to say."

The University did not rehire Mrs. Dixon, and it did not respond to any of the other demands made by the sit-in group. The University refused to grant amnesty, and it refused to negotiate with the people who were inside the Administration Building. But it also refused to call in the police, and it rejected the idea of cutting off the building's heat and electricity. In fact it took no public action whatever, but simply waited, and after fifteen days the invaders left the building of their own will. Some of them were later suspended or expelled after disciplinary hearings. A few months after the sit-in Richard Flacks was found in his office drenched in his own blood. He had been savagely beaten and slashed by a man he later said had come to his office posing as a newspaper reporter. Flacks had suffered severe injuries but fortunately survived them. He said he did not know the man who attacked him and could offer no motive to explain the attack; as of this writing the man has not been arrested or identified. Flacks also announced that he would accept a post at another university. His colleagues in the sociology department had declined to grant him tenure at the University of Chicago.

And so it ended, or appeared to end. For the time at least. *"I did it, and my doing made a difference."*

5

the Freedom Surfer

In his classroom at the University of Chicago, Joseph J. Schwab likes to practice what he calls "the art of recovery," or the definition of real issues. One day after class he practiced this art on the Bettelheim-Flacks debate.

Schwab said: "When we juxtapose Bettelheim's statement that some people are paranoid and don't belong in college with Flacks' statement that they do belong because some of them intend to have university careers, it's one little piece of the art of recovery when you realize that these two people are not speaking to the same question at all. Bettelheim is talking about the students' psychological belongingness. Flacks turns around, ignores that, and talks about merely the fact that they intend to have a university career. If Bettelheim were really to join the argument with Flacks, Bettelheim would say: 'But my point is that they don't have the temperament, at this time at any rate, to have an academic career.' And Flacks, if he wanted to join the argument, would have to say: 'But I'm talking about a modification of the career to fit the kind of temperament they have.' Now that's a very different kind of analysis from saying simply that they disagree. They're really disagreeing on two different matters, and they have not joined the argument. I know they were interviewed separately. If they had been together, though, the chances are awfully good that Bettelheim would have continued to psychologize the problem—and that Flacks would have continued to socio-careerize the problem."

And what is the synthesis?

"You mean the solution? There is no solution. What you're looking for is not a synthesis but a joining of the issue, so that Bettelheim would stop and say: 'What kind of people would be appropriate to the kind of career Flacks is talking about, and are these people maybe appropriate?' And Flacks would then say: 'Given the kind of personality that Bettelheim says, are they appropriate to the career they're setting out on?' And *then*, finally, they might join together in looking at a third problem, which is: What kinds of careers are important and what kinds of personalities are desirable? Instead of getting stuck on the hassle about who these kids are like and whether they're appropriate to a career that we've already mapped out for them."

Schwab's advice may be good, but it is doubtful the two men could ever join the argument themselves. Bettelheim sees American society as fundamentally All Right, and Flacks sees it as fundamentally All Wrong. That is the deeper basis of their disagreement, and it probably precludes any reasoned discussion of particular issues. Flacks himself appeared to recognize this when he noted the "curious fact" that Bettelheim's analysis of Nazism led Bettelheim and the radicals to totally different interpretations of the contemporary political picture. It might be argued that Bettelheim knows a real dictatorship when he sees one, having lived under one, and therefore has a more realistic perspective. But relativity begs the question, and the same argument could be turned around to suggest that Bettelheim's experience of a greater evil prompts him to accept a lesser evil that other men find intolerable. More to the point, Bettelheim and Flacks to a considerable extent were actually saying the same thing—were in fact describing the same phenomenon. Both men were discussing the effects of a prolonged adolescent moratorium, and both men were saying that the moratorium has created serious problems for many young people. This brings us back to the question that we left hanging at the end of the third chapter.

The question has been located. We can now ask: Is the adolescent moratorium *unduly* prolonged? Is it "good" or is it "bad"? And what in any case should we do about it?

Bettelheim obviously feels that the prolongation is undue, and he emphasizes the psychological stress it produces. This stress does indeed exist. There was considerable evidence of it, for example, during a late-night rapping session in the student union at Lawrence University in Appleton, Wisconsin. A number of students had gathered, and they were talking about Keniston's youth theory. Most of them thought Keniston had accurately described them: they were psychological adults and sociological adolescents. Among them were an eighteen-year-old boy we will call Judd and a nineteen-year-old girl we will call Molly.

Judd was a handsome, dark-haired young man: Boston Irish. He was a science student, he said, and he planned to major in oceanography. He was clean-shaven and neatly dressed in casual clothes, a black silk bandanna knotted at his throat. Molly was a short, sullen-looking girl given to long periods of introspective silence. She was a theater major, she said, and maybe she wanted to be an actress.

Judd grinned and said: "Our parents are paying to destroy their culture. They're doing it every time they send one of us to college. And year by year they pay a little bit more for college, and they pay a little bit more to destroy their culture. In another ten years, maybe twenty years, there isn't going to be much left of this culture. Because people like Molly, people like me, and some of the other people here are radical enough to destroy it. We're *going* to destroy it." To which another boy replied: "I don't think they're paying to destroy society when they send us to a place like Lawrence."

"Yes, they are," said Judd. "My father is. He was the true depression success story, you know. Went through college under the GI Bill and worked his way up to top management in this executive training program. So when I look at him, I have to admire him for his intelligence and his drive and everything, and he respects me for my supposed intelligence. But we have a verbal deal. Now, he's a liberal—conservative liberal, I like to call him —but we had this deal that until I was eighteen my political views and so on would not cause him any trouble. I took part in no peace marches, I did not picket or protest and so forth, and for this I was allowed to live at home with a fair amount of personal freedom. I was—uh—subsidized in my learning. But from eighteen on I can do anything I want. I can get arrested and stuff, and this won't bother him, as long as I get out on my own and so on. You know. It's: 'You get arrested and it's your problem. I don't want to hear about it.' And for this, you know, I will be processed through college. So he's actually paying to have his culture destroyed. Don't you see?" The other boy shook his head and said: "But he doesn't know it." "Subconsciously he knows it," said Judd.

Molly talked about her own parents. "You know," she said, "they *insist* to me invariably that they *never* asked themselves who they were. That they never even made an attempt to—uh— go through the philosophical underground to—uh—you know, to rise above it." They had lived through the depression, and somebody suggested this might be the explanation. But Molly just couldn't see it. "I find it very hard to believe," she said. "Because I don't know *anybody* who hasn't been at one time, you know, in the depths of philosophical despair. You know: *faced* themselves and said, okay now, what's it all about?" One of the boys said: "My stepfather grew up in the depression. And you know behaviorism. They really identify with that dollar. I can understand that." But Molly could not. "Why can't *they* understand?" she asked. "If *my* father knows what it really is to be hungry—and I doubt it—why doesn't he see that it's still going on? Why can't he see that there are some people who never got out of that depression? And that gets down to why I'm a radical. There has to be a change. And I *want* it. And I know I'm *right*."

The talk became less brave as the evening wore on. Molly had been quiet for a long time. One of the boys said: "I know what I'd like to do, but I've got nothing I want to do for the next year or so." Molly responded: "I've got it really narrowed down. Like I should make my final decision, you know, within the next month." She thought for a moment and added: "That's not quite true. It's like I have to make a one-thing decision, and I'm not so sure I want to do that now. I mean, is it necessary to say: 'Well, I'll do the same thing the next day and the next day and the next day'? Do you have to define your place in society in those terms? I mean, could I be—and it's just a question—but could I be like a sociological adult whose place in society is doing a different job every year?"

"Not if you're talking about brain surgery," said a premedical student. "And that's my problem, I guess. I'd like to be a doctor. I have a deep interest in the human body. And yet sometimes I feel a definite pressure on me. You have to get the grades so you can go to medical school. Sometimes I would like to just take off a term and do something. But you can't. The problem is, sometimes you have a strong feeling you want to become a doctor, say, but then other times you think, well, hell, maybe I don't want to. But you can't really quit and say to hell with your studies. It's real antagonistic. It kind of tears you apart." Another boy said: "I know chemists who have flunked out—or just dropped out, you know, with no degree—and then they go out and create something. Like this one guy created a new nylon polychain that was, you know, endless or something like this. An amazing breakthrough. And he doesn't have a degree. As far as the academic society is concerned he'd be invalid for teaching, and he'd be invalid to get a job. But now he's a research consultant, you know, and holds a chair in chemistry—but no degree, all of his degrees are honorary; they were given to him, you know, after he discovered this endless nylon chain."

Judd had listened with interest. "On this matter of loafing," he said. "I guess four times a year I seriously consider forgetting the whole thing. Especially in the summer, I turn into a surf bum. I mean I really copped out last year. I worked two months loading trucks so I could have all the money I wanted when I came back here to school. But after that I just copped out completely and spent my whole time at the shore. I didn't even know about the riots at the Chicago convention. I was fed up with the whole thing before that, because I knew McCarthy wasn't going to get it, so I went to the ocean, and I didn't find out about the riots until I wandered into a surf shop for the first time in a week, and after that I was willing to cop out for the rest of my life. I figured for every day I work I can cop two days on the beach, and that's my father's one great fear. He's afraid I'll take the ultimate cop-out and end up on the North Shore in Hawaii. That's really tempting. If it was like California or the North Shore I wouldn't have to work at all. I could go there and I'd be able to bum enough, just living with other people and sleeping on the beach. But on the Eastern Shore you have to take a car down, and if you don't have the car you get arrested. It used to be that you could sleep on the beach, and I could have somebody just drop me off, and I could travel all up and down the Maryland-Delaware-Virginia coast, and all I'd need was a little food. But now they patrol the beach—they even patrol the dunes. Fishermen can stay all night, twenty-four hours a day, and if they go to sleep it's fine for them. So we tried bringing poles, and that worked for a while, but finally they caught on to it. I mean, you have a pole and a surf board—there's something wrong. So it's a bad situation. But this one time I was talking about—I think the only thing that brought me back was walking into the surf shop that day. I had a quarter in my pocket, and I needed wax for the board. So you're still relating to your technological culture, no matter what you do. But I figured with a bar of wax, if I stayed on the island it would be another four or five days before I needed a coat of wax again, and I wouldn't have to bother with people another four or five days, and that's all that was really concerning me. But this guy in the shop had a television set, and he said look at that, and here were several cops beating this guy to a pulp with nightsticks. And I said, you know: 'Well, Prague, Czechoslovakia.' No. Chicago. It was a little disheartening. So I invested ten cents in a newspaper, and I thought about it a long time, and then I decided to come back here in September.

"I guess my oceanography is a compromise with having to be some portion realistic. Like a competition surfer. In surfing, you know, there's supposed to be three schools. There's the freedom surfer who completely drops out and in many cases is a head—you know, a real head—and the freedom surfer just lives to surf, and whatever happens in between sets just kind of happens. The plastic surfer is a guy who's down for the weekend, then goes back to his nine-to-five job. The competition surfer, he gets paid by a manufacturer; he's in between. The competition surfer has found his groove—he wants to surf, but he wants to make money too, so he's found his thing. But you have to admire the freedom surfer for being able to cop out completely and really be himself. And I'd say there are many people in the freedom school who are easily far better than this year's world champion —but they just don't give a damn. They've lost something. I mean, they give up something to be what they want. And the thing they give up of course is hope. So I guess you'd have to say they're unrealistic. But I don't know. Some days I don't feel I really belong here. I say to myself some days: 'Well, are you going to drop out and surf—or are you going to try and contribute something to society by being an oceanographer?' And I don't think I've really decided. I'm torn at the fork of a road. But there are days when I feel I really should be somewhere on a wave, not worrying about anything."

Judd said he might go inside his head, as he put it. He said he was planning soon to take LSD for the first time. Maybe that would help him decide.

The point of all this hardly needs to be belabored. Adolescence is just as painful as it always was, and extended adolescence is probably a good deal more painful. Toilet training in a sense has been prolonged into the twenties, and it hurts. Bettelheim was right. If anybody still doubts it, let him read Dotson Rader's revealing autobiography, *I Ain't Marchin' Anymore!* (after the song by Phil Ochs). Rader took part in the Pentagon march and the Columbia University uprising. He tells of "the pain of being outside," and he writes, at the age of twenty-six: "Color me Red. And brave. Unadmitted my manhood, like so many other New Leftists, was tied intimately to the image of myself as nascent revolutionary. . . . My manhood was profoundly connected with dissent. . . . in a country whose System emasculates young men, street disorders, seizures of buildings, dislocation, confrontation, the tempting of violence had become rituals of manhood. . . . Violence was wanted. I hungered for it. I wanted to fight in front of my chick. To prove myself. . . . Not to belong. A feeling as ordinary and sentimental as that. A conviction of failure before a beginning, a gnawing sense of loss. While all men are conscious of alienation, what I think was different about us is that we attempted to fix blame." But public demonstrations created merely the illusion of power. "Triumph was beyond us. Incapable of power, our lives were diminished to gesture." Columbia was the first time in Rader's life that he felt effective. At the Pentagon, he and his friends had wanted the troopers to fire on them. "We wanted a response to *us*. Any kind."

Bettelheim was right. And probably Erikson is right too when he rejects the notion that a sociological adolescent can be a psychological adult. By definition, this would appear to be impossible within the context of our Calvinist culture. To some extent at least, we all need to be told who we are; like Tinker Bell we need a certain amount of public applause to establish our value if not our existence. Initially we need parental approval, and failure to receive it may lead in some cases to infantile autism; later we need the approval of the wider society, and failure to receive it may lead ultimately to a kind of social autism. So young people do suffer in this situation, and some of them as we have seen suffer more than others; for various reasons, some are more susceptible to the trauma of *Sturm und Drang.*

While all this is quite clear, what it means is less clear. We must take a deeper look at the problem, from the standpoint of the individual and the standpoint of society.

First the individual.

There is a less elegant phrase for storm and stress. We used to refer to this phenomenon as "growing pains," and the emphasis was usually on the growth factor: the pain was just the symptom, or rather the price of the growth. Talking about Daniel Offer's non-turmoil adolescents, Keniston said: "It would seem to me at least that some degree of *Sturm und Drang* is probably essential to psychological development. It's true that modal or typical teen-agers often do not show the kind of turmoil the literature says—quote—ought to be there. But there are different ways of interpreting that. My own would be that in fact there are many people who have what one might call a very incomplete adolescence, in the psychological sense, and that these are people who by and large do not go through that process of questioning or in some cases rebellion or challenge that I think is almost a prerequisite for some kind of complex and rich adulthood. I have a notion of what one might call a kind of individuation and personal complexity, or differentiation of personality if you will, which presupposes in my view a period in which one analyzes or works through many of one's early suppositions. And I at least would feel that possibly those who haven't experienced any of this in their own development—well, one would question whether they've developed. So to speak."

Offer's modal adolescents do bring to mind the observation of the matron at a cocktail party, in a *New Yorker* cartoon: "One never hears about the 90 per cent of American youth who are law-abiding, clean, and studious, and don't concern themselves with war, bigotry, and human rights." Nor was Offer's choice of communities a particularly happy one, from a certain point of view. Park Forest after all was the home of William H. Whyte's *Organization Man.* Offer was asked frankly if he liked these modal young people. "Oh, yes," he said. Were they creative? "Well, creativity is an interesting question. How many creative people are there—you know, altogether? I think they are as creative as the person next door, you know. They are average—some of them are bright, some of them are not so bright." Are they boring? "No. They are interesting people. They have a tremendous sense of humor. Some of them are extremely bright—but a few, a very few."*

It is not very productive to ask what Keniston happens to like or Offer happens to like; they would agree that this can hardly be a final test of anything. On the other hand, the subjective element is difficult to eliminate. What we need perhaps is some basis for comparison of their views, and for this we can look to those cultures where turmoil is either absent or exceptional. In Samoa, for example, Miss Mead found a marked lack of neurosis but also a marked lack of individuation: "a low level of appreciation of personality differences, and a poverty of conception of personal relations." She noted what is obvious: "important personalities and great art are not born in so shallow a society." Closer to home, Bettelheim observed a similar situation in the Israeli kibbutzim. The kibbutz-reared young people displayed an "emotional flatness" that Bettelheim was hard put to evaluate. They were all that the ghetto Jew had not been. They were committed to "an entirely different Sachlichkeit, a literal-

---

* This business of intelligence deserves at least a footnote. Much is made of the fact that the radical students for the most part appear to be intellectually gifted and have records of high scholastic achievement. As the sociologist Seymour Martin Lipset has pointed out, however, this also is true in general of conservative activists as well as moderates involved in student government. But conservatives on the whole do not view the university as an agency of social change, and therefore they are not as likely to be involved in campus-oriented political activities. "This means that, on any given campus, or in the country, the visible forms of student politics will suggest that the student population as a whole is more liberal or radical leftist than it actually is. Since conservative academic ideology fosters campus political passivity, one should not expect to find much conservative activity among students, and the absence of such activity need not signify the absence of a conservative temper among some, or perhaps many, students."

ness, a matter-of-fact objectivity which has no place for the emotions." A member of the founding generation said of them: "Let's say they're more realistic, mechanistic, objective than we are; less humanistic, less involved." As noted earlier, they also failed to develop distinctive personalities—and Bettelheim detected a truism: "The more egalitarian a society, the more all are equal." The kibbutz child is probably much happier than a child his own age in American society. "But not having to resolve a crisis of great depth as regards industry versus inferiority, he again has no need to develop great inner resources to weather it. Nor will his personality deepen for having resolved such a conflict successfully. . . . The existential despair that seems to haunt Western society, the kibbutznik escapes: despair about oneself or the world, about the fact that life has to end, and that it has little meaning or purpose." But the kibbutznik escapes at a price. "In terms of Erikson's model, despair is escaped at some cost to personal identity, emotional intimacy, and individual achievement." The Israeli pioneers visualized a brave new world in which personal freedom would be combined with a folk society of comrades. But their dream like all dreams was only partly realized. The more closely knit they became as a group, the more it cost them in personal identity. Bettelheim reacted to all this with mixed emotions. He decided he would worry more if all Israel were composed of kibbutzim. Speaking of the second generation, he concluded:

Knowing nothing of apartness, they are content with satisfactions not destroyed for them by having to fight for a sense of belonging. Neither must they strive for an individuation that might compensate, through a rich inner life, for what is absent from their group life. They feel no need to push ahead, but neither do they have the impulse to push anyone down. While such people do not create science or art, are neither leaders nor great philosophers nor innovators, maybe it is they who are the salt of the earth without whom no society can endure.

What are we to make of this? It is clear, as Erikson has said, that a prolonged adolescence enables many individuals to realize inner potentials that might otherwise have atrophied—to accomplish much that they would never have attempted without the moratorium. And it is clear, as Adlai Stevenson once said, that there are no gains without pains. But it also is clear that the moratorium can be abused, and that the pains for some people far outweigh the gains. For some people it is prolonged to a fateful degree, and Erikson has sounded frequent warnings to this effect. I asked him, however, if he thought there was any evidence that the moratorium in general has been unduly extended—from the standpoint of society as a whole. "It's a very difficult subject," he said, "because this moratorium takes such a different form, you know, depending on the historical period. But today there's no doubt there's almost an endless moratorium. If anybody over thirty doesn't count, that means the only important part of life would be the one before that—and that becomes a kind of unlimited moratorium because it has no transition to the future or anything like that." But this too is a subjective reaction—merely one man's opinion—and inevitably in fact the question of due or undue shades into cultural subjectivity. "It's all relative to the culture," said Erikson. "That's just the point. It depends on what you're after, and also the historical period. In Israel right now they may need this kind of person that Bettelheim describes." In America right now we may need an altogether different sort of person—Keniston's youth, for example—but Keniston's youth, on the other hand, would certainly be out of place in Samoa.

Ultimately, then, it is necessary to ask if all standards of judgment indeed *are* wholly relative to a particular culture— which of course would imply that there *is* no purpose in life, in the sense of an evolutionary goal for mankind as such. Or is it possible instead that the human race has some sort of universal destiny to fulfill, some rendezvous to keep, or some ideal state of existence that all men should strive to attain? In short, is there a Kingdom of God to achieve—with or without God? And if so, is this kingdom to be sought in the present or the future, on this earth or among the stars, in human happiness or human achievement? Is the idea to make the world a comfortable dwelling place, or is the world to be viewed as Teilhard's machine for progress?

These considerations must be deferred to later chapters. In the meantime it is possible to deal with our question on a more immediate and pragmatic level. The extension of adolescence is a fact in this country, whether we like it or not, and the moratorium in the future is likely to become longer rather than shorter. So we can start with this fact. Schwab has criticized Keniston and Erikson for making what is the standard or what ought to be. That may or may not be justified, but it would certainly seem good sense to make what is the standard at least of what *is*. Bettelheim in many respects has made a brilliant diagnosis of the problem; he has eloquently described the traumatic effect of the moratorium upon many young people today. And he plainly has great empathy for these people. But his greater concern seems to be with their reaction to the trauma and the damage they might be permitted to do to the established society; his prescription then arises from this concern, and it is in essence a very simple one: the tormented adolescents must be firmly put down whenever their screams grow too loud. Beyond this Bettelheim has nothing to suggest except a return to past rituals—presumably football rallies and beer parties. Even if this were a good idea, it has against it the fact that it will not work. And it is not a good idea. It is not really important that Bettelheim feels this way; again, he is one man. Unfortunately he appears to reflect the thinking of many adult practitioners who would treat the symptom instead of the disease.

But if Bettelheim is correct in assuming that the young have a need to assert their early manhood, it will not satisfy that need merely to treat them as children in need of discipline; they need walls to push against—and those walls now and then should give way, or the young people may stop pushing altogether. But they are treated as children, and thought of that way. Discussing this over a beer recently, Edward T. Hall said: "You know, we used to talk about college men. Then it was college boys. And now it's college kids. I remember reading one of the early diaries on the opening of the West; it mentioned that a wagon train was led by 'a man of fourteen.' I guess somebody fourteen could be a man then, and know all he needed to run a wagon train—which was plenty—because he had good models, and he could see people doing it, and it was taken for granted that he was a man. But we keep introducing new metaphors into the situation. We created children, and then we created adolescents; we created students in a classroom, and we call them college kids. They're supposed to act in certain ways. And one of them of course is quiet."

George Wald was thinking along the same lines one afternoon. The Harvard University biologist, who won the 1967 Nobel Prize in medicine, was waiting to address a rally opposing an anti-ballistic missile system. He sat in his hotel room, in a warm ray of sunlight, an innocent smile on his face, and he said that college students today are not children; they are a new breed of cats. "I think there are two things in this situation," he said. "On the one hand, we've passed through—and I should say roughly ten years ago was the peak of it—we've passed through an absolutely first-magnitude revolution in American education. American education has come over a great divide, and the heart of that revolution was in the high schools—not in the colleges but in the high schools. Suddenly the high schools began to educate, to a degree and on a scale that they'd never done before. It was the result of a whole complex of things. Sputnik was part of it. There was an intellectual movement to this that James Conant and Admiral Rickover were pushing. There were various programs for retraining the teachers under federal sponsorship, so that high school teachers who frequently spent their vacations working in gas stations suddenly could take their families to some nice place and earn still more money being retreaded and learning their material. The schools of education were beginning to relax a little on those technique courses, and teachers were beginning to learn content. But the thing that put teeth into the whole business—more than all these other things put together—was the advanced placement program, the realization that if a student in high school had a certain kind of course made available to him he could do the first year of college work in high school, and this saved a year of his life, and a year of support for the parents, and so as this got going parents all over the country began insisting that that kind of instruction go into the high schools. And I realized about ten years ago—really about eight or nine years ago— that the freshmen who were coming to Harvard were a new breed of cats. I'd never seen their like before. They're amazingly learned. And it's that that got me to volunteer—the first time in the history of Harvard that anybody had volunteered for the freshman course. About eight years ago I started a new introductory course in biology, realizing that something new had to be done for these kids who are now ever so much better informed— more used to doing intellectual work, more eager to do it—than ever before. So that's one element in the situation. I think people don't get any brighter with the passage of time, but they're better educated. So it was a new deal. But the other thing grew too."

He had talked about the other thing in his celebrated speech in Boston in the spring of 1969, the speech that almost overnight had made him an admired spokesman for many college students all across America.

"These young people," he said, "are facing an absolutely new situation, the like of which has never existed before in human history. And that's what I was directing the talk to mainly. Ten years ago if you asked a kid in college how he'd like to see himself twenty years hence, he might tell you: 'Well, the way things are going, I'll have a decent income and a house in the suburbs and maybe two cars, and my kids will be in a good private school, and I'll have a certain status in the community.' You don't get that response any more. Those things don't seem particularly good to the present students. They don't see that as an end in life. They see that it hasn't done much for their parents. And there's something much worse than that. And that is if you really push matters far enough—and there you really have to push, and they won't even tell you frequently, no matter how hard you push—they're not sure they'll be physically in existence ten, fifteen, twenty years hence. And nobody can be sure, and the more expert the person you go to, the clearer that becomes. So they really are a generation that isn't sure it has a future. They don't see that future, and they sure don't want what their parents got. I think the present scene is so gloomy, has such poor prospects that are apparent for the future, that there are only two kinds of attitudes toward it: despair, in which case you cop out—or anger. And it's anger that keeps a lot of people going. It's anger that keeps me happy. And I think that the mood of the students is a mixture of anger, frustration, and disgust." Wald's smile faded. "It's a poor life they're being handed. And they're just seizing on any immediate issue, something that they can do something with, with all the adults around them perfectly helpless and not knowing which way to turn. But the whole thing is a yell for help."

Wald possibly overestimates the fear of world destruction; there was probably more of that a generation ago. The future is a long way off, and it seems more likely that the young people feel rather that they have no present. But Erikson for one certainly agrees with Wald that students today are better prepared for responsibility than they ever were before—and precisely at a time when they are denied any opportunity for responsible participation in the society, not to mention their own educations. "They are maturing earlier, physically, than they ever did before," said Erikson. "They also are better informed than they ever were before. If then specialization keeps them in school, let's say into the middle twenties, that is exactly what they object to. So that's why they are, I think quite rightly, wanting to have more responsibility now." He agreed with Bettelheim that students seem more interested in changing the environment than changing themselves. "That's right," he said. "That's anyway an adolescent phenomenon; they complain that the world does not fit their expectations. But right now I think there is a quite rightful insistence, if they have to study that long, they should be permitted to play the role of adults already during their study time. I think this is right."

Schwab and other educators turn a deaf ear on demands for equal student power in the administrative process—partly on the basis of inexperience and partly because students move on and do not have to live with their mistakes: they would not feel the real "pinch" of decision-making. But Schwab has a number of suggestions to reform the curriculum and to create a greater sense of academic community. Among other things he would eliminate early commitment to a major field of study and would allow for diversity of study in the senior year before graduate specialization; he would revive the concept of the teaching fellow, but at the undergraduate level, to serve as a link between students and faculty; he would encourage students to design their own metacurriculum of noncredit courses and would arrange for students to serve as "apprentices" to administrators in government and industry, to learn how decisions actually are made. Professors would become students again and take courses outside their own disciplines; for example, a science professor would be enrolled in an English course and learn Shakespeare with the undergraduates, and a humanities professor would study astronomy.

Many similar ideas to stimulate more student-faculty collaboration are detailed in Schwab's book *College Curriculum and Student Protest*. They are good ideas, as far as they go. But the social critic Paul Goodman, for instance, would undoubtedly dismiss them simply as fresh examples of social engineering— and therefore as "uneducational in principle." Goodman also rejects the idea of Student Power, however, and suggests that its advocates should stop and ask themselves whether they are authentically students at all. What they should be demanding perhaps is a more open entry into society. "And there *is* an authentic demand for Young People's Power, their right to take part in initiating and deciding the functions of society that concern them—as well, of course, as governing their own lives, which are nobody else's business." This is a much more fundamental approach to the problem than the Band-Aid reformism proposed by Schwab and others. Goodman, who is a brilliant man, is basically opposed to the whole idea of direct teaching in schools, which is a concept some Irish monks developed in the seventh century "to bring a bit of Rome to wild shepherds." He has pointed out that only in the last century in industrialized countries did a majority of children receive such teaching at all, and only in the last few decades was formal schooling extended into adolescence and further: in America in 1900 only 6 per cent of the population went through high school and one-fourth of 1 per cent went through college. Now we have more than seven million college students, and the number grows.

The schools have isolated society from its problems, and "vital functions of growing up have become hermetically redefined in school terms: community service means doing homework, apprenticeship is passing tests for jobs in the distant future, sexual initiation is high school dating, and rites of passage are getting diplomas." The motivation for the behavior of a five-year-old is geared at least fifteen years in the future. In the absence of an adult culture a youth subculture naturally develops. Goodman's bold solution is to eliminate most of our high schools and to cut back drastically on schooling in general— "because the present extended tutelage is against nature and arrests growth." Only 10 to 15 per cent of the young people actually thrive on it anyway, according to James Conant. (Significantly, while more than 90 per cent of Daniel Offer's modal adolescents planned to attend college, only 4 per cent indicated that reading or studying was the activity they most enjoyed.) The chief method of learning would consist of incidental education— taking direct part in the ongoing activities of society—and college training in general would follow rather than precede entry into the professions. "There is no essential reason why law and medicine are not better learned by apprenticeship," Goodman says. After all, it is by incidental education that an infant learns the abstractions of language—an incredible accomplishment, learning to talk—and as a general rule the young learn very easily within the environment. "A child who can't count can always make change for a dollar." It would be necessary of course to develop rules of licensing and hiring that are realistic to the actual work, eliminating mandarin requirements. "We must design apprenticeships that are not exploitative. Society desperately needs much work that is not now done, both intellectual and manual, in urban renewal, ecology, communications, and the arts, and all of these could make use of young people." Adolescent years might be devoted to public service, and all adolescents in any case should be guaranteed a living—to insure freedom of option and freedom of criticism. According to Goodman, the present cost of high schooling would almost pay for this. "Our aim should be to multiply the path of growing up, with opportunity to start again, cross over, take a moratorium, travel, work on one's own." Academic schooling of course could still be chosen by those with academic talents, "and such schools are better off unencumbered by sullen uninterested bodies."

In important respects Goodman's vision is a description of medieval society, before the Schoolmen took over. Philippe Ariès tells us that children in that period—including the rich—were sent at an early age to serve as apprentices in the homes of others. In fact, all education was conducted by apprenticeship—except at the Latin school, which was intended solely for clerics. At about the age of seven, children would start their lives in another home and would learn there a trade or possibly the good manners of a knight. This helps explain the mingling of children and adults that Ariès has remarked upon. The young and the old were constantly brought together by trade and craft in everyday life— the little apprentice mixing the painter's colors, the little page attending his general on the field of battle. "In short, wherever people worked, and also wherever they amused themselves, even in taverns of ill repute, children were mingled with adults. In this way they learnt the art of living from everyday contact." The family as we know it could not exist under these conditions, and it is no accident that the family and school education developed at the same time: "This evolution corresponded to the pedagogues' desire for moral severity, to a concern to isolate youth from the corrupt world of adults, a determination to train it to resist adult temptations." Thus our modern civilization was established on a scholastic foundation, "and time would steadily consolidate it by prolonging and extending school life."

To some extent it might be possible to view childhood, adolescence, and protracted adolescence as extensions of natural evolution. In this connection the zoologist N. J. Berrill has related human brain size and intelligence to an extended growth period. The maximum size of a child's head at birth is determined by the width of the mother's pelvis, and eventually in the evolutionary process the obstetrical limit was reached. Thus the "problem" arose—how to produce individuals with brains relatively much larger than those produced at birth? An egg or embryo can attain larger than average size in only two ways: it can grow faster, or it can grow for a longer time. "In fact it can even grow more slowly and still end up larger if only it keeps on growing." The mammals produced their young in litters, which meant that "the slowest to develop and the last to get out were the losers." But during the arboreal stage—up in the trees—a mother could safely handle only one offspring at a time. So there was now an opportunity for a longer period of growth after birth. "With each small increase in adult brain size the time between birth and puberty also lengthened. It had to, just to make the larger brain. And step by step, each one infinitesimal as each generation succeeded the last, we took our distinctively human path. Our long infancy, drawn-out childhood, prolonged youth and delayed puberty are simply the means by which our big skulls and voluminous brains could be attained, and the prolongation of life as a whole is its consequence." As far as the latter goes, modern health care has now stretched even further the period between conception and death. Rather than add unwanted years at the end of life, however, Berrill suggests that it might make more sense to extend the period of youthful development—to slow the rate of growth and thus postpone puberty to the age of twenty or even thirty. "Puberty at thirty would mean menopause at ninety and death from old age at one hundred and fifty." And even if we did not actually live a longer time, our youth would last much longer.

Maybe the New Biologists are already working on this. If we have not yet managed to delay puberty itself, however, we have certainly stretched its psychosocial extension. And while Berrill's concept may be comforting for those who like to take the long view, the fact remains we are in trouble at the moment, both psychologically and sociologically. There is no hope that society will act on Goodman's proposals. "Against all evidence," he admits, "people are convinced that what we do must make sense, or is inevitable." But some of the young people themselves in effect have acted upon Goodman's proposals, in reaction to what we might call the Oz syndrome. The Scarecrow was convinced he had no brains until the Wizard presented him with a Testimonial, and the Cowardly Lion did not feel brave until he was awarded a Medal. But many of the young have decided the Wizard is an old phony, and they at least can do without his blessings. Diplomas and degrees have lost much of their magic; some talented people are opting now to enter the society without them, and this is probably a good sign. But most middle-class adolescents are still caught in the web, and adult society has to decide how it will react to the violence of their struggle. We should take an interest, if only for the reason that it might portend the future. If a workless culture really is in the economic tarot cards, we may be watching a preview of our own response to enforced leisure and nonproductivity.

The scene is often pathetic. The widespread interest in witchcraft and astrology, for example, is no doubt motivated in part (but not wholly) by youth's sense of helplessness. As one student told the sociologist-priest Andrew M. Greeley: "I'd sooner feel that my future was being shaped by the stars or by the turn of the cards, because these would represent powers that would be more concerned about me than either my draft board or the Pentagon." Or more to the point perhaps, powers that can be influenced and controlled—if you know the right spell to cast. Surely we can offer our young people something better than this.

And surely we must, for their own good and our own. Bettelheim has written about those concentration camp inmates who were described by their fellow prisoners as "moslems," men who displayed schizophrenic-type behavior; what marked them off from their fellow inmates was their inner feeling of utter helplessness: the fact that they had given up all hope. In the same sense, according to Bettelheim, for childhood schizophrenia to develop "it is enough that the infant be convinced that his life is run by insensitive, irrational powers who have absolute control of his life and death." So too perhaps with the young radicals. At the moment they are causing us a good deal of pain and aggravation, and concern is expressed that their acting-out behavior will become more extreme than it already is. Maybe it will. But ultimately another possibility also should concern us: if they are wholly frustrated and disregarded, they too may give up their anger and their hope—and this may well be the greater danger in the future. We have already mentioned the possibility of social autism. This would result if radical dissent were to end in the kind of total alienation that characterizes those young people who are attracted to the psychedelic drug movement and the Leap to the East. That is to say, the hippies. This has already occurred in many individual cases, and there is some reason to believe that the infection is spreading even now to the New Left in general—as we will see further on.

What can be done? A reduction in the voting age would be a sensible gesture, but only a gesture; elimination of the draft would make even more sense, in so far as the draft has been a major factor contributing to forced college enrollment. Beyond this, it might help if we were to stop just a moment and hear the young people out. Because they are saying some good things. They are a potential source of effective social criticism, and the quality of their criticism will determine the ultimate *social* value of the adolescent moratorium. It would be a serious mistake to assume that the pressure for humanist reform is wholly or even fundamentally represented by the youth rebellion, and a serious mistake to believe that the young people themselves can effectively solve any of the problems they have identified. They cannot. In the end, as Wald has said, the only answer to student unrest is adult unrest. Nor is youth the wave of the future; contrary to popular belief, the median age in America is increasing rather than decreasing. But the young can help, if we let them, and they are in a unique position to examine the society and to challenge its abuses. From a transpersonal standpoint, therefore, the moratorium should be assessed in terms of its fruits for life. If the moratorium indeed is a product of the technological economy, and if it has resulted in a great deal of personal suffering, it also has produced a Greek chorus of protesters who have the time and freedom to bite the hand that created and feeds them.

This hand needs biting.

the cMan with Four cAces

Thoreau never used the term national priorities, but he did spend a lot of time wondering how to calculate the true cost of an investment. He was thinking about this one day when a friend said to him: "I wonder that you do not lay up money; you love to travel; you might take the cars and go to Fitchburg today and see the country." Thoreau insisted it would be quicker to walk than take the train, and he told his friend:

"Suppose we try who will get there first. The distance is thirty miles; the fare ninety cents. That is almost a day's wages. . . . Well, I start now on foot, and get there before night; I have traveled at that rate by the week together. You will in the meantime have earned your fare, and arrive there some time tomorrow, or possibly this evening, if you are lucky enough to get a job in season. Instead of going to Fitchburg, you will be working here the greater part of the day. And so, if the railroad reached around the world, I think I should keep ahead of you."

Thoreau concluded that "the cost of a thing is the amount of what I will call life which is required to be exchanged for it, immediately or in the long run."

More than a century later the French economist Bertrand de Jouvenel was pondering the merits of building a hypersonic transatlantic plane. He estimated that a supersonic plane would more than double present speeds, while a hypersonic plane would multiply speeds perhaps five times beyond that; thus by 1984 we should be able to fly from London to New York within forty minutes. The transatlantic passage in 1820 had required twenty-five days, and in 1838 the ship *Great Western* had cut that to fifteen days. So the economy in time achieved by the *Great Western* was ten days; that of the supersonic plane more than three hours; that of the hypersonic plane less than three hours. On a time graph from 1820 to 1984, then, the speed curve would rise by ever larger amounts—and the time-saved curve would rise by ever smaller fractions. Which led de Jouvenel to conclude that the social benefits of faster travel would be well below the opportunity cost: "that is, the social benefits which might be conferred by an alternative use of equivalent resources." And he suggested that public support for technical innovation should depend on the relevance of the innovation to improvements in the quality of life.

De Jouvenel was certain that nobody would dispute the principle. It was not his impression, however, that such logic would influence the actual decision to build a hypersonic plane—which of course will be built. This may bring to mind the story of the test pilot who radioed: "I'm lost, but I'm making record time." It also serves to illustrate a fundamental criticism of technology that is summed up now in the popular observation: *Our priorities are out of order.*

Of course they are out of order. Everybody knows that. But the explanation is rather more complicated than the bare fact suggests, or at least is less widely recognized or agreed upon. There are a number of ways to approach the problem, but the starting point invariably is John Kenneth Galbraith's study *The*

Affluent Society, first published in 1958, and its central concept of an economy whose private sector is consistently enriched at the expense of its public sector. So let us start from there too. Galbraith himself recently reviewed and updated his book, and his line of argument can be summarized as follows.

The end of World War II saw a "market revival"—a return to grace of the American free-enterprise system. The public was weary of wartime controls, and the voters in 1946 elected the most conservative Congress in modern history. The result was a drastic reduction in public spending—except for spending to contain communism—and even liberals for the most part went along with the conservative trend. The liberals fell back on Keynesian fiscal policies designed to maintain a satisfactory level of employment and production. The idea was for the government to spend more money when the level fell (but without raising taxes), and then to make up the deficit by cutting its spending when the level had risen again. Thus the role of the state could be kept to a minimum. The liberals previously had been committed to public spending for public services; they still felt that such services should be provided, but their primary emphasis now was on maximum production.

The conservatives at first regarded the Keynesian system as subversive, even when it provided for a minimal degree of state interference. They later came to accept the same system under conditions that provided for an enlarged state role in the economy. Keynesian policy in effect was underwritten by big defense budgets resulting from the Cold War and later the Korean War. (As Buckminster Fuller put it, the military told Congress it could buy or die. Congress decided to buy.) Such budgets became habitual. They were acceptable to the liberals because they bolstered production (and contained communism). They were acceptable to the conservatives because they contained communism (and bolstered production). Everybody was happy.

Except Galbraith. A Keynesian disciple during the New Deal years, he began to agitate now for a larger investment in public services. He warned that continued neglect of the public sector could result in a social eruption; it also seemed clear and basic that some expenditure was necessary to remove the waste products that were created by the production system. Or so it seemed. The matter came to a head during the Kennedy administration in a debate on tax policy. There were two alternatives: to reduce taxes and thereby to stimulate the GNP with an increase in private income, or to maintain taxes and spend the money for social purposes—"education, urban renewal, and improved welfare standards." Galbraith supported the second alternative, and lost. Taxes were lowered in 1964.

Looking back on *The Affluent Society* more than a decade after it appeared, Galbraith decided he had made one serious error in the book: understatement. It could hardly be argued that years of expanded production had reduced social tensions. Galbraith concluded that "even the most stalwart conservative who dares not venture out in the street at night and hesitates on occasion to drink the water or breathe the air must now wonder if keeping public services at a minimum is really a practical formula for expanding his personal liberty."

When *The Affluent Society* was first published, Galbraith's critics asserted that he had overstated our affluence and overlooked the fact that millions of Americans suffered in grinding poverty; it was featherheaded to talk about cutting production when so many people were out of work and needed jobs. Galbraith felt these critics had not read him well. Such a philosophy, he said, would postpone forever any effort to correct the imbalance between the two sectors of the economy; if you had to wait until the whole population reached a certain minimum standard of living, that standard itself would constantly rise with the increase in overall wealth. You would be chasing the horizon. More to the point, the critics had failed to recognize the real reason why so many people stay poor—the reason in fact being our continued underinvestment in education, housing, health, and other services that might help to lift people from poverty. It seemed to Galbraith that the critics were saying that we cannot do anything about poverty until nobody is poor.

This in essence then is the Galbraithian thesis: America is privately affluent and publicly poor. Our priorities are out of order. Again, this is widely recognized now; but those who contemplate the fact are often attended by a sense of bafflement and frustration. Consider the following quotation: "The United States and the Soviet Union now possess—for the first time in history—the technology and productive capacity for extending . . . benefits to all men. Think of the important and beneficial work that the United States and the Soviet Union could undertake with the vast sums now being spent on instruments of war. Why, it staggers the imagination! We could use that wealth to help the two-thirds of the world that is afflicted with poverty, hunger, illiteracy, and disease." Indeed. Those were the words of President Lyndon B. Johnson, who dreamed of a Great Society and awoke to the harsher realities of Vietnam and Watts. What happened to the dream? The obvious answer might appear to be the Vietnam War itself—but the obvious answer could easily mislead us. As George Wald remarked: "Vietnam is just an incident. It's a terrible incident, and we'll get out of it, but that in itself won't change things very much." The Nixon administration was barely in office before the Secretary of Defense was telling us that an end to the war could not be followed by any major cuts in military spending. Melvin R. Laird declared in an Armed Forces Day speech to the Military Order of World Wars: "A drastically reduced defense budget will not provide adequate national security in the world in which we live." In turn, the rationale for this kind of statement was explained—in part—in another address made some years earlier:

"The present tensions with their threat of national annihilation are kept alive by two great illusions. The one, a complete belief on the part of the Soviet world that the capitalist countries are preparing to attack it, that sooner or later we intend to strike. The other, a complete belief that the Soviets are preparing to attack us, that sooner or later they intend to strike."

General Douglas MacArthur said that at an American Legion meeting in 1955. And undoubtedly the arms race is predicated in part on a mutual sense of fear and distrust. Both sides have been rattling for a long time now, of course; the Cold War has continued for almost a quarter of a century, and neither side has struck—which might suggest to some that the intention to strike is in fact an illusion. Surely some good opportunity must have presented itself somewhere along the line, if the intention were really there. Unfortunately each side has given the other ample cause to distrust it, and this rules out any simple solution to the problem. The problem is compounded, moreover, by the possibility that another factor exists that has nothing to do with national security—a factor that the inventor and all-round genius Buckminster Fuller has referred to as *the socialism-avoiding subterfuge*.

The reasoning here is not hard to follow. We have discovered that a substantial amount of federal spending has a salubrious effect on employment, production, and the GNP. Therefore it is necessary to justify that spending. And it does not really matter what the money is spent on: it could be invested in social services or the production of Hula Hoops, just so long as it creates more jobs. In theory, that is. But spending to provide social services is socialism—which we all know is wicked and un-American—and the taxpayers in any case would not support a large investment to help people who are not willing or able to make Hula Hoops themselves. But they will support a similar investment that can be justified on the basis of an external threat to national security or prestige. They will pay tax dollars for defense, and they will pay for a race to the moon—if you can convince them that the trip to the moon is really a race after all and is not intended merely to advance human knowledge (Columbus certainly was not bankrolled for that purpose). So the end results of socialism are achieved without resorting to socialism—without appearing to at any rate—and the subterfuge has succeeded in its purpose. The liberals perhaps are not all that sure that socialism is wicked, but, as Galbraith notes, they will go along because the system fits their Keynesian concept of maximum production as the basic antidote for social ills. And within this system the sky is the limit, both literally and figuratively. According to de Jouvenel's figures, for example, four-fifths or more of America's government-financed Research and Development (or R&D) expenditures are for purposes of international power politics and national prestige: defense, space, and atomic energy. Senator J. William Fulbright estimates that the United States since World War II has spent roughly ten times as much on warfare and related requirements as it has spent on human welfare, and Marcus Raskin of the Institute for Policy Studies puts the actual figure for military spending since 1945 at $1,300 billion. He also estimates that we have spent $100 billion to prop up foreign dictators who had no popular support in their own countries. This often was required to permit our own military presence overseas.

We are talking now about the military-industrial complex, as the late President Eisenhower's speechwriter Malcolm Moos described it—or more precisely the military-industrial-university-labor union complex. Some would call it a conspiracy, but it would be difficult to demonstrate that an actual conspiracy is involved, in the sense that a group of men initially sat down somewhere together and planned the whole system. We simply are not that well organized, for one thing, and it is more likely that the complex developed in Topsy fashion; according to Galbraith's analysis it was "the result of a long series of steps taken in response to a bureaucratic view of the world." It is, after all, the function of a military bureaucracy to foresee any possible threat to the national security, and the military itself cannot be faulted for doing too well what it is supposed to do. If you are looking for spooks in a dark room, you are almost certain to see some, and in any case it is not the job of the military to protect the country from its own excesses: that is or should be the function of the civilian government. Once it had come into existence, however, such a system would tend to perpetuate itself. This indeed has happened. And now the system is under attack.

A number of factors have provoked this attack, among them the unofficial détente with Russia and the riot-generated pressure for domestic reforms. But the resistance is considerable, and this is hardly surprising; military production is now about 10 per cent of America's total production. Discussing this problem, George Wald said: "When one speaks of turning these huge sums of money from armaments to meeting human needs, it isn't going to be easy, because you can't plant these human needs—housing, better schools, better education, cleaner air and water, cleaning up the cities. None of that makes a multi-billion-dollar defense contract that you can put in some plant in Texas or California or wherever. It's a special kind of business. And there is another feature that is very serious. It's also a no-risk business, unlike every other business in America. The government does most of the investing. It will even build the plants and then turn them over to the people running them. If the estimates are off by 100 per cent, the Defense Department, as we now know, cheerfully pays out. It's a no-risk business. So people aren't going to get out of this just spontaneously. The heart of the problem is in the profits. If you're promoting some enterprise or suggesting some enterprise that has big contracts in it and big profits, you promptly have a big lobby in Washington, and you're at the elbows of congressmen all the time. Now, the people don't have a lobby. So how are we going to get pressure in Washington for pure air and water or for better schools or for any of these things that we want so much? You know the threats that are brought on to push these other programs through. You get people scared to death, as at present our administration is scaring the whole country to death—so they'll permit these other pressures to operate. But the heart of the whole thing is a fantastically lucrative business. My heavens above, it's the biggest business in the country. And everybody one way or another is feeding at that trough. But we're ambivalent about it, you know. I think there's an enormous ambivalence. Because it's threatening our lives. It's not only threatening our lives in the future, it's spoiling our lives in the present. And when I think of the people who are profiting from this—they're not devils, they're just people. And I think if they don't feel strange about this internally, as I'm sure they do now and then, there is another vulnerability, and I put a lot of hope in that. And that's their kids. They have kids. They're spoiling the lives of their kids. They're spoiling the present lives of their kids and threatening them with early extinction. And the kids are telling them about it. And they have to live with that. And that's the soft spot, I think. I think a lot of these people—even people who are making huge profits out of armaments—would be glad to see a way out of it."

There is in fact increasing evidence that defense is no longer the lucrative business it once was—that its profit margin is perhaps only half that of American industry as a whole—and that many defense contractors would be glad to see a way out of it for purely financial reasons. As the political scientist George E. Berkley points out, for example, the no-risk situation that Wald talks about was more the case in the 1950's, before Robert McNamara moved to change Defense Department contracting policies from a cost-plus to a fixed-fee basis. Fixed-fee contractors could no longer count on a guaranteed profit if the actual cost of their project did not meet their quotation. And with the influx of war orders that began in 1965, says Berkley, many companies found themselves forced into uneconomic production practices, including extensive overtime and the overutilization of plant and machinery. Several other factors have made defense contracts less attractive than they once were, from a profit standpoint, and probably the most important of these is inflation. As the economist Barbara Ward Jackson puts it, "War is the most inflationary of all exercises," for military spending "puts no goods or services back into the economy to mop up the wages and salaries it distributes." In the end, then, economic self-interest may convince us that large military budgets are the worst possible form of concealed socialism—a threat not only to peace but also to the dollar. Heavy investment in social services would be an ideal alternative. A more likely prospect, however, is increased government investment in air transport and in other areas of advanced commercial technology that require federal subsidization.

A question arises. How does one account for the vast program of arms spending in Russia? Surely the Russians have no need for a socialism-avoiding subterfuge. No doubt the Russian military budget results in part from a (legitimate) fear of our own intentions, not to mention the mounting tension with Red China. But again, there may be another factor involved—something roughly equivalent to the military-industrial complex in this country—and this factor has been pointed out by Andrei D. Sakharov. Sakharov is the Russian equivalent of George Wald. A physicist, he is often described as the father of the Russian hydrogen bomb, and in recent years he has emerged as an articulate social critic who has challenged the Russian establishment with great courage. He has spoken out forcefully against neo-Stalinism and Russian military policy, calling on his country and America to join together in a humanist crusade to rescue the world from starvation and destruction. He has demanded intellectual freedom within Russia; he has criticized the biological engineers, and he has warned that technological pollution could destroy the planet.

In widely circulated writings, Sakharov has been particularly critical of his own country's bureaucratic elite, and has attributed the arms race in part to their "ossified dogmatism." He insists there is no effective defense against a massive rocket-nuclear attack, and he suggests a Russian-American moratorium on "senselessly expensive anti-missile systems." Beyond this he asserts that the world by 1975–1980 will face "a sea of hunger, intolerable suffering and desperation, the grief and fury of millions of people." This will provoke a wave of wars and hatred and a world-wide decline in living standards. There must be a concentrated program of economic and technical assistance for the underdeveloped nations, and this will not be possible until we have eliminated the "egotistical and narrow-minded" approach to international relations. "It is impossible as long as the United States and the Soviet Union, the world's two great superpowers, look upon each other as rivals and opponents." Sakharov said there must be significant changes in the foreign *and* the domestic policies of the two countries. "It is necessary to change the psychology of the American citizens so that they will voluntarily and generously support their government and world-wide efforts to change the economy, technology, and level of living of billions of people. This of course would entail a serious decline in the United States rate of economic growth. The Americans should be willing to do this solely for the sake of lofty and distant goals. . . . Similar changes in the psychology and practical activities of governments must be achieved in the Soviet Union and other developed countries." Sakharov proposed that the aid program should be financed by a fifteen-year tax equal to 20 per cent of the national incomes of the developed countries. Among other things, the imposition of such a tax "would automatically lead to a significant reduction in expenditures for weapons."

Sakharov's observations have been published in this country under the title *Progress, Coexistence, and Intellectual Freedom,* edited by Harrison E. Salisbury of the *New York Times.* Salisbury for his part contested the idea that the aid plan would slow our rate of growth and suggested instead that it "might well touch off the greatest economic boom in American (and world) history." However that may be, Sakharov is provocative in his criticisms of military spending and his constant jabs at the Russian bureaucracy that was the despair of Lenin's final days. He thinks capitalism and socialism have fought to a draw in regard to their potential for economic productivity, but he adds: "The development of modern society in both the Soviet Union and the United States is now following the same course of increasing complexity of structure and of industrial management, giving rise in both countries to managerial groups that are similar in character. We must therefore acknowledge that there is no qualitative difference in the structure of society of the two countries in terms of distribution of consumption." To accomplish economic reform, he indicates, one of the first orders of business in America and Russia must be "increased public control over the managerial group."

Salisbury has cautioned that "Sakharov is not the Kremlin." Nor of course is Wald the White House. Sakharov moreover appears to be in serious difficulty with his government at the moment, and this voice from Moscow could well be silenced. But Wald carries a copy of Sakharov's book with him wherever he travels, and he appears to share Sakharov's stated conviction that ultimately "victory is on the side of the humanistic, international approach." Wald said: "I think the important thing is to realize that people all over the world want just what we want. They want freedom. They want freedom of speech, and they want to see some sort of future before them. They want to be relieved of armaments. They don't want to feel a constant threat. They don't want to be pushed into the army. All over the world. And exactly the way American students feel, that's the way the Russian students feel; exactly the way American scientists feel, that's the way the Russian scientists feel. And Sakharov was telling us all about it. The point is, we and Soviet Russia by now are alike as two peas. Every guy we have in the government, in the Pentagon, has his opposite number in the Russian scheme of things. Those guys understand one another very well, and the only block between them if they sat down at a table together would be a language block. They are as alike as peas, and just as there are big industrialists in this country who see not only their wealth but their prestige and power in big armament contracts, so there are industrial commissars in Russia who are in exactly the same boat, and they love to make those nuclear weapons just as much as the people here who are in love with that kind of thing love to do it. But just as in this country, there are opposed forces at work, and the question is: Which side wins out?" Wald recalled the statement by the Secretary of Defense—America should "disarm from a position of strength." He said: "So this is a game. It's a game played by governments, and it's beginning to bother me very much to realize that it's a game that the ordinary people in these countries feel oppressed by. I think these people would get along very well together and understand one another very well. But just notice how hard it is to make a contact. Just notice how nicely walled off I am from making contact with Russians, with Chinese, Cubans, and various people who—I am told—would be on the opposite side of the fence. And they are walled off by their government from making that contact with ordinary Americans. I think this is a game played by governments, and it's a game of power—political power and wealth and prestige—and it seems very reasonable and as though it were paying off for the people who are playing the game. But it's pretty hard on the rest of us."

That is one analysis. The problem is not Vietnam; the problem is the military-industrial complex that began to take shape in this country in the years following World War II. But other critics take the analysis a step further and suggest that the basic problem is neither a particular war as such nor even military spending as such. For example, Christopher Lasch. He was sitting in his home one night, scratching his head and chewing thoughtfully on the ice that was left in his drink. He said: "The phrase military-industrial complex tends, it seems to me, to *conceal* the real nature of the problem, which is that it's a class problem, and not one that can be analyzed in terms of any particular interest group. In other words, it isn't just people who make bombs and airplanes and have too much interest in Congress. It's people who make anything. It's people who make lipstick."

In a word, capitalism.

According to this view, the starvation of the public sector is a direct consequence of the nation's production system. That system is geared essentially to produce private products for private consumption, and thus by its very nature is unable to support an adequate program of social services.

So says the socialist. To understand his criticism, let us look first at the case that is made *for* maximum private production. Let us start with the position of a fairly orthodox Keynesian economist such as Leon H. Keyserling.

In a paper criticizing Galbraith and calling for increased output, Keyserling argues that such production must serve many purposes in addition to personal incomes and outlays. He then offers a long list of social needs that range from education and transportation to housing and urban redevelopment, and he asserts: "All of these things are paid for, in the final analysis, not with money but with production." To which a puzzled socialist might reply: "But how will the production of soda pop and chewing gum pay to rebuild our cities?" Keyserling is ready with the answer. This will be paid for with a part of the "economic growth dividend" resulting from increased production. To explain this further, Keyserling cites the proposed "Freedom Budget" that he helped to prepare in 1966 for the A. Philip Randolph Institute. With "appropriate changes in policies," our total national production (in 1965 dollars) could rise from the $718 billion figure reached in 1966 to a possible high of $1,140 billion in 1975. Over the nine-year period 1967–1975, then, this would provide a level of production averaging annually $228.5 billion higher—and aggregating $2,056.5 billion higher—than if total production during the nine years remain at the 1966 rate. The aggregate figure $2,056.5 billion is the economic growth dividend for the nine-year period. Using only *one-fourth* of this dividend we could by 1975 reduce the numbers of those in poverty from more than thirty million to about two million; we could meet all the goals of the "Freedom Budget" and build a better America for all of its citizens.

In an effort to "prove" his case for more production, Keyserling first points out with some satisfaction that the real economic growth rate under the Democrats was lifted from a 1953–1960 annual average rate of 2.4 per cent to a rate of 4.8 per cent during 1960–1966 and a rate of 5.1 per cent during 1962–1966. "There can be no doubt," he wrote, "that the years from 1961 forward, under both the Kennedy and Johnson administrations, have registered substantial economic and social gains." But then he adds glumly that even these impressive growth figures were "not enough to avoid retardation of practically all of the Great Society domestic imperatives." In fact, the social programs provided "have been in almost all cases lamentably small." And this in Keyserling's eyes offers "the best empirical proof" that the GNP needs to be pushed still higher.

One might wonder just what it is that Keyserling actually proves. The idea of course is to collect a part of the economic growth dividend in taxes, and then to use that income to pay for social services. We have already seen, however, that the triumph of Keynesian economics resulted instead in a tax reduction. And the social services were not provided. Nor have they since been provided.

Keyserling complains that the tax cut was not in fact a "properly construed" application of the Keynesian approach. Almost half the cut was allocated to benefit corporations and high-income individuals who were already saving and investing too much; the problem was compounded by an "erroneous" policy of tight money and rising interest rates designed to combat inflation; an inordinate investment boom in producers' durable equipment "got entirely out of hand" and outboomed the rise in GNP by more than two to one; the trend in federal public outlays relative to the size of the economy continued downward, and ultimately in fact "the unbalanced boom sparked by the ill-considered tax reductions was succeeded by a very sharp diminution in the rate of economic growth." It is possible of course that Keyserling's interpretation is valid; it is possible that a policy of economic growthmanship would have worked quite nicely, if only the government had followed his advice to the letter. But the socialist would insist that such a policy is predestined to get out of hand—or rather is out of hand to begin with.

Presumably a fantastic increase in production would at some point create enough surplus to pay for social services. But only at some sacrifice to a still further increase in production. In other words, it would be necessary at *some* point to stop and say: That's enough production for the moment—let's rebuild the cities and succor the poor. But if our basic concern is the GNP—if it is our eternal goal to increase the GNP—that point by definition will never arrive. How can it? Thus the truth of the saying, the rich get rich and the poor get poorer. The gap between them continues to widen, and the richer the rich are, the poorer by comparison are the poor; the poor have further to go to catch up, and the problem of poverty becomes increasingly harder to solve. As for employment, it is possible to debate the notion that automation is actually reducing the total number of jobs—at the present time at least. But any new jobs generated by technology are likely to require skills that the poor do not have, and the general increase in private affluence will not help the poor in any way to attain those skills.

But the rich get poorer too. They just don't notice it at first. Their environment deteriorates, and angry people threaten their peace of mind. Sometimes the angry people kill them or steal their milk. Thus the socialists (and others) argue that the affluent sector fails to recognize the enormous social costs of private production—the so-called hidden or external costs. For example, the political economist Wassily Leontief has observed that market prices more often than not represent an incomplete picture of the real costs of production and the true benefits derived from the consumption of various goods. "The market price of a car, for instance, may reflect correctly the amounts of labor, capital, and of other material resources used in its production; the price of gasoline and oil reflects the cost of running it. But the no less real costs imposed on other people by the use of the car— increased air pollution and greater congestion of traffic lanes, for example—are, as a rule, not included in the price, and thus the prospective owner does not take them into consideration when he buys the car."

The attorney and industrial consultant Leland Hazard would add to the price list: the cost of policing streets and highways, running traffic bureaus and traffic courts, providing morgues and hospital and ambulance services for the dead and injured. Lasch also would extend the list. He said: "At this stage in its development the system of corporate, large-scale, semi-private capitalism more and more relies on the state to support it by performing all kinds of essentially unprofitable activities. And the automobile industry is a nice example of an industry which has to be subsidized publicly—you know, in the form of roads, in the form of urban renewal: a whole ramifying series of public activities that go on, the effect of which is to ruin the social, physical environment but which are necessary to the maintenance of a system that increasingly has to produce goods that people don't really need—that is, cars and so on." Thus Congress in 1956 established a Highway Trust Fund to finance what eventually will be a 41,000-mile interstate highway system costing perhaps $55 billion to $60 billion, and the fund is self-perpetuating—fed at present by a four-cent federal tax on every gallon of gasoline sold. The more roadway there is, the more cars there are; the more cars there are, the more gasoline is consumed; the more gasoline is consumed, the more roadway there is. As the industrial editor A. Q. Mowbray put it in *Road to Ruin*: "A perfect closed loop calculated to keep smiles on the faces of the highway builders."

We have heard Herbert Marcuse assert that the technological carrot results in a paralysis of criticism: the consumer is the prisoner of his needs and is sated to the point of apathy by the flow of material goods. A major criticism of Marcuse is that he overestimates the degree to which the production system actually delivers the goods. It might be more accurate to say that Marcuse himself fails to appreciate the hidden costs involved, but—as indicated—this also can be said of the average consumer, including the average working man. Marcuse also has made a case that the working man is alienated by his own automaton role in the production process; but again, Lasch and others feel that the worker is probably far more distressed by the hidden costs, although the source of his distress continues to elude him.

Lasch crunched on a sliver of ice. He said: "You can talk about the allegedly oppressive conditions of industrial work and how the worker doesn't have any say in the product and so forth, and how he's treated as a cog in a machine—all that, which is more or less true. But it doesn't have any kind of concrete meaning, because it doesn't confront real problems. If you're talking about the traditional blue-collar working class, that itself is diminishing in size and I suppose eventually will disappear altogether. But it still is obviously very central now, and I think it's as discontented and unhappy as can be—not from any generalized malaise, but because these people have very specific things that make them unhappy. There are things like their neighborhoods being threatened with imminent destruction—either because they're being bulldozed out of existence or because Negroes are moving in or because of a combination of these pressures. Their schools are deteriorating. The cities in which they live are deteriorating. The whole environment is deteriorating. And of course nobody pays any attention to *them*. Other people move away, and they have to stay there and live with it. So I think these are the real and immediate issues. And I think the problem comes from the fundamental tendency in this kind of society, where on the one hand the private sector is flourishing and on the other hand all public facilities are falling apart. So what this means for working-class people is that they only feel the oppressiveness of the system in their private lives—in their neighborhoods, or in their capacity as consumers, if you can distinguish that from what they do at work. At work they're pretty contented, because they don't perceive the relationship between what happens to them at work and what happens to them when they go home."

What happens at work in many cases is the production of a tremendous amount of junk.

What constitutes junk of course is a subjective judgment. But it might be defined here as a product or service that is less necessary for ultimate survival and well-being than some other product or service—or, more precisely, something that is produced *instead* of something else that *is* necessary for survival and well-being. From the viewpoint of growthmanship, however, the intrinsic value of the product is less important than the act of production. The producer is also a consumer, and his consumer demands will result in still more production. Production also is stimulated by advertising, which seeks to create new demands, and the nature of these demands once more is of secondary importance. As a Bell Telephone commercial informs us: "Now even though you don't need three phones you can afford them." And you should buy them after all, because the purchase of additional phones will create more jobs and more consumers to buy whatever it is that you produce. Maximum production and consumption then are the foundation on which the economy ultimately will prosper by creating a surplus of wealth to meet all our priorities; beyond that, however, production and consumption have become a way of life—an end in themselves. As Erich Fromm has expressed it, the modern American has been transformed into *Homo consumens,* the total consumer. "He spends his time doing things in which he is not interested, with people in whom he is not interested, producing things in which he is not interested; and when he is not producing, he is consuming." He is, in short, "the eternal suckling with the open mouth." And he is not happy. Consumption is a salty drink.

This view is shared by many young people, the children of affluence. Molly and the others were talking about it that night at Lawrence, and Molly said: "I guess my parents during the depression didn't have a lot of things they wanted to have, and everybody worked together then to get the bread, to buy the nice things that kept everybody together. And yet, it was not easy. And I get a lot of feedback on this deal from my parents. 'We decided we're going to give our child all the things that we never had— whether *you* like it or not!' And I know damn well that if I went home and, you know, said something that they weren't too eager to hear—I know that somehow or another my father would bring it around to what did I *want?* You know, materially. To make me shut up. And he's very upset by the fact that this doesn't sway me. Because this is his bag. If a father decides he wants bread for his family, okay; that's understandable. I can see that. But in a lot of cases it's way beyond, you know, giving them food. It's lots and lots of *stuff.* And why? Somebody asked me once why The Who gets a kick out of wrecking hundreds and hundreds of dollars' worth of equipment—this band called The Who, and every time they do a show they kick in their amplifiers and slam their drum sets around: hundreds, thousands of dollars' worth of equipment. And they get subsidized by a company. It's like they don't have to pay for it. But they really delight, you know, in smashing up the *materials* which are creating their art, and still have music. I don't know. As far as the indulgent parent is concerned—the twentieth-century American mother—she's simpering around saying: 'Go ahead, do whatever you want—but it'll kill me.' This is a really typical thing, I think. This is a lot of the reason why I buy half my clothes at rummage sales and why I left home and moved to the Near West Side of Chicago for a while. Then it began to hit me what a conversion reaction this was. They didn't have money so they wanted me to have it; they wanted me to have it so I didn't want it. So I said, wow, this isn't it. Because there's things it can get me, like an academic education. And so here I am again, getting an education, and they're paying for it. But even so. I saw a couple years ago in the so-called hippie movement, there was a real grub thing to it; there was a real anti-bread thing to it. Now I'm making an assumption that people didn't just say that; they're actually trying it. I mean, they're not just wearing blue jeans that are worn out because they put them in the washer and washed them fifty times the day they bought them; I'm making the assumption that they're wearing blue jeans because they're practical, and they last a long time. I mean, they actually decided there was something more than saying, you know, let's spread the bread around; there's also giving some of it up. There's so much bread floating around. And it's being used to kill people. And a telephone in every room with a twenty-five-foot extension cord, and send three men to the moon. All right, maybe this *is* just a part of the old conversion reaction. But you walk out from all this—electric can openers and knife sharpeners—and then you find out what it is to be very, very hungry. And okay, when I was brought up I had a little vacuum cleaner, and I had a little machine I could push a button on and it would pat me on the head and say, you know, you're a good girl. But I know—because I rebelled from this and went to see—that there are rats biting babies in the city of Chicago, and there are children eating laundry starch to stay alive. And it's not very pretty. And my mother, you know, is probably right *now* pushing a button on her electric knife sharpener. And I don't give a damn because I don't want one, but I mean—and it's part of the reaction, and I admit it—but I think that technology and all of those conveniences are a lot of shit when you start to look at what is happening to people who are hungry."

Yes, that's right. Molly is a spoiled brat, and the vaude-ville team of Frank and Milt Britton were smashing their equip-ment long before Molly threw her first tantrum, and poverty is not when you do your shopping in thrift stores. Poverty is when you know the bread isn't out there if you change your mind and want it, and the anti-bread movement lacks that one essential element that is necessary to understand why a depression gen-eration has a passion for possessions, a compulsion to acquire: it lacks the numbing sense of inescapability. From the mouths of spoiled brats, however, are coming some questions that need to be answered. And these questions would be valid even if the poor were not with us.

How much is enough?

Do we work to live or live to work?

Could we live without working—and what if we had to? What would we do if there was nothing to do?

A necessity to face these issues may ultimately be forced upon us by the production system itself—a possibility that has been raised most prominently perhaps by the economist Robert Theobald and by the Ad Hoc Committee on the Triple Revolution, which in 1964 drafted a widely discussed memorandum on cybernation and human rights. Cybernation is a combination of automation (in which human energy is replaced by mechanical energy) and cybernetics (in which human thought is replaced by computer thought). "This results in a system of almost unlimited productive capacity which requires progressively less human labor. . . . Potentially unlimited output can be achieved by sys-tems of machines which will require little cooperation from human beings." Negroes and teen-agers have been the first to discover that the labor force can no longer absorb them, and except in service industries there will be no significant creation of new jobs in coming years; there is consequently developing in America a permanently jobless and impoverished class. Cybernation without question could eliminate poverty both at home and abroad, but this is prevented at present by an outmoded industrial system in which job-holding is the basic mechanism by which economic resources are distributed. The jobless are crippled consumers, and the goods and services they need are not produced. This income-through-jobs distribution system is the main brake on cybernated progress. It follows therefore that "the major economic problem is not how to increase production but how to distribute the abundance that is the great potential of cybernation." The traditional link between jobs and income is breaking down. The economy of abundance could sustain all citizens in comfort; because of cybernation "society no longer needs to impose repetitive and meaningless (because unnecessary) toil upon the individual." National policy in the past has been more concerned with the welfare of the production process than the welfare of people; our policy in the future should be to free all people from unfulfilling labor and to encourage "new modes of constructive, rewarding and ennobling activity." Every individual and family should therefore be provided with an adequate income "as a matter of right." Beyond this, the economy as a whole must be directed in the future by planning institutions under democratic control. "Planning by private bodies such as corporations for their own welfare does not automatically result in additions to the general welfare." The democratic requirement therefore is planning by public bodies for the general welfare. "A principal result of [such] planning will be to step up investment in the public sector."

So said the Ad Hoc Committee, whose members included such people as Gunnar Myrdal, Michael Harrington, Linus Pauling, and Theobald. Theobald has since continued to beat this same drum with considerable energy, insisting that the cybernated utopia is not only desirable but inevitable. It will come despite our bumbling, and despite the emotional resistance to it that is inspired by the Protestant Ethic. According to Theobald, the Protestant Ethic had to be inculcated in the working man early in the nineteenth century to keep him on the job. People had a tendency to quit working the moment they had made enough to satisfy their basic needs, and for the industrial revolution to succeed it was necessary to convince them that their dignity depended on a job. But the Protestant Ethic "is proving highly undesirable in the second half of the twentieth century," and it is both "unjust and dangerous to socialize an individual to believe that he can achieve satisfaction in a job and then deny him the possibility of finding a job." But fortunately "attitudes are already shifting from a desire for further increases in wealth to a desire for self-realization." Young people and others are coming around to the Ad Hoc point of view.

Not Charles E. Silberman and the editors of *Fortune*. Their book *The Myths of Automation* is in large part an assault on the Ad Hoc position, and it presents sophisticated arguments to rebut the Ad Hoc statistics on unemployment and automated progress. For example, the "myths" about automation developed in the early 1960's "because the spread of the computer happened to coincide with an extended period of unemployment." There was no cause-and-effect relationship. The teen-agers, for instance, had the bad luck to flood the labor market at a time when there was already an oversupply of adult workers due to an influx of married women; the teen-ager who looked for work was competing not with a computer but his mother. Silberman's diagnosis was familiar: "the economy has not grown rapidly enough." We need more GNP to increase the aggregate demand for labor. Theobald in a recent publication dismisses all this with a footnote. "Even those," he writes, "who most vigorously deny the importance of the immediate impact of automation and cybernation accept that its long-run effect will be to replace people by machines." And to establish this he quotes a sentence from Silberman's book: "Sooner or later, of course, we shall have the technical capability to substitute machines for men in most of the functions men now perform." *Dirty pool, Theobald.* The sentence quoted is followed immediately by the observation: "But the decision to automate would still be an investment decision—

not a scientific decision. . . . In the last analysis, men will not be replaced by machines because widespread substitution of machines for men would tend to reduce the price of the latter and increase the price of the former, thereby creating a new optimum combination of the two." Human labor, in other words will be cheaper in some cases than machine labor, and business firms in such cases will continue to hire men. According to Silberman. But that seems rather a slender straw, taking the long view, and Theobald perhaps is correct in his footnote conclusion. "The debate has been narrowed to a question of the time span involved: there is no longer any real question about the reality of the development."

Silberman and Keyserling are economic soul brothers when it comes to one important point. The solution to our problems is seen in terms of increased production, whether that increase results from human labor or cybernation; the only real argument involves the method of distributing the new wealth to be produced. This essentially is a futurist analysis, and as indicated it poses fundamental questions concerning the nature of man, the meaning of growth, and indeed all of the basic assumptions that underlie Western concepts of progress and evolution; we will try to deal with them later. In regard to our immediate situation, however, most humanist types are more interested in the distribution of our present wealth—and some of them think it would be instructive if we all gave some thought to the implications of Sputnik.

The early successes of the Russian space program were accomplished by an almost baroque technology far inferior to our own. As Galbraith has wryly noted, these incredible achievements were not a result of great national wealth expressed in terms of automobiles, depilatories, and deodorants; the Russians obviously were making more purposeful use of their resources. Not necessarily better use, we should add. Russia's space ventures seem more ill-considered even than our own, in view of the urgent social needs that exist in that country, and they add weight to Sakharov's complaint that Russia too is controlled by an irrational bureaucracy. America reacted to Sputnik with alarm. (Remember all those old jokes about Russia claiming to have invented everything from the hot dog to the electric light? You stopped hearing them after 1957.) We looked with particular alarm at our school system, assuming that must be the source of the trouble, and significant reforms were instituted. But our chief reaction was to rush into space ourselves, to beat the Russians. Something like this very often occurs in a metropolitan newspaper office after a first edition has been published and the editors have a chance to compare their product with the first edition of the competition newspaper. The editors discover that the competition has devoted its banner headline to a story they have played back by the want ads and comics; their first instinct is to change the play in the next edition and give their banner to the competition story. The same drama of course is taking place simultaneously in the city room of the other newspaper. When the second editions appear each newspaper may well have reversed itself in response to the other. That is known as news judgment.

While the Russians may have their own priorities out of order, Sputnik did demonstrate that a society can achieve a goal if it believes that goal is important, and it will do so with the resources at hand. This is what Buckminster Fuller really meant when he said Congress was told to buy or die and it bought. In fact, the advance of science and technology has actually been based on the increased ability to do more with less: real wealth consists not of gold but the mastery of the physical and the conversion of energy (a fact Fuller drives home by pointing out that all the gold stores in the world could never account for the trillions of "dollars" spent on the development of the airplane). The moral here is simply that Americans right now could meet all of their social needs—if they thought that was important. To do so it is not necessary to goose the GNP any further; the only real problem is to convince Americans that it is important, and that the solution depends not on further economic growth but on an immediate transfer of priorities from the private to the public sector. Also a diversion of funds from the military-space programs.

As this is written, Pentagon counter-strategy appears to center on a *mea culpa* tactic of self-accusation. The top brass is telling the lower brass—and the public—that the public obviously is fed up with military inefficiency and mismanagement. The public is up in arms over the misuse of its hard-earned tax dollars and even now is demanding drastic cutbacks in spending. And the public is right! The level of performance has been intolerable. Unfortunately, all of this comes just at a time when the Russians may be making a renewed effort to achieve military and technological superiority; the situation is parlous, the prospects grim, the outcome in doubt—despite our best efforts they might well surpass us. It therefore behooves the military to see the error of its ways and atone for its sins, wipe the slate clean, and turn over a new leaf. Not a dime must be wasted; not a nickel. The confidence of the public in its military establishment must be restored; the survival of America could easily depend on it.

This in essence is a response to the kind of timid criticism that used to be made when the Army purchased a warehouse of left shoes or the Navy contracted to buy two warehouses of mustache wax. It assumes that the issues are efficiency, waste, and duplication—that the public wants to be reassured it will get a bang for a buck, as the saying once was. But these are no longer the issues. The more serious critics, for example, are not simply asking if a proposed weapon or system is efficient; they are not asking if it will work; they are asking if we *need* to build it, or if it might make more sense to spend the money on schools or housing. This kind of criticism in turn has evoked a more subtle response, and we are starting to hear warnings now that substantial reductions in military and space programs would slow the pace of technological progress. Aside from their immediate applications, these programs contribute to our technical knowledge as such—our technological base—and in doing so they also generate new products and jobs in the civilian economy. Therefore beware. These proposed social programs may be worthwhile enough—of course they are worthwhile—but people should understand that investments in that area will not produce the same kind of self-generating dividends: they will not create as many new jobs, and they will not add to our overall technical capability. So says the whispering voice. And to a certain extent the argument is valid, especially if you accept the idea that more jobs are the basic answer to our urgent social problems. But this argument on the one hand is a rather cynical admission that the socialism-avoiding subterfuge really does operate in the economy, and on the other hand it merely brings us back again to the Keyserling rationale for increased production. If you accept that rationale, the argument is sound; otherwise it is not sound. If it is not sound, what then must we do? Realistically there must at some point be an arms agreement with Russia; any meaningful cuts in viable weaponry will not be made unilaterally, and it would be wasted effort to push for that. Beyond this the public can insist that any further military expenditures be rational: that they actually increase our security in case of attack and not be intended merely to maintain a level of investment. The space program could be submitted to the same scrutiny.

Galbraith and others think the issue is serious enough to elect a President on next time. It certainly is serious, but as already indicated it may not in itself be the fundamental issue. A large reduction in military spending would undoubtedly be followed in the next breath by a widespread demand for tax relief—especially if the government's anti-inflationary programs should turn out to be overly successful and contribute to a serious recession. In the latter case a tax cut probably would make sense. In the long run, however, the fundamental challenge is to overcome the mystique of increased production and then to commit a major share of our resources and energies to the solution of our social problems. As a first step to accomplish this, three main courses of action are now frequently proposed.

First, a revolution.

That would be fun. Suggest it sometime to one of America's peasant workers while he is mowing the lawn outside his home; if it will cure crabgrass he might go along with it. But it is rather interesting that Sakharov for one has rejected this solution. "There are, of course, situations where revolution is the only way out," he writes. "This applies especially to national uprisings. But that is not the case in the United States and other developed capitalist countries." His reasoning is pragmatic. To begin with, the presence of millionaires in America is not a serious economic burden because of their small number. Sakharov adds: "The total consumption of the rich is less than 20 per cent, that is, less than the total rise of national consumption over a five-year period. From this point of view, a revolution, which would be likely to halt economic progress for more than five years, does not appear to be an economically advantageous move for the working people. And I am not even talking of the bloodletting that is inevitable in a revolution." Another advocate of growthmanship, it seems. If nothing else, however, this should serve to remind us that the old Bolsheviks were not romantic students; nor were they afflicted with myopia.

The other alternatives are (2) reformation of the Democratic party and (3) creation of a fourth party. The first of these is favored by Wald, for example, on the theory that Congress already contains a nucleus of right thinkers—some of them Democrats and some of them Republicans. "So I think what we need is a realignment of parties in this country. You put together those liberal Republicans and the liberal Democrats, and you've got yourself a party. And then you take that coalition of reactionary Republicans and reactionary Southern Democrats and Wallacites, and you've got the other party. And that would make an interesting political situation." In a weirdly logical variation on this theme, the economist Kenneth Boulding has suggested a coalition of the New Left and Radical Right based on individualism and their mutual antipathy toward the federal bureaucracy. But Raskin and others call for a fourth party and remind Wald of the abortive attempt by the Democratic Study Group to take over the Democratic party during the Eisenhower period; in the end the only thing taken over was the Democratic Study Group, and who in any case has led us to our present situation if not the liberal Democrats themselves? Lasch said: "The kind of party which would emerge out of that realignment—which may well take place—would be a reformist party which really didn't want to change anything. I mean it would be a Kennedy-type party." Lasch was in favor of a socialist fourth party when he wrote *The Agony of the American Left,* but he had changed his mind for the moment. He explained: "In the long run, if anything's going to change, it seems to me it will have to be a socialist party—and not the existing one either. But a number of things have to happen before any mass socialist party can emerge. And one of the things—certainly not the only one—is that there'll have to be some ideas—some theory, some strategy. In other words, the kind of thing we were talking about before. People will have to be able to make theoretical connections between the sphere of work and the sphere of consumption—a very detailed analysis of those things. But I don't think a party's main function is analysis and theory, so I think it's too soon even to think about parties."

Which brings us to a more basic question.

Assume that the New People have somehow come to power. They have the best intentions and a strong public mandate to correct the present system. What might they do to set matters right?

Classical socialism can hardly be the answer. Nationalization of major industries would not in itself solve anything at all; on the contrary, it would probably result in the kind of state bureaucracy that exists today in Russia. So many young Communists in this country are Maoist and anti-Russian because they resent Russian bureaucracy as much as they do the American version, not to mention Russia's foreign policies, and they feel that the Soviet leaders have betrayed the people's revolution: thus they turn to China on the dubious assumption that the Chinese leaders remember their Marx and Lenin better. Nationalization would not necessarily result even in a change of managers—just a change of employers—and for all practical purposes the managers of many big corporations are already working for Washington. What matters in the end is not so much the ownership of production as the *nature* of production. In this connection a rather interesting proposal has been made by David Braybrooke of Dalhousie University, whose reasoning goes somewhat as follows. The day may come when citizens will express a desire for fresh air, clean water, and well-planned cities. As individual consumers they cannot purchase these things themselves, but they can express their demand collectively to their elected representatives. Washington responds (of course) and is now in the market for social goods and services rather than bombs and bayonets; so do state and local governments. The law of demand and supply takes over. The corporations diversify their output and their sales efforts and start to seek out government contracts for the production of these "public goods." Governments are simultaneously active on the other side of the market. "As the private corporations invent and promote public goods on the supply side, governments at various levels would be busy inventing them on the demand side, and seeking out firms capable of producing them." Firms would compete vigorously to design and provide anti-pollution systems, recreation centers, parks, and museums. They would try to create new demands through advertising—but this time on behalf of public goods. "A crucial feature of the envisaged development is that it does not leave everything for the government to plan and organize in the public sector; it would make private corporations engines of progressive public policy."

Being realistic again, Braybrooke's plan has in its favor the fact that the nationalization of American corporations is about as likely to occur as sexual Prohibition. He correctly states that the left has failed to exercise its imagination about the future of private corporations, which are not going to fade away. "Is it to be imagined that social progress can be carried on ignoring them? To do so, if it were feasible at all, would flagrantly waste human and organizational resources." But the point here is not that this idea has any special merit or that it will work; in fact it will not work. And that is the point. It will not work because it is predicated upon a demand that does not exist. This in turn simply underscores, in heavy pencil, the fact that any shift in priorities from the private to the public sector depends ultimately on the national will and a major shift of values within the private sector. Without this, there is not a prayer of success for any plan, theory, idea, or strategy. As Paul Goodman nicely puts it: "American society would have to be about human beings rather than the Gross National Product." Goodman adds: "But all this amounts to a religious conversion and seems hopeless. It is possible that we cannot have such a conversion without convulsions; unfortunately I do not hear of any convulsions that would lead to the relevant conversion."

Lift your finger, Mr. Goodman. It is resting now on the pulse of the problem.

A conversion in fact is precisely what is needed.

A majority of Americans are obviously convinced that our present pattern of production and consumption is fundamentally All Right. Nothing much will change unless they come to see it instead as fundamentally All Wrong. And it would be easy to share Goodman's pessimism on this subject—if for no other reason than our continued consumption of cigarette smoke. The popularity of this product suggests that it is not enough merely to demonstrate that a reordering of our priorities is necessary and critical—that it would work to everybody's advantage and may be essential to our national survival. The American Tobacco Company simply changes its name to American Brands and we all light up again. Anybody got a match? But there is some basis for optimism when we recall the actual nature of conversion—as referred to earlier—and the fact that the process leading up to it occurs at a subliminal level, not apparent to the subject or to those who observe him. It is possible that new psychic energies are in motion below the surface of awareness, and it is necessary then that all those concerned should continue to push against that leaning wall. As Tolstoy's story indicates, it could fall some-day as the result of a convulsion that is not even relevant. Or there could be an earthquake.

But now the mirror turns dark again.

Prophets far more pessimistic than Goodman warn us that a change of heart will not change reality, and already we are too late to save ourselves. We are rushing toward madness and disaster, and there is no way to stop. The humanist criticisms we have listened to so far have been directed primarily at the *uses* of technology—at the system of production and consumption and those lunatics who control the system (namely us). It is time now that we listened to other critics who would tell us that *nobody* controls the system; when a certain level of complexity is reached the system starts to control itself, and ultimately it goes out of control altogether. The problem is not in the system as such; nor are we the problem. The problem is technology itself. Technology has become an independent force, and this force will crush us.

The most prominent spokesman for this point of view is probably the French social historian Jacques Ellul, whose book *The Technological Society* has attracted considerable attention in this country. Ellul describes man as a slug in a slot machine; he starts the machine going, but after that he no longer partici-pates in the operation. And the machine once started cannot be checked or guided; to imagine so is vanity, and man's humanity is lost in the process. "Everything today seems to happen as though ends disappear, as a result of the magnitude of the very means at our disposal." Worst of all are the scientists themselves, blind sorcerers who utter only the emptiest platitudes when they stray from their specialties. Some optimists think they have rediscov-ered a humanism to which the technical movement is subordi-nated, but they are pious dreamers; the best we can hope for by the end of the century is a world-wide totalitarianism which will allow technology its full scope: "a dictatorship of test tubes rather than of hobnailed boots." It is not quite clear how Ellul knows all this, but he tells us it is so—and you cannot help but feel that Ellul would be deeply disappointed if his predictions failed to prove true. He is a captious critic, and often a ridiculous one. For example, we read in *The Technological Society* that the technological society would never allow publication of a book such as *The Technological Society*. But it is necessary to take quite seriously the point of view that Ellul represents. So let us take another look at the technological machinery to see if there is anybody at the controls—and if so who. Once again, the best place to start is Galbraith.

Galbraith in his more recent writing has addressed himself to the question of power, and where it is located in the modern economy. In the early days of the Republic the decisive factor in production was *land,* and power belonged to the men who owned land: such Virginia gentlemen as Washington, Jefferson, and Madison. Labor was abundant, and agricultural equipment required very little capital investment; only land was in short supply, and therefore land was most important. In the nineteenth century, however, the new mechanical inventions expanded the opportunities for the employment of capital. For a time it was asserted that there was no real locus of power in a competitive market; but Marx soon set everybody straight on that point: power belonged to those who controlled the supply of *capital.* The wealthy landowners were thus dethroned by the big bankers and financiers: men such as J. P. Morgan and Andrew Mellon. And then in recent decades, within the large corporations, there was evidence of a shift of power from owners to *management.* At least where the managers were able to maintain profits, stockholders became increasingly impotent. Marxians argued that the change was superficial—that power still resided in capital. But meanwhile another development was taking place. Capital in the last century was not in surplus, and it owed its power to that very fact. Today capital is abundant. As one result there are no more famous bankers who are widely known outside the financial community. Power has passed now to a new factor in production: to organizational structure, or what Galbraith has referred to as the technostructure of the modern corporation. Thus the power of an organization is its *organization*. A complex organization is difficult to create, but once created it takes on a life of its own; it becomes a synthetic personality which consists not of one mind but of many specialized minds that supply the organization with the information it requires. The technostructure is so complex it cannot depend on the whims of the market, and it is so powerful that it has reduced the power of the market; customers are persuaded to buy what the technostructure has decided to sell—and these customers of course include, at the top level, the federal government. But, as noted, this power resides not in one individual but in many individuals with specialized knowledge—and these individuals moreover are not normally found at the top of the corporate hierarchy; the people with the information are more likely to be middle-level experts. So the decision-making power has passed from the individual to the group and also has moved deep down into the company where it is beyond the reach and competence not only of owners but of any individual. To a considerable extent it also has passed to the *universities*, which are the source of supply for these highly trained specialists. That in part is what Richard Flacks was complaining about some chapters back. Galbraith is more charitable. He writes: "I am not completely sanguine as to the way the educational estate will employ its new influences; the faculty meeting is not an utterly encouraging precept. But neither is a trend in influence toward the educated to be wholly deplored."

It would certainly be a gross oversimplication to say that these people are running the country at the moment; the country is a big place where many interests clash. But these are the people Zbigniew Brzezinski was talking about—the meritocrats of the technetronic society—and they wield enough power to upset a good many other people, including many general intellectuals of a humanist persuasion. This no doubt can be attributed in part to jealousy. The elite specialist pats the general intellectual on the head and tells him that unfortunately the specialty in question is beyond his comprehension—which often enough is well calculated to send the general intellectual running off in a pout to play games with the radical students, who don't like the bad specialist either. But it goes much deeper than that. The same specialist, for example, may also be called upon to testify before Congress—where he might claim esoteric knowledge of the need for a new weapons system (one he happens to be selling). And this could cost us a lot of money. Beyond that, it is asserted that the elitist problem-solver produced by modern technology is moving America in directions that are "strongly anti-democratic." That argument has been pursued at considerable length by John McDermott in the *New York Review of Books*.

Noam Chomsky called the meritocrats the New Mandarins. McDermott calls them the Altruistic Bureaucrats and defines technology as referring fundamentally to "systems of rationalized control over large groups of men, events, and machines by small groups of technically skilled men operating through organizational hierarchy." He points out that the evolution of the democratic ethos in Europe and America was based to a great extent on the development of a popular literacy that destroyed the gap in political culture between the mass of the population and the ruling classes. With the development of the printing press, the common man learned first to read the Bible—and later Tom Paine. But the new technology creates its own politics, and it also in so doing creates its own technical computer language that the specialists alone can speak and understand. It is an exclusive language, as Latin once was. The result is a decline in popular literacy in terms of our ability to grasp the social and political implications of technology. In this sense technology contributes to an erosion of the democratic ethos, and it provides the basis for a new class conflict in the society. It also contributes to the growth of social irrationality and explains in part the emotional response of many young people and others who protest the course technology appears to be taking. If the specialists lay claim to a higher rationality, what is there left to fall back on if not raw emotion?

It remains to be asked if these experts themselves are

actually in charge of anything. From one point of view they are more the victims than the masters of complexity. Fuller likes to point out that the extinction of various species in the evolutionary process has resulted invariably from overspecialization; an animal designed specifically to cope with one set of conditions cannot adapt to drastic change in the environment. To Fuller the human specialist is nothing more than a "brain slave" who does very well what he is programmed to do, and men who have sought power in the world have always followed a cardinal principle: divide and conquer. Thus the tyrant king had a simple solution whenever he noticed a bright young man who might eventually develop his own taste for power; he made that man a specialist. Power, then, is reserved for the comprehensivists—the men who employ the specialist brain slaves to carry out their grand schemes. Galbraith in this connection has dismissed as "pure vanity" the notion that the achievements of modern science and technology are the work of some new race of intellectual supermen. He writes: "The real accomplishment is in taking ordinary men, informing them narrowly but deeply, and then devising an organization which combines their knowledge with that of other similarly specialized but equally ordinary men for a highly predictable performance." This might suggest that the real power resides with the men who have the organizational ability to recruit the specialists and establish these complex structures—as Alfred Sloan put General Motors together. Once established, however, the organization runs itself; the power then resides in the organization as such. The people who constructed the organization are no longer important. And they no longer have any power over it. The organization will do what they intended it to do—but they cannot tell it to do something else.

This sounds very much like the description of a bureaucracy.

Edward T. Hall was talking about this. He said: "Sloan figured out what it was that would make General Motors work, and he put it together—and as far as I can tell they've been afraid to tamper with it ever since. Bureaucracies have inherent in them that, once you get them started, they will then continue to do that which they were designed to do—only more so. They're like beavers that have to build dams. And we've got the Corps of Engineers here, for instance. You can't stop them. They build dams all over the damn place. I mean, even if they're evaporating more water than they're saving, they'll still build dams. Logic has never stopped a bureaucracy yet. And the function of bureaucracies is to preserve themselves. Parkinson said a lot of this stuff presumably tongue in cheek, but it's absolutely right about the way bureaucracies function. So a lot of the problems in the world today are problems that stem from the fact that we've developed a whole series of bureaucracies, and we don't know how to control them. And the only way to control a company that I can think of is to put it out of business. You can't go in and reason with the president of the company or the chairman of the board and say: 'Look, you just simply have got to stop making DDT.' Their only answer would be: 'How are we going to meet our dividends?' So how do you deal with the problems the world is facing today—literally the degradation of all of life? How do you deal with the irrational? Because that's what it is. The kids are absolutely right when they say we're completely nutty, we're off our rockers. They're absolutely right, because there isn't anything rational about anything we're doing right now."

One answer to Hall's question has already been proposed by the Ad Hoc Committee: our problems can be solved through planning by public bodies under democratic control. This of course would not be possible unless there had first been a public conversion, and the national will now called for a massive effort to meet our social needs. Assuming that government was given such a mandate, the allocation of our resources might be controlled any number of ways. As indicated, the nationalization of major industries would not be necessary. If the people were willing to pay heavy taxes for social programs, as they now pay heavy taxes for military and space programs, there would be less income available for private consumption—and the law of supply and demand would automatically reduce the production of junk.

Many of the junk producers would be either forced out of business or forced to change the nature of their production. If government encouraged private industry to produce the public goods, as Braybrooke suggests, these firms might switch to that kind of production. Government in some circumstances might find it more economical to produce the goods directly, but the main objective in any case would be to change not the ownership of production but the *nature* of production.

There are at least two major objections to this idyllic picture, and both of them have been raised by the economist Martin Bronfenbrenner. It is easy to speak of a central planning agency that is under democratic control; it may be much more difficult to ensure that the control in fact will be democratic or will remain that way for any length of time. As Galbraith has pointed out, an important factor in the market revival after World War II was the publication in 1944 of Friedrich von Hayek's influential book *The Road to Serfdom.* The thrust of that book was that state economic planning leads inevitably to dictatorship and servitude. Bronfenbrenner and others feel that Hayek's argument has never really been answered and thus remains to be conjured with. This problem is all the more vexing in view of the mounting demand for participatory democracy and a greater local voice in decision-making.

The second objection is related to the first. In creating a central planning agency, would we not be creating just one more bureaucracy—indeed a bureaucracy to end all bureaucracies? Bronfenbrenner reminds us, for example, of the impressive failures of central planning represented by China's Great Leap Forward and various of the Russian and Indian Five-Year Plans. The reason for such failures supposedly was explained at the turn of the century by the Italian economist Enrico Barone, who demonstrated mathematically that a central Ministry of Production could never anticipate or integrate the vast multitude of factors involved in the operation of the overall economy; the law of supply and demand was inherently superior to any form of state planning, and always would be.

Bronfenbrenner concedes that this objection is no longer as valid as it used to be. He points for example to the revolutionary advances in gathering statistical data and also to the improved theories and techniques for processing such data: input-output analysis, linear programming, economic-stability analysis, and computer simulation of economic processes over time. And the radio-directed taxi driver is a good example of technology's increased ability to "put the right man in the right place at the right time." The computer is the basic piece of hardware in this information revolution, and Fuller in fact has described the computer as the ultimate answer to virtually all of man's problems—including the problem of specialization and the problem of war. According to Fuller it was always a fantastic joke to suppose that politicians could ever solve the problem of war. Nor will the problem be solved by demonstrations or peace marches. War is caused by the simple but fundamental fact that there is "not enough to go around." And computers in time will end the problem by producing a technological cornucopia—a horn of plenty from which will flow more than enough to go around for all the world. Beyond this the computers eventually will make the human specialist obsolete. No longer required to absorb great masses of detail and esoterica (all stored in the computer memory banks), all men in the future will be free to become comprehensivists like Fuller and can deal exclusively in general systems theory. They can turn their attention to "integrative patterning" and to "powerful generalization." Marshall McLuhan in the same sense has asserted: "As *any*thing becomes more complex, it becomes less specialized. Man is more complex and less specialized than a dinosaur." According to the Mazda mystic, prophet of the Electric Age, a perfect example of this is the computer-programmed automatic machine. For instance, such a machine equipped with grippers, benders, and advancers can make eighty different kinds of tailpipe in succession—just as easily and cheaply as an earlier machine produced eighty tailpipes of the same kind in the pre-electric and mechanical stage of technology. The computer-programmed machine has the flexibility of the human hand. It will eliminate specialization in education, and ultimately it will eliminate the world of work. In so doing it will make learning itself our principal form of production and consumption: all men in the future will "learn a living." Each man will be called to the role of artist.

This cheerful view of the computer will not go unchallenged in the following chapter. But let us assume for the moment that technology someday will enable us to solve all our economic problems. This promise would not satisfy Jacques Ellul and others who still insist that technology is a force that controls us far more than we control it; while it may provide us with material abundance, mankind in the process will be wholly dehumanized. Since there is nothing it cannot do, there is nothing that will not be done in its name. It commands us: that which can be done must be done. Thus it leads predictably to a certain kind of world that is predetermined by something inherent in technology itself: to a scientific dictatorship and—as part of that —to behavioral manipulation and genetic engineering.

This idea has been under examination by scholars participating in the Harvard University Program on Technology and Society, a ten-year project described as the most comprehensive study ever conducted on the social impact of technological change. The program will not be completed until 1974, but a preliminary report was released in 1969 by the project's executive director, Emmanuel G. Mesthene. According to Mesthene's report, the unrestrained exploitation of technology has resulted in widespread social problems. But these problems are due much less to "some mystical autonomy" that is exercised by technology, and are due "much more to the autonomy that our economic and political institutions grant to individual decision-making." Mesthene concluded: "The negative effects of technology that we deplore are a measure of what this traditional freedom is beginning to cost us."

Anthropologists would go a step further than this. Our political and economic institutions are merely the surface manifestations of something else that lies much deeper—something we are hardly yet aware of. As Hall put it: "We're just in the process of discovering this tremendous substratum that the anthropologists call culture. All men have a culture, but a culture for the most part is something that you have without ever knowing that you do have it. For example, man probably talked for thousands of years before he knew that he talked—because he didn't have words to talk about talking. And there was a certain point when some genius discovered that man talked, and to use our expression he began to rap about it. And this was the big revolution, because it was no time at all until men started to develop writing systems, and that changed everything. And the situation we're in now is very much comparable to the one in which man discovered that he talked. We're discovering culture. And all culture does is just simply control your life, and it molds everything that you are. Our technology and our religions and our philosophies and our written music are the things that most people call culture. Well, they're not culture at all. These are the extensions of this other base that lies underneath." It is culture that determines a man's perception of reality, and his language is a part of that culture; it is culture that made it impossible for a Hopi Indian to imagine a corn stalk existing any place that a corn stalk did not actually exist. But in our culture we talk of something like technology, as if technology were a thing that exists in reality: as if we had nothing to do with our own perception of it. Or uses of it. We fail to perceive that our perception of it is based to a considerable degree on the fundamental assumptions about reality that are a part of our cultural system. Hall said: "We have no control over what it is that we are until we learn what the system is. And then we can control it. But we have treated our philosophies as though they were life—and we're doing the same thing with technology, and you can see this in Fromm's writing and in other people's writing. Technology is treated as though *it* were the thing we had to handle. Because of course it's producing all this poison. And it's treated as though we couldn't do anything about it."

Cultural anthropology exposed the fallacy of Freud's biological determinism, as we have seen. Economists in the same sense are now taking a fresh look at the idea of technological determinism, and they are using cultural comparisons to evaluate the actual impact of technology. Thus a team of North American economists was assigned to find out why the growth of the British economy has lagged since World War II. They decided that Britain needs "growth via increased efficiency," but they paused to ask: "Are we not proposing growth and change in a society where don and docker alike prefer leisure and stability?" De Jouvenel recalls Marx's assertion that the most advanced country offers the less advanced the image of their future —and then goes on to compare modern Japan with the Britain of Marx's day. Japan in terms of per capita income has caught up with Marx's Britain, but Japan bears little resemblance to Victorian England. Modern Spain in turn has almost the same per capita income as Japan, but not much else in common. De Jouvenel asks: "Will you explain the enormous differences between Victorian England, present-day Japan, and present-day Spain wholly by differences in social values and attitudes?" If so, he says, you abandon entirely the notion that "as Technology goes, so goes Society." Boulding asks why the modern breakthrough in science and technology occurred in Europe rather than in China, since the folk technology of China was clearly superior to Europe's at least until the seventeenth century. "China clearly had the technology to explore the world and to expand its culture, and the fact that it did not do so is almost certainly due to the value systems of its rulers, which favored withdrawal, stability, and staying at home." Not so the value systems of Portugal and Spain.

Boulding proposes that the interaction of values and technologies is simply too complex to sort out: "a hen and egg problem in n dimensions." He goes on to suggest, however, that the thrust of technology is presently creating a *superculture* that is worldwide in scope. This is the culture of skyscrapers, expressways, and airports—"all airports are the same airport"—and it has not only a common ideology (science) but even a common language (technical English). It is a Coca-Cola sign on a remote mountain in the Canary Islands and a rusty beer can floating in the Gulf Stream current; it is a mushroom cloud rising over Red China. According to Boulding, all the major problems in the world today revolve around the conflict between this emerging superculture and the traditional cultures on which it impinges. The superculture does not appear to generate its own values to support it, and the only countries to adapt to it are those with strong traditional cultures and therefore strong ethical systems. Japan has been able to adjust to the superculture; in China the superculture has virtually destroyed the older culture.

So says Boulding. There is depressing evidence that he could be correct, despite the examples previously cited. It does seem that the more a country industrializes, the more it resembles the United States of America. But this does not mean that the future is closed, and it does not mean that Ellul's nightmares are the shape of things to come. On this point the last word must go to de Jouvenel.

It is silly to suppose that everything that can be done will be done—because it is not possible to do everything at once. A man comes to a fork in the road. If he goes one way, he cannot go the other way at the same time—and the course he takes may make it impossible for him to return again to the same fork. He has made a commitment, and it could be permanent. Similarly, an advanced industrial country is constantly engaged in research and development. In the process, de Jouvenel has pointed out, it inevitably develops a huge backlog of available techniques— ideas that *could* be put into operation. But first there must be a selection, and after that an operational investment. R&D expenditures have multiplied at least twenty times in the last twenty-five years, and operational investment has not kept pace. Nor could it. The backlog is overwhelming, and it continues to grow. Thus the rule: "as much more becomes technically feasible, much less of the technically feasible can be *embodied* in socially operational plant and equipment." To change the analogy, we are like customers in a supermarket; we have only so much money to spend, and there is only so much we can carry home. What we buy will depend upon our tastes—or our values—and unhappily we are not at the moment giving enough thought to our shopping list. But the decision at least is our own. In de Jouvenel's opinion, the age of technology is an age of opportunity. "No generation has been more free to lay the foundations of the good life," he writes. "But we shall not be free if we do not become aware of our freedom."

Perhaps we are free and perhaps we are not. But the only way to find out is to act as if we were, and this is why Ellul's morbid counsel is finally worthless and worse. What purpose does it serve? If we are doomed we are doomed, and if we are not doomed it would be folly indeed to assume that we were. Nor does it serve any purpose simply to suspend judgment on the matter, since judgment in this case cannot be suspended. As William James once again has pointed out, not to act is to act. A man retires on a bitter cold night and wonders if he has left the window open; if he "suspends judgment" and goes to bed, he has acted on the assumption that the window is closed. And if we go to sleep suspending judgment on whether or not technology can be bent to the shape of our dreams, we are acting on the assumption that it cannot.

This does not mean we are compelled to accept what may appear to be the present direction of technological change. On the contrary, it means we are not compelled to accept it.

There are those who will not accept it. And they have their reasons.

7

the Virgin and the Computer

One of Arthur C. Clarke's science-fiction stories concerns two computer engineers from America who were hired to install an automatic sequence computer in a Buddhist lamasery in Tibet. The High Lama explained that his monks had been busy for three centuries compiling a list that would contain all the nine billion names of God. When the list was completed the world would end, but the High Lama had calculated this would take another fifteen thousand years if the monks continued to work by hand. The engineers installed a Mark V computer. They supervised its operation for three months and then left the lamasery to return to America. As they rode down a winding mountain trail they looked up at the clear night sky. One by one the stars were going out.

Some humanists seem to think that computers really will blow out the stars. The computer to them is an infernal machine, a hated symbol of technetronic rationality. This reaction to the computer is itself symbolic of an anti-rational element that often appears in today's social protest movement. It is often dismissed simply as irrationality rather than *anti*-rationality. But there is an important difference. The latter in fact represents a conscious rejection of reason by many dissenters who claim a "moral intuition" that is superior to computerized logic. A feminine intuition, if you will—and this regardless of the sex of the dissenter. It might help us to understand this development to refer to a theory that Erich Fromm introduced some years ago in connection with the Oedipus myth.

Fromm suggested that the myth had nothing to do with incestuous rivalry but referred instead to an ancient conflict in Greece between matriarchal and patriarchal systems of society. This idea is based largely on J. J. Bachofen's analysis of Greek mythology. Bachofen in 1861 had proposed that sexual relations originally were promiscuous, which meant that a child's consanguinity could be traced only to the mother; women in consequence were respected as the source of life and law, and they ruled both the family and society. There is evidence indeed that the Olympian gods were preceded by a religion in which the supreme deities were mother goddesses. After a long struggle, however, the men took over and established a patriarchal society and a patriarchal religion.

According to the Fromm-Bachofen thesis, matriarchal culture tends to emphasize blood ties, ties to the soil, and passive acceptance of all natural phenomena; patriarchal culture is characterized by respect for man-made law, by rational thought, and by the effort to change natural phenomena. The patriarchal principle is one of order and authority, obedience and hierarchy; in the patriarchal system the main virtue is obedience to authority. The matriarchal principle is one of love, unity, and peace; the mother extends her love to her own children and to all of life; the idea of man's universal brotherhood is rooted in the principle of motherhood. Fromm wrote: "In the matriarchal concept all men are equal, since they are all the children of mothers and each one a child of Mother Earth. A mother loves all her children alike and without conditions, since her love is based on the fact that they are her children and not on any particular merit or achievement; the aim of life is the happiness of men, and there is nothing more important or dignified than human existence and life." In short, matriarchy is humanistic. Patriarchy is authoritarian and hierarchical, and the central theme of the Oedipus myth is the attitude toward authority: "the myth can be understood as a symbol not of the incestuous love between mother and son but of the rebellion of the son against the authority of the father in the patriarchal family."

The poet Robert Graves also has played with this thesis, but its historicity is very doubtful. There simply is no serious evidence that women at any time actually ruled in Greece. And as for the supposed respect that was accorded to women because of their childbearing role, Bachofen perhaps never knew that the female contribution to reproduction was recognized only after the invention of the microscope; men had assumed that women provided merely a comfortable nest for the male sperm, and it was not until 1827 that the female ovum was discovered by the naturalist Karl Ernst von Baer. But this by no means rules out the existence of a fundamental antagonism or tension between maternal and paternal views of the human condition, and in fact the notion goes back to Plato's concept of a female eros and male logos. This same idea was developed by the philosopher F. S. C. Northrop in his classic study *The Meeting of East and West.* Northrop was intrigued by what he called "the female metaphysical principle" in the Catholicism of Mexico. He remarked upon the adoration of Mexico's patron saint, the Dark Madonna, Our Lady of Guadalupe. Her divinity was not mediate through Christ; the Mexicans appeared to worship her as divine in her own right, and Northrop proposed that the Virgin represented the female eros: "the emotional, passionate, metaphysical principle in the nature of things." Christ on the other hand represented the male logos: "the rational, doctrinal principle, formalized explicitly for orthodox Catholicism by St. Thomas Aquinas." But it was the Virgin who for the most part inspired the devotion of the high-spirited Mexican Catholics.

The original Catholic orthodoxy had been based on the Platonism of St. Augustine, a religion of passion which emphasized the female eros in the nature of things and the emotional love of God. But St. Thomas followed the science and philosophy of Aristotle and thus emphasized the male logos, maintaining that the good life is controlled by reason and the rational knowledge of God. Northrop wrote: "This is the reason why the emotional, passionate person in the Christian Church's symbolism is the female Virgin and why the doctrinal, rational person in its symbolism is the male Christ, representing the unseen, because only rationally known, God the Father." But Plato unfortunately had "quite arbitrarily" branded the emotional female principle as evil and the male rational principle as good (a consequence perhaps of knowing Socrates' wife). "This is why one destroys orthodox Christianity when one attacks reason, why the Protestant Church does not allow the Virgin in its symbolism at all, why it tends to be afraid of vivid colors, the passions and the emotions, and why the Catholic Church, when orthodox . . . always insists that the Virgin is not divine immediately in her own right, but only mediately because she is the purely earthly mother of the Christ." Northrop was writing during a period when Catholicism was experiencing a revival of neo-Thomism, and there have since been many changes within Catholicism and Protestantism, but the main thrust of his argument remains as valid as it was in 1945.

Freud's views of individual and social development were strictly authoritarian and patriarchal, but there also has been a matriarchal school of analysis represented among others by Otto Rank. We have already mentioned his theory of the birth trauma as the basis of all later anxiety, as well as his influence on Fromm. Rank believed that the birth trauma results in a perpetual desire to return to the mother; in the primal horde the function of the father was to prevent the sons from acting on this desire. The

British psychiatrist James A. C. Brown has summarized Rank's theory as follows: "In a patriarchy the ruler is the one who prevents return to the mother, and the primal anxiety of the mother is transformed into respect for the king or ruler. Increasing masculine domination results from the desire to exclude women in order to keep repressed the memory of the birth trauma, but periodically the wish to return to the mother asserts itself and revolutions against masculine dominance occur. . . . In Christianity, the Son becomes God and the primal mother Mary, while the primal father is the Lord of Hell. The crucifixion is a punishment for rebellion against the Father and is followed by resurrection—that is, birth." Similarly, the British analyst Ian Suttie held that the basic fear is loss of mother love and that man's social acivities all arise from the basic need for such love. He wrote: "I think that play, cooperation, competition, and culture-interests generally are substitutes for the mutually caressing relationship of child and mother. *By these substitutes we put the whole social environment in the place once occupied by the mother.*" In turn, failure to receive the love that is desired may result in an inferiority complex, in schizophrenia, in persecutory attitudes toward society, or in acting-out behavior that is intended to attract attention: "You must love me or I will bite you."

A rather curious example of patriarchal-matriarchal conflict was provided some years ago in a study of the symbolism of editorial cartoons in the *Chicago Tribune*. Analysis of the cartoons indicated that the *Tribune* had a collective Oedipus complex (Frommian variety). The noble virtues, such as thrift and patriotism, were invariably personified by stern-looking father images: an Abraham Lincoln, a George Washington, an Uncle Sam. The deadly sins, such as government spending, characteristically were represented by a heavy-breasted slattern in a Dogpatch barnyard who carried a naked child under each arm and had dollar signs all over her tattered clothing. Mom the Earth Goddess was obviously a Democrat.

Another example is William Bolitho's reaction to America's first hippie, Isadora Duncan. Bolitho was fascinated by Miss

Duncan, and his well-known portrait of her in *Twelve Against the Gods* expresses his admiration of her adventuresome spirit. But he was clearly annoyed by Miss Duncan's habit of sponging off people who had money. Thus he fumed when she casually asked a woman with sixty millions to write her a check for fifty dollars, and he wrote: "It was a matter of simple justice to her; those that have must give. And in this, this essentially social, if not socialistic, anti-Nietzschean conception of the rights of the poor, an indefinite number of men might not concur. How many women in their hearts, I do not know. The concordance, in fact, between the form into which the modern state is undeviatingly proceeding everywhere, and the womanly, as distinct from the masculine social ideal, cannot be quite accidental. Somewhere at the end of it is the State, the great provider, husband for every woman and father to every child; an interesting research for day dreamers. And, if it is so, or approximately, the adventurous, unsocial, masculine life is destined to take on even more rigorously the character of a revolt."

In the hall of dynamos, as we have seen, Henry Adams was inspired to view technology as a force—a force that was wholly new in the universe. The forty-foot dynamo became a symbol of infinity: "one began to pray to it." The newly discovered radium rays "were a revelation of mysterious energy like that of the Cross." But Adams at Lourdes had also recognized another force—the force of the Virgin and of Venus: the force of woman. At Lourdes this force still seemed as potent as X-rays, "but in America neither Venus nor Virgin ever had value as force—at most as sentiment." Americans had never been truly afraid of them. The Woman had once been supreme in the world, when she was a goddess because of her force: "she was the animated dynamo; she was reproduction—the greatest and most mysterious of all energies; all she needed was to be fecund." But evidently America was ashamed of her and she of herself; why else was she strewn so profusely with fig leaves? The monthly magazines had created an American female that Adam would not have recognized. Sex in the past had been strength; but the Puritans knew that sex was sin, and in America only Walt Whitman and a few others still insisted on the power of sex. You could see this power in the naked Aphrodite of Praxiteles, and you could see it in the creations of Michelangelo and of Rubens, but Saint-Gaudens instinctively preferred the horse as a symbol of power. Or a railroad train. The typical American man had turned his mind and hand to mechanics; he had his hand on a lever and his eye on a curve in the road; he could not run his machine and a woman as well. So the woman was emancipated—that is, she was left to find her own way. And the whole world saw her trying to find it by imitating the man; she must, like the man, marry machinery, and in doing so become sexless like the bees. The Virgin-Venus had been the greatest force the Western world had ever felt. But now for Adams there was no other choice: "he turned from the Virgin to the Dynamo." He had to. "An American Virgin would never dare command; an American Venus would never dare exist."

That was in 1900. Seven decades later there is reason to believe that a Venus does exist now in America, and that much of the current reaction to technology is an expression of her matriarchal values. Summarizing a number of studies, for example, Seymour Martin Lipset finds the following pattern: leftist activists tend to be the offspring of permissive families characterized by a strong mother who dominates family life and decisions; conservative activists tend to come from stricter families in which the father plays a dominant role. The conservative activist students tend to fear such emotions as pity and compassion for the oppressed, while the leftists, "more likely to have been raised in female-dominated families, are more prone to be open expressively toward 'feminine' concerns."

Lipset has a caveat. A disproportionate number of the leftists are Jewish, and Lipset wonders if the differences described are not simply the differences that exist between Jewish and Protestant families. To prove that child-rearing practices play an independent role in the determination of political choice it would be necessary to compare students *within* similar ethnic, religious, and political-cultural environments. "I think that question has been fairly adequately answered now," said Keniston. A number of studies have compared Jewish activists and non-Jewish activists. "And they showed that exactly the same variables distinguished the gentile activist from the non-activist. In other words, it's not being Jewish that's the factor; it's the way you're brought up. And it happens that more Jews are brought up in a certain way than gentiles are; but if a gentile is brought up that way too—that is, in a humanist family that emphasizes these values—then he too is just as likely to become an activist."

Keniston in his *Young Radicals* himself reports evidence of "an unusually strong tie between these young men and their mothers in the first years of life." This close maternal tie in turn "seems to have evolved into an unusual responsiveness to the mother's wishes, especially with regard to academic achievement." And the maternal pressure for academic performance was considerable. Involvement with the father on the other hand was ambivalent. The father in many ways was highly respected, but in other ways was seen as "unsuccessful, acquiescent, weak, or inadequate." The mother was the more active and vigorous partner within the home, and the father's greatest strength lay outside the family, in his work. There also in many cases was a sense of disappointment that the father in his own life had not been able to comply always with the ideals he had expressed to his children: that he was "unwilling to act on his perceptions of the world." It seems probable, Keniston concludes, "that in many activist-producing families the mother will have a dominant psychological influence on her son's development." Keniston adds:

As a group, activists seem to possess an unusual capacity for nurturant identification—that is, for empathy and sympathy with the underdog, the oppressed and the needy. Such a capacity can have many origins, but its most likely source in upper-middle-class professional families is identification with an active mother whose own work embodies nurturant concern for others. Flacks's finding that the mothers of activists are likely to be employed, often in professional or service roles like teaching and social work, is consistent with this hypothesis. In general, in American society, middle-class women have greater social and financial freedom to work in jobs that are idealistically "fulfilling," as opposed to merely lucrative or prestigious. As a rule, then, in middle-class families, it is the mother who actively embodies in her life and work the humanitarian, social, and political ideals that the father may share in principle but does not or cannot implement in his career.

Discussing this recently, Keniston said he later found evidence in his group of a somewhat stronger relationship with the fathers: "that is, a positive and warm relationship of identification, although with a number of qualifications in terms of the extent to which the fathers had not actually lived out the values they had taught their sons." But he added: "I think the general point is correct—that patriarchal society is eroding, and that what might be called matriarchal values are coming more into the ascendant. This goes along with certain things that Feuer said—I mean some of what he said, not most of it; but some of it is right, about the de-authoritization of the older generation, particularly of the fathers, under present circumstances, all over the world. So I think that indeed authority is being challenged, has to be challenged, in a time of rapid social change. Now, it's very difficult for me to say that humanitarianism or peace or interracialism are paternal or maternal values. But on the other hand it's clearly true that for humanist youth many of the old notions of masculinity are not an attractive ideal any more, and that there is much more acceptance of what were traditionally considered—and this has to be put in quotes—'feminine' qualities of gentleness, empathy, sympathy, compassion, love, tenderness, and so on."

Flacks agreed. "This is a broad change in American society," he said. "I think it's irreversible. I think it fits with the kind of advanced technological society we have that male and female roles in the family are less distinctly defined—that there is much more equality within the family. But I think anybody who claims this pattern is distinctive of kids who are in active rebellion is kidding himself. I think it's a prevalent pattern throughout certainly the middle class. I mean, I don't see this business of egalitarian families and blurring of sex role differences in the family as being necessarily a direct cause of political activism or political protest. In other words, I think that *most* middle-class suburban families today have these characteristics—where the mother is the central figure for the children, and the father is in many ways less central." But suppose then that two of these typical suburban families were found living next door to each other; one of them produces a radical and the other produces one of Daniel Offer's modal adolescents. How would Flacks account for that? He said: "Probably the main difference would be that the family which produced the radical was more interested in political affairs— more discussion of politics, more concern over what was happening in the outside world—and probably also was more intellectual in that they read more books, talked more about books, and their recreation had to do with the arts and intellectual affairs rather than the outdoors and sports and so on. I think we did exactly the kind of study that you propose there, and I think that's essentially the finding that we had."

Offer in fact reported that a majority of *his* subjects also felt much closer emotionally to their mothers than they did to their fathers—at first. By the time they were ready to enter college, however, they tended to identify more with the fathers, and in many cases they had begun to feel a sense of awkwardness or estrangement in their relationships with the mothers. Talking about this, Offer said: "I don't mean to be critical of Keniston. Well, maybe I do. But he has his own conceptualization of the warm parent, and with all due respect, you know, he doesn't give you anything you can test. So it's a methodological question. But I might say—and this is a guess—that Keniston's mothers are overly involved in their children. They smother the children and won't let go." He twined his hands together and said: "I like to use the analogy of the two hands. If you have parents and children who are very strongly tied together—not necessarily symbiotically, but obviously too much so—then in order to separate them you need a lot of strength, and you have to pull them apart." He tugged with his hands. "But if you have a relationship which is good and smooth and mutually satisfactory, then to separate is relatively easy." And his fingers slipped apart. "The mothers in my group were possessive, but they could let go. They don't want to separate, but they know they have to separate. It's very painful for them, and it's very slow: it takes them many years, I think. But they can do it when they have to."

A related criticism was expressed by Jarl Dyrud and Daniel Freedman. We have already suggested the possibility that some radical students may attempt to establish a separate identity by outradicalizing their liberal or radical parents, and we have mentioned that the radicals often appear to resent a parent who does not always practice his own preaching. Along these same lines, Keniston writes that it seems probable "that many activists are concerned with living out expressed but unimplemented parental values." Citing studies by Frederic Solomon and Jacob R. Fishman, he proposes that many activists are "acting out" in their demonstrations "the values that their parents explicitly believed, but did not have the courage or opportunity to practice or fight for." Now see how the same basic observation can be interpreted to imply something much less innocent. Said Dyrud, in reference to Offer's subjects: "This is not data, but I have the fantasy that the nonturmoil kid who shares *overt* goals with his parents will develop the means to achieve them—and, since these are congruent to his parents' attitudes, the program will run fairly smoothly. But in these other families I had the impression that, even though the mother was warmly related to the radical child, whose means were very good, he nevertheless had overtly developed a *covert* goal of the parents. And I think that's why he went so far with it. In other words, he was living out the disappointments of his parents—acting out the unfulfilled, megalomaniacal fantasies of the parents rather than the reasonable expectations of the parents. And even though the

the Virgin and the Computer
169

child is a very competent child, it's a bad program. If your goals are overt they are tempered by reality and experience, and they become attainable, and the means can be developed to reach them. But if you have covert goals which are never tested in that way they remain unrealistic and unattainable." Freedman picked up the point. "That's right," he said. "Untested by the parents. And what you see if you watch the kids is a testing of these covert goals on behalf of the parents: 'What's going to happen *if*?' So they are testing consequences in reality at the expense, I would say, of the stability of the whole society, at a time when reality-testing at this level should be much more modulated. Because somehow or other in this identification with the covert goals— the untested goals of the parents—they never stop to ask certain questions. For example, this criticism that the parent copped out. Well, what was the real option for the parent? What were the consequences if the parent *didn't* cop out? That they don't know about."

Dyrud said: "You know, there's an odd congruence between the parents' covert fantasy and the child's attempts to meet it. I mean, these parents who come and warmly support their child who is sitting in. They come very close to the attitudes of other parents—inhibited parents—whose children are acting out sexually." Freedman offered an example of this. He said: "These attitudes are transmitted to the child by a system of signals. The best case I ever saw of it involved a young girl I saw in a clinic. Her problem was acting out in promiscuity—getting pregnant all the time. And what was her history? Whenever she came home from a date her mother would go into the bedroom with her and look at her panties. Now if you come home from a date and have your panties inspected—well, what's the message to the girl? 'What is most interesting between you and me?' And these are the way these signals come. It doesn't take any magical reading. So I'm sure we could find ideal scenarios going on in these radical homes, let's say, which also tell what to do. If I sit at the table and verbally slay the President with excellent facility, I don't know what message that gives. It must give some message.

I don't know if that's the way it actually happens. But it ain't mysterious, I'm sure."

Evidence to support this suspicion is easily adduced. Parents of radicals are quoted in *Time* magazine: "I'm proud of Nick's involvement. Perhaps he's doing what I didn't have the guts to do." "I don't always agree with Mike, but I admire him. . . . He's one of those Americans who's not thinking about himself. He's an idealist." An eighteen-year-old draft resister was recently freed from a four-year federal prison term when he tearfully confided to a judge that he did not register for the draft because his mother would not let him. So let us acknowledge that this factor may very well exist in some cases, at the pathological edge. It is something that we should be aware of—a precautionary footnote—and the individual might want to consider it in evaluating his own motivation and conduct. But again, it is dangerous to extrapolate from clinical experience and therapeutic examples. Nor does it serve any purpose in evaluating the social impact of a mass phenomenon: in this case the widespread assertion in the society of matriarchal values and goals. Whatever the final judgment may be then, let us turn now to a consideration of these values and their possible effect on American culture.

Various cultures historically have emphasized one of the two principles, the patriarchal and the matriarchal. Thus one speaks of Germany the Fatherland; but it is Mother India and Mother Russia. America for its part is symbolized by a patriarchal Uncle Sam—but also by Columbia, who lifts her lamp beside the golden door and offers her love to the tired and the poor, the homeless and the tempest-tossed. If there is now a humanistic revolt in this country it may in a sense be represented by a shifting of emphasis from Uncle Sam to Columbia, from the patriarchal to the matriarchal, from the rational to the intuitive, from scientific values to spiritual values, from the authority of the father to the more permissive and democratic attitude of the mother. This in turn may explain in part the so-called blurring of the sexes. A humanistic young man, stressing matriarchal ideals, is not likely to conform very well to the American stereo-type of crew-cutted, jut-jaw masculinity. That stereotype for many people has always been difficult to live with, and it probably has contributed to such aberrations as the male transvestite: a man who from time to time likes to put on female clothing and act like a woman. Transvestites say they are not homosexuals, that transvestitism has nothing to do with physical sex. Said a middle-aged stockbroker: "It's just that there are times when I feel I have to express the feminine side of my nature. So I slip into a dress, and I vacuum the house or something." According to one theory, transvestites as little boys were coddled and dressed in skirts by mothers who had really wanted daughters. Said another transvestite: "It wasn't that way at all. It was my father. He used to pick me up and kiss me and love me. And then when I was about ten or so I realized that he had stopped that—except with my sisters. All I got was a slap on the back if I hit a home run. I thought if I was a girl he might still love me the way he used to. They don't have transvestites in European countries where they don't see anything wrong when a father embraces his son and shows his affection in that way. In France the gen-erals even kiss you when they pin a medal on you." A Jewish interviewer once asked a transvestite: "What can you do as a transvestite that I can't do?" The transvestite said: "I can go to a movie and cry." "But *I* can go to a movie and cry too," said the interviewer. "That's because you're Jewish," said the transvestite. Which seemed to rattle the interviewer a bit—but was probably true. Jewish culture does not regard emotion and compassion as strictly feminine qualities; a man who can weep is no less a man, and a man who cannot may be something less than human. The same of course is true of other cultures; you can make your own list. The point is, however, that American views on this subject appear to be changing—especially among the young. Keniston said: "One sees a lot of people today who are not transvestites and who are fairly secure in their masculinity who are perfectly happy to go to a movie and, you know, cry. And I think that's something that fifty years ago would have been much harder for a man to admit."

But the implications of this development go far beyond a few tears shed at the movie house. We have suggested that the female eros may be responsible in part for an anti-rational reaction to technology and the formal logic of science. The Virgin and the computer. What is the basis of their conflict, the nature of their quarrel?

Richard N. Goodwin, a former presidential assistant, has pointed out that you can ask a computer whether you have the military capacity to accomplish an objective, and the computer will answer either "yes" or "no." The computer will never say: "Yes, but it is not a good idea." One reason for this has been mentioned by Sakharov, who follows Norbert Wiener in warning of the "very real danger" that results from "the absence in cybernetic machines of stable human norms of behavior." Sakharov cautions that computer advice "may turn out to be incredibly insidious and, instead of pursuing human objectives, may pursue completely abstract problems that had been transformed in an unforeseen manner in the artificial brain." This may be perfectly true, but it verges on the popular fear that computers are not to be trusted because they are "inhuman." In one sense, though, they are all too human, and this may represent the greater danger and a more fundamental reason to distrust them. For example, it might be argued that a computer could be programmed to supply the answer Goodwin wanted—if enough data were fed into it. But in fact—to guarantee accuracy—you would have to know the answer beforehand in order to select the relevant data. And this is true in the case of any rational judgment based wholly on a "logical" consideration of factual evidence. It is the eternal fly in the ointment of the scientific method. As the distinguished scientist Lecomte du Noüy has said, "the sanest judgment is always questionable because it is impossible to assemble all the elements required to give it an absolute value." This really is the heart of the problem. The scientist never has all the facts at hand;

he must always operate on the basis of incomplete information. Thus he is always plagued by the possibility that his decisions will have unforeseen consequences.

The sociologist Peter Rossi was chatting about this one afternoon in connection with liberal demands for instant programs of social reform. A liberal himself, he was making the point that even well-intended actions can lead to unanticipated problems. "For example," he said, "in the 1930's a major cry of the liberals was better housing for the poor—not anticipating that public housing would become a ghetto for the most unorganized elements of the poor, a dumping ground for the unwanted. Which wasn't what we had in mind. Or a liberal mortgage policy for the poor. We didn't anticipate it would create suburbs. So you get very skeptical about the consequences of reform, and more appreciative of the wisdom of existing institutions."

Another example was provided by the installation in highrise apartment buildings of elevators that are summoned by heat-sensitive call buttons that respond to the mere touch of a finger. As a safety precaution the elevators also were equipped with electric eyes to prevent the doors from closing on anybody who was entering or leaving the elevators. But convenience and safety turned out to be a potentially lethal combination. This was not discovered until later, when fires occurred on the upper floors of some apartment buildings. Firemen found that in some cases the heat of a fire summoned all the available elevators to the burning floor. The doors slid open, and the residents jammed into the elevators. But the smoke blocked the electric-eye beams, and the doors would not close. The residents could not ride down in the elevators, and the firemen could not ride up in them. Et tu, Otis.

A related objection to scientific rationalism is that science necessarily distorts reality by oversimplifying it—using gross statistics to create an artificial average. As an example of this, Carl Jung said that a scientist might weigh all the stones in a bed of pebbles, divide the total weight by the number of stones, and thus determine that the "average" stone weighed 145 grams. But it is possible that none of the stones would actually weigh 145 grams, and the average weight in any case would not give you any idea what the pebble bed really looked like. Jung was tempted to state as an axiom of reality that "the real picture consists of nothing but exceptions to the rule, and that, in consequence, absolute reality has predominantly the character of irregularity." Jung added:

At the same time man, as member of a species, can and must be described as a statistical unit; otherwise nothing general could be said about him. For this purpose he has to be regarded as a comparative unit from which all individual features have been removed. But it is precisely these features which are of paramount importance for understanding man. If I want to understand an individual human being, I must lay aside all scientific knowledge of the average man and discard all theories. . . . Scientific education is based in the main on statistical truths and abstract knowledge and therefore imparts an unrealistic, rational picture of the world in which the individual, as a merely marginal phenomenon, plays no role. The individual, however, as an irrational datum, is the true and authentic carrier of reality, the concrete man as opposed to the unreal ideal or normal man to whom the scientific statements refer.

"The world is much richer in detail than science can possibly suggest," agreed Rossi, who at that time was director of the National Opinion Research Center. "The whole development of science is a kind of rape of experience, forcing people into simple molds. I'm sure there must be individual differences on the molecular level which if molecules could complain would make them resentful of chemists. Of course science simplifies, because it has to. But let's not confuse the simplifications of science with living as an individual. It would be a mistake, for example, to choose a wife on the basis of a statistical prediction formula—a great mistake. Based on background similarities of a gross variety you might be perfectly matched by a computer and hate each other on sight. Or vice versa. If I'd consulted a computer about my own wife I would never have married her, which would have been a serious error. We can only make gross predictions about a mass of individuals—based on religious background and so forth—and the errors of prediction are really quite large. In a way it's like physics. We know how gas molecules behave, but not any specific gas molecule. We also know how Catholics behave, in general, but we never know what any particular Catholic is going to do—when he steps into a polling booth, for example."

Rossi was referring to the fact that the so-called laws of nature are derived by applying the statistics of chance to a vast number of particles; at the atomic level, however, individual particles appear to behave in a completely chaotic manner—as if they had free will. This has been seized on to support the argument for human free will, but a number of physicists such as David Bohm have suggested there may be a deeper level of causation, as yet undiscovered, that would also account for the behavior of an individual particle. Rossi acknowledged this theory, but added: "Philosophically, however, I believe we will always find some kind of irreducible capriciousness in the world. I like to believe that anyhow. I don't like to contemplate a world where you could have a completely accurate, deterministic social science. That would take an awful lot of fun out of life; it would take a lot of fun out of child-raising, for example: the way it is now, there's always the mystery of what's going to happen next year. Once it's happened you can maybe explain it all right, but it's interesting to watch it unfold. As a scientist I'm perfectly willing to live with a certain amount of uncertainty, and as an individual I delight in it."

A final objection to computer logic has to do with the manner in which facts are selected for analysis. As Theobald has pointed out, a scientific experiment may often be structured to exclude what it does not wish to perceive; or as Fromm has said, the particular facts chosen for computer analysis "can be untrue by their very selection, taking attention away from what is relevant." Or worse yet, from what is sane. Fromm reminds us that logical thought is not rational if it is merely logical. "Paranoid thinking is characterized by the fact that it can be completely logical, yet lack any guidance by concern or concrete inquiry into reality; in other words, logic does not exclude madness." It might be more correct to say that paranoid thinking is logical after a point; that is, a paranoid chain of thought becomes logical if you accept the major premise on which it is based. For example, I once wrote a series of newspaper articles on illegal wiretapping by private detectives. As a result, a number of readers came to the newspaper office to ask for help. They complained that they were under electronic surveillance, spied on by neighbors or by alien creatures from outer space; many of them were under the impression that their radio and television sets were listening to them and watching them, rather than the other way around. A middle-aged salesman was convinced he had been followed for years by Greta Garbo. A spinster pursued by sex fiends would undress only in a dark closet, she said, and since her bathroom was bugged by television she had not bathed for several years. The way these people lived and the elaborate precautions they took made perfect sense—if you accepted the premise that they were in fact being spied upon. If you accepted that, they were the most logical people you could ever hope to meet. Similarly, our defense spending is perfectly logical if we accept the premise that the Russians at any time may develop a capacity to destroy us without suffering intolerable damage to themselves; or it is logical if we accept the premise that world peace is best achieved by increasing our own capacity to destroy the Russians more effectively than we can already destroy them. Then the Secretary of Defense is entirely rational when he describes the ABM as "a building block to peace." And the President is rational when he rejects the establishment of a Department of Peace on the ground that we already have a Department of Peace—consisting of the Department of Defense and Department of State. If we did set up a Department of Peace, as the President pointed out, this might lead some people to think that these other departments were *not* a Department of Peace. It would not be logical.

(In other days we were less logical but possibly more honest. We used to have a War Department and a Secretary of War—as well as war bonds that later became defense bonds and then savings bonds. If our language is going to keep pace with our logic, they will have to become peace bonds.)

But against such logic the female eros asserts itself. In effect and in fact it shuts its ears and refuses any longer to "listen to reason." One of the best examples of this is provided by Noam Chomsky in his book *American Power and the New Mandarins.* Chomsky writes that he felt increasingly uncomfortable when he took part in debates on the Vietnam War. He goes on to explain, in a passage that is worth quoting at some length:

I remember reading an excellent study of Hitler's East European policies a number of years ago in a mood of grim fascination. The author was trying hard to be cool and scholarly and objective, to stifle the only human response to a plan to enslave and destroy millions of subhuman organisms so that the inheritors of the spiritual values of Western civilization would be free to develop a higher form of society in peace. Controlling this elementary human reaction, we enter into a technical debate with the Nazi intelligentsia: Is it technically feasible to dispose of millions of bodies? What is the evidence that the Slavs are inferior beings? Must they be ground under foot or returned to their "natural" home in the East so that this great culture can flourish, to the benefit of all mankind? Is it true that the Jews are a cancer eating away at the vitality of the German people? and so on. Without awareness, I found myself drawn into this morass of insane rationality—inventing arguments to counter and demolish the constructions of the Bormanns and the Rosenbergs. By getting into the arena of argument and counterargument, of technical feasibility and tactics, of footnotes and citations, by accepting the presumption of legitimacy of debate on certain issues, one has already lost one's humanity. This is the feeling I find almost impossible to repress when going through the motions of building a case against the American war in Vietnam. Anyone who puts a fraction of his mind to the task can construct a case that is overwhelming; surely this is now obvious. In an important way, by doing so he degrades himself, and insults beyond measure the victims of our violence and our moral blindness. There may have been a time when American policy in Vietnam was a debatable matter. This time is long past.

Chomsky then describes a newspaper photograph showing a girl holding a baby sister who had been wounded by American helicopter fire directed on a hamlet in the Mekong Delta. He writes: "I cannot describe the pathos of this scene, or the expression on the face of the wounded child. How many hundreds of such pictures must we see before we begin to care and to act?" A logical book review editor offered this book to Arthur Schlesinger, Jr., one of the New Mandarins described therein and an arch rival of Chomsky. Schlesinger in his review referred to the passage about the photograph and wrote: "The incident could hardly have been more horrifying; but it simply does not by itself justify political conclusions. Would the photograph of German children in Dresden or Hamburg wounded by bombs from allied planes have led Chomsky to argue that we should stop the war against Hitler? In short, logic prescribes that the case against the Vietnam war must be established—as it easily can—on other grounds than the tragic fact of the killing or maiming of innocent bystanders. But Chomsky has no particular regard for logic."

Schlesinger neglected to mention that the raids on Dresden and Hamburg have been widely criticized as senseless atrocities—possibly the worst of World War II. The two raids created ghastly fire storms that killed perhaps 130,000 persons in Dresden and 50,000 in Hamburg, compared to about 71,000 killed at Hiroshima. Dresden in fact has been described as the greatest single massacre in European history, and there is room for doubt that either raid contributed significantly to ending the war against Hitler. But whether they did is not the point, nor are we concerned here with the specific issue of Vietnam as such— whether or not our intervention there is legitimate or necessary. Richard H. Rovere may have come close to the point when he wrote a few years ago that "there is building up in this country a powerful sentiment not simply against the war in Vietnam but against war itself, not simply against bombing in Vietnam but against bombing anywhere at any time for any reason, not simply against the slaughter of innocents in an unjust conflict but also against the slaughter of those who may be far from innocent in a just conflict." Schlesinger to the contrary, this suggests that "the killing or maiming of innocent bystanders" may in fact constitute excellent grounds for ending a war—or not starting one in the first place. Such a sentiment of course can be described as romantic, impractical, and unrealistic; it certainly has no particular regard for logic, and it will not put an end to war. It surely will not. But it is equally true that wars will never end without this sentiment. Which brings to mind the little girl in Carl Sandburg's poem *The People, Yes,* who saw her first military parade and remarked: "Sometime they'll give a war and nobody will come." Another case of female reasoning. It is the essence perhaps of the antagonism between Chomsky and Schlesinger: *eros contra logos.*

Eros serves us well when it opposes itself to logic that is based on paranoid fictions. It also serves us well when it opposes itself to logic that is based on statistical distortion of human complexity—for example, the logic of urban renewal. It was a woman, Jane Jacobs, who first called public attention to the kind of bulldozer rationality that fails to recognize the importance of cultural variety in urban neighborhoods; her book *The Death and Life of Great American Cities,* published in 1961, offers a brilliant defense of such variety, and it has provoked the wrath of the pebble weighers. Edward T. Hall too has criticized the demolition of ethnic neighborhoods or enclaves by urban renewal planners who seem blind to the fact that they are destroying more than buildings. He has pointed out that such enclaves historically have served an essential function in the American city, providing a haven in which rural people could comfortably and successfully make the transition to urban life. Moreover, different cultural and ethnic groups have developed complex social sytems which are related in a very intimate way to the physical structure of the enclaves: hallways and stores, streets and churches. These social systems in turn represent almost the only aspect of urban life today that is not calculated to alienate people and drive them apart; but they are demolished along with the buildings, and the results are often appalling. One study showed for example that the destruction of an entire neighborhood in Boston's West End caused a significant number of Italians there to become deeply depressed; their world had been shattered, and they appeared to lose much of their interest in life. "We're trying to save the buffalo," said Hall. "We're more careful now not to wipe out a species. But we still think nothing of wiping out a way of life for an entire group of people. This is more than the quality of life. This is life itself. What is life about after all unless it's relationships with other people—all the seemingly inconsequential pieces that go to make up the fabric of existence?" At the root of this problem is the idea of the Melting Pot, our consistent refusal to accept the reality of uniquely different cultures in a heterogeneous society. As Hall put it: "Negroes, Indians, Spanish Americans, and Puerto Ricans are treated as though they were recalcitrant, undereducated, middle-class Americans of northern European heritage instead of what they really are: members of culturally differentiated enclaves with their own communication systems, institutions, and values." Thus we miss the richness of diversity, and help to destroy it. We impose upon diversity the smothering sameness of the technological superculture; we deal with human needs on the basis of a logic borrowed from science: a logic that treats people like gas molecules. And when the bulldozers arrive the people say "no." They cannot articulate their objections; they cannot put into words what the machines would take away from them; they can only say "no." Which of course is not rational. They are not reasonable people. Just ask the urban renewal planners, and they will tell you just how unreasonable these people can be.

Once again, eros serves us well when it opposes itself to a logic that is based on psychological determinism. Rossi said that he hated to think of a world in which it would be possible to have a completely accurate, deterministic social science. But Rossi is not B. F. Skinner, and in fact there are many scientists for whom such a world is a pleasure to contemplate. In addition to protesting some of the uses of technology, matriarchal humanism therefore finds it necessary also to protest what amounts in some cases to a technological definition of human identity.

Erikson and others have said that a firm sense of personal identity requires at least some sense of autonomy: a feeling that the individual somehow is acting on his own, not simply being acted upon. But science has tended very often to deny that autonomy. Charles Darwin in the nineteenth century proposed that man is an animal; in turn the physics of that era proposed that the physical universe is a vast machine that follows a cosmic edition of *Robert's Rules of Order*: a clockwork mechanism whose movements are wholly predictable and predetermined, the product merely of cause-and-effect relationships. Freud put the two concepts together and made man a wholly predictable animal. As James A. C. Brown put it, referring to the principle of causality: "Freud was the first to apply it to the study of personality in the form of a literal and uncompromising psychic determinism which accepted no mental happenings as 'accidental.' " Now, in this century, behavioral psychology has gone one step further and made man a wholly predictable machine—studying the human being as if he were an object or a thing. Or more often than not studying rats, not men, and then projecting the results to provide an explanation of human behavior—producing what the novelist Arthur Koestler has called a "ratomorphic" view of mankind.

It is necessary to distinguish between clinical behaviorism and experimental behaviorism. The former has developed new methods to deal with crippling neurosis and in so doing has provided a significant alternative to psychoanalysis. A good example of this is "The Case of the Frightened Tram Driver," as reported by the British psychologist H. J. Eysenck. The tram driver in question had developed an almost incapacitating fear of human blood; even a nick while shaving was enough to upset him. An analyst might have spent several years inquiring into his childhood experiences, trying to discover the source of the phobia. But the man consulted a behaviorist who was not really interested in the reason for the phobia; his concern was to cure it. So the driver was submitted to a series of interviews in which he was hypnotized and shown progressive amounts of human blood, starting with a faintly blood-tinged bandaged. In a comparatively short period of time the patient "could visualize a casualty ward full of carnage and not be disturbed by it." Two days before his last session he saw a man struck down by a motorcycle. "The victim was seriously injured and bleeding profusely. The patient was quite unaffected by the blood, and when the ambulance arrived, helped to load the victim on to it." (It might be argued that the therapy produced an insensitive monster, but at least the poor man can shave himself now.)

Behavioral therapy for the most part utilizes a system of punishments and rewards, or aversive controls and positive reinforcers. As an example of the former, a behaviorist friend has successfully treated homosexuals by showing them photographs of homosexual perversions and then subjecting them to an electric shock; as an example of the latter, he has procured experienced female prostitutes to introduce his patients to heterosexual pleasures. It might appear that the behaviorists treat symptoms rather than diseases, but they insist that their patients do not simply develop new neuroses to replace the old ones; on the contrary, removal of a neurotic symptom will usually produce an overall improvement in the patient's total personality. There is considerable evidence that these claims may be justified, and it would be difficult to object to therapeutic methods that relieve human suffering.

Humanism's quarrel is with experimental or academic behaviorism which degrades human dignity and lends itself potentially to social engineering by meritocratic technicians. For example, one aspect of behaviorism is S-R, or stimulus-response research. This supposes that a given stimulus will always produce a given response under similar conditions, and that careful study of the reaction patterns will provide an inclusive explanation of human activity. As for the human personality that responds to the stimulus, that is merely a ghostly figment of the romantic imagination—what the Oxford University philosopher Gilbert Ryle described as the "ghost in the machine." The machine of course being the human organism. (Which made Koestler so angry he wrote a whole book to refute the notion.) B. F. Skinner is the leading exponent of this deterministic theory; he does not strictly speaking consider himself an S-R psychologist since he tends to view behavior as more fluid in nature—"it isn't made up of lots of little responses packed together"—but he does insist that the behavior of an organism is wholly determined by the external environment. "As far as I'm concerned the organism is irrelevant either as the site of physiological processes or as the locus of mentalistic activities." The behaviorist Clark Hull once wrote that "for the purposes of analyzing behavior, we have to assume that man is a machine." Skinner for his part has said that if machine means a system that behaves in an orderly way, "then man and all the other animals are machines." He has described emotion as "the probability of engaging in certain kinds of behavior defined by certain kinds of consequences." Thus anger is a heightened probability of attack, fear is a heightened probability of running away, and "love is a heightened probability of positively reinforcing a loved person." This kind of talk tends to produce in humanists a heightened probability of vomiting, and in fact Skinner has wondered aloud about the kind of violent reaction he provokes: "I've often asked myself what's eating these people." That indeed is a very good question, and Skinner perhaps should think on it some more. If man really is a machine, why should he resent it so much when somebody calls him a machine? That seems a very curious way for a machine to behave.

But the question of free will is not the real issue here; the fact that B. F. Skinner happens not to believe in free will is after all a matter of small consequence, harmful to no one, and the worst it could lead to is a loud argument. The real issue involves the possibility that conditioning techniques developed in the behavioral laboratories might ultimately be used to manipulate mass behavior—that man in the future will be treated as a machine, and perhaps in the end will be transformed into something very closely resembling one. As indicated earlier, the really serious threat would be an alliance of molecular biologists and behavioral psychologists in a technetronic program designed to relieve social tensions by the alteration of man's genetic structure and psychic processes. This might be accomplished by a combination of genetic engineering, aversive controls, positive reinforcers, drugs, and the electrical stimulation of brain centers. The result could well be the Cheerful Robot that C. Wright Mills used to talk about. Skinner in fact has already outlined his own concept of such a "planned utopia" in a novel he had the colossal temerity to title *Walden Two*. It would be based almost exclusively on positive reinforcers. "The alternative to punishing people who behave badly is to build a world in which people are naturally good." Skinner acknowledged there was "a real danger here," in that behavior might be controlled to a point where any opposition to the controls would not be possible. "When people are being pushed around, controlled by methods which are obvious to them, they know who and what is controlling them, and when things become too aversive, they turn against the controller." But the use of positive reinforcement might make it difficult to identify the source of control. "Even though you are inclined to revolt, you don't know whom to revolt against." Which might suggest that the time to revolt is now, while the potential controllers can still be identified and resisted.

The revolt in fact has started, and Wald and Sakharov have joined it.

Wald said, in reference to genetic engineering: "Learning about DNA, that's a marvelous and proud achievement. The more we know about it the better. But immediately then one transposes that knowledge into a technology and says we'll begin to manipulate human genetics and guide the future course of human evolution—and that's *all wrong*. I would say that just as we have operated in the past with a legal principle of the inviolability of human life, we are now going to have to erect a legal principle of the inviolability of the human germ plasm—the hereditary material. It may be that certain instances will arise in which one will be willing to permit certain things to be done over that barrier. But the barrier should be high, and any such effort should have to meet that barrier and overcome it." Sakharov warned of the new methods that might be used to manage the norms of behavior, "the strivings and convictions of masses of people." He said: "It seems to me that we cannot completely ignore these new methods or prohibit the progress of science and technology, but we must be clearly aware of the awesome danger to basic human values and to the meaning of life that may be concealed in the misuse of technical and biochemical methods and the methods of mass psychology." And he added: "Man must not be turned into a chicken or a rat."

In response to behaviorism and Freudianism there has also emerged now a so-called third force—*humanistic psychology*. The Brandeis University psychologist Abraham H. Maslow has been a leading spokesman for this movement.* An angry and tangible ghost, Maslow has called for "a new image of man." Just as humanism puts man and man's needs at the center of concern, humanistic psychology rejects any concept of mankind that is based on the physical sciences or on studies of the lower animal orders. Its central concerns also are man and man's needs: "the need for love, for friendship, for dignity, for self-respect, for individuality, for self-fulfillment." Maslow does not believe you can explain these needs and aspirations by studying

* —which we have discussed in some detail in *The Private Sea* (1967).

rats and electrons. A great many other scientists have not believed this either—but it must be counted a significant development when a major scientific system arises to oppose the logic that man is a machine, or that man could be managed in the manner of machinery. Maslow and others have even started to talk about something called "transhumanistic psychology," which takes into account man's religious experience. Maslow indeed has asked for a new science that will resacralize and respiritualize our concept of human life. He wrote recently: "I am denying the whole modern history of science which has from its very beginning claimed the need to be value-free, value-neutral, value-rejecting. . . . The world of objects and the world of things *is,* in a sense, value-free. However, human beings are *not* value-free; they live by values, they live for values." And he urged his fellow scientists to join the humanists in "a rejection of the tendency to technologize, to make something value-free, merely a matter of technique."

One can almost hear Skinner asking, "What's eating that man?" Indeed, Skinner has said that his concepts have "nothing to do with the interests of the humanists." Skinner goes on to say:

. . . we see that the humanist and the behaviorist have different conceptions of man and the nature of man. But if it is the goal which matters, rather than the conception, then I feel that the weight of evidence is all on our side. For example, in education we can specify materials and methods which bring about the changes in the student we want to bring about—and in a very effective way, much more effective than the person who thinks of the student simply as an individual whose wishes must be respected, who must make decisions, and so on. He may make decisions, but the forces which lead him to do so must be taken into account. People who have most respected the student as an individual have at some time or other confessed to a need to arrange conditions which lead him to want to do what he wants to do.

Well, as a matter of fact the conception *does* matter—and to people such as Maslow it matters very much. As far as the conception is concerned, however, the evidence probably does not weigh very much on either side of the argument; Maslow can no more prove that man is not a machine than Skinner can prove that he is a machine. But again, this aspect of the quarrel has very little to do with evidence or with formal logic—as far at least as the humanist is concerned. Skinner may be arguing from the standpoint of evidence—a very shaky logos in this case —but Maslow's reaction essentially is an emotional rejection of such evidence, the eros refusing to listen or accept. As we suggested earlier, and as Skinner himself implies, the goal in this instance probably does matter more than the conception—and the goals of the behaviorists and the New Biologists can be criticized both on rational and intuitive grounds: a combination of logos and eros. For example, Skinner might be asked how he knows what the student wants to do; he might also be asked who the *we* are who decide what changes "we want to bring about." Those are logical questions and rather important ones. Behaviorism in fact is wide open to rational attack, and one of the best criticisms of its conditioning techniques was formulated by a man who never heard of B. F. Skinner or behaviorism either. Mark Twain once observed: "We should be careful to get out of an experience only the wisdom that is in it—and stop there; lest we be like the cat that sits down on a hot stove-lid. She will never sit down on a hot stove-lid again—and that is well; but also she will never sit down on a cold one anymore."

Another fundamental objection to human engineering involves the possibility referred to earlier of unforeseen consequences. These occur, it was said, because the scientist necessarily operates on the basis of incomplete information. Of course he must operate that way, and there would be less cause for concern if all men of science were as circumspect as Sakharov and Wald; but they are not, and that is the problem. We have mentioned the proposal by the Columbia University physicist Gerald Feinberg that mankind adopt as its final goal the creation of a universal consciousness. This idea is spelled out in Feinberg's book *The Prometheus Project,* which deserves as wide a reading as possible. It should be read as a warning, for it represents the pathological edge of scientific rationality: logos gone loco. Feinberg, for example, begins with the statement that there is no plan or pattern to evolution; it follows logically from this premise that there is no such thing as an inherent human nature, and man therefore is free to determine his own psychic and genetic future. Feinberg does not tell us how he arrived at this premise; maybe he read it in Sartre. In any case, he goes on to state that natural selection is no longer the most desirable method for producing change; among other things, it works too slowly. "Hence there is no reason why we should wait for evolution to bring about those changes in man that we desire. If we can only agree on our goals, our technology can do the rest. . . . It may be that a revision in man's psyche would be more relevant to human happiness than any transformation of the environment." As a first step Feinberg suggests that "the most rapid progress will be made in the area of machine consciousness and in producing links between man and machine." Of course there is always a possibility we might make an "irreversible" decision: "the human way of life may change so drastically that there is no realistic possibility of returning to the previous way." So we had better be careful: "we had better know the consequences of what we are doing." And how do we "know" the consequences before they occur? Well, "it seems possible to determine in advance when some action may have irreversible effects and, at least in broad outline, what these effects would be." Feinberg adds: "We might define as a part of progress any development that enables us to accomplish something we could not do before, whether or not we choose to do it in practice. . . . We will not know what we can achieve until we try." Precisely. And what if we happen to choose the wrong goal for mankind? Feinberg replies: "I do not think that it will be held against us that we planned on the basis of the best information we had."

This man is at large and has three degrees. It would be

possible of course to debate him on logical grounds, to dispute his premise and to argue against his conclusions; but there also is something beyond logic that tells us, as it told Wald, that this is *all wrong*. And this something could well be man's salvation.

The Virgin and the computer. Erikson too has recognized the basis of their quarrel, and he has made an interesting proposal to reconcile their differences. He began by noting that woman's potential contributions to our male-dominated society have yet to be determined, and he wondered how her "specific creativity" might be fully utilized—not only in the home but in industry and education, government and science. He asked: "Do we and can we really know what will happen to science or any other field if and when women are truly represented in it—not by a few glorious exceptions, but in the rank and file of the scientific elite?" It is possible they might open whole new fields of inquiry which the masculine mind cannot so much as conceive; there could well emerge a female science, or a female branch of the sciences. Following that line of thought, Erikson said: "I am reasonably sure that computers built by women would not betray a 'female logic' . . . the logic of the computers is, for better or for worse, of a suprasexual kind. But what to ask and what not to ask the monsters, and when to trust or not to trust them with vital decisions—there, I would think, well-trained women might well contribute to a new kind of vision in the differential application of scientific thinking to humanitarian tasks." To continue the thought, the women might also be asked to decide whether cloning people is a good idea, or patching together an uncle and niece; they might decide whether it is necessary in a given situation to go to war in order to defend the national interest or honor; they might be put in charge of the Red Telephone, or the Washington-to-Moscow Hot Line. Lecomte du Noüy said that man must use his reason, "but he will perpetrate fewer errors if he listens to his heart." Or in this case perhaps, his wife.

Not all women would agree with this. The economist Sonia S. Gold, for example, has disputed Erikson's implication that women have a special "nurturant capacity" and therefore should concentrate on the nurturant goals of the society or seek nurturant employment within the economy. "Historical evidence," she writes, "would seem to indicate that both men and women have concurred and participated in the nonnurturant behavior of society and have also carried out specialized nurturant functions. . . . The sharp division of the society into nurturant and nonnurturant activities and environments, with sex role differentiation sharply maintained on this basis, is really a matter of ideologic preference." Which raises the question: is there in fact a unique feminine identity?

Freud thought there was one, and he thought it was inferior. He suggested that women from childhood on are dominated by envy of the male penis; as Susan Lydon has written, he cast them in the role of "mutilated males." He also insisted that a sexually mature woman must experience vaginal orgasm rather than clitoral orgasm. This made her sexual pleasure dependent upon the male organ—and further served to emphasize her inferior status. But the widely publicized research conducted by Dr. William H. Masters and Mrs. Virginia E. Johnson has now demonstrated that all female orgasms are centered anatomically in the clitoris—that vaginal orgasm does not differ anatomically from clitoral orgasm. This means then that a woman's sexual pleasure is not necessarily dependent upon the male, and knowledge of that fact has further served to "liberate" her from masculine domination. Erikson's research also has led him to conclude that women are not mentally preoccupied with something that is not there; rather, they have a secure and satisfying awareness of "inner space": in a word, the womb. Thus little boys in school tend to draw pictures of towers, outdoor views of houses, and other exterior scenes; little girls are happy to draw doorways, rooms, and other interior scenes. Which indicates "a shift of theoretical emphasis from the loss of an external organ to a sense of vital inner potential." But Erikson has followed Adams in suggesting that woman's so-called emancipation may prove to be an illusion if it merely offers her the right to be more like men; he continues to believe she has a specific creativity which has yet to be defined. However that may be, it does appear that many women today are acting more like men—just as the men for their part are acting more like women. Erikson has said there is obviously developing "a new balance of Male and Female, of Paternal and Maternal." This in turn might suggest that eros and logos are not mutually exclusive: that the values we have discussed here are not so much matriarchal values as *human* values. It should be remembered that reason and emotion were also in the past personified by two male gods, Apollo and Dionysus. And while there may now have occurred a welcome shift of emphasis from one to the other, it is possible also to overcompensate.

Joseph Schwab, for example, was talking about the attitude of the youth who says that he could enter the society if he wanted to—but he doesn't want to because he doesn't like the society, and therefore the society must change before he will enter it. "What the hell does this mean?" asked Schwab. "Which likings is he working from—the ones he had as a baby before he'd been weaned, or the ones after he'd been weaned but before he'd had a martini, or the ones he had when he picked up the *Playboy* philosophy and thought that a simpleminded nerve-end hedonics was life? How far has he got the competencies and used them to look at his wants? Does he really mean *want*? I suspect that he does, just as a child says I want it, I want it, whether it's there or not and whether it's possible or not." In other words, it is possible to confuse eros and id, or moral intuition and purely selfish emotion. But an action can also be selfless and still be immoral—a point we will return to shortly.

Christopher Lasch said: "I think humanism is inseparable from the idea of rationality, so I can't see a revolt against rationality as humanism, even though it may choose to adopt some humanist rhetoric. I think there *is* a revolt against humanism going on—from all sides—and this is the worst thing. That is to say, a revolt against the idea, against the very delicate, fragile sort of growth that's taken place in the last four or five hundred years, in spite of capitalism, and in spite of everything else: just the idea that people somehow can comprehend their situation

and shape the whole environment—cultural, physical—to needs
that people can recognize somehow as human needs. That's what
I mean by humanism. And that's why I think it's inseparable
from the idea of using reason, because reason is the tool by which
you attempt to control the environment. It seems to me this idea
is now under attack from technocrats, who are certainly emi-
nently rational in their ability to control technology but who don't
seem to have much sense of putting it to any kind of human
purposes. But I think, you know, that humanism is also under
attack from all kinds of irrationalists—among others, the sort of
New Left cultural revolutionists. The whole attack on reason,
on authority, disciplined use of the mind—this has gone very far.
I think there are probably lots of reasons, but the immediate one
surely is that rationality, in the form that we observe it, has gone
sort of mad—it's irrational—and I suppose that's a very difficult
thing to attack from a point of view which still tries to argue from
the central points of reason—because the answer to that is:
'How with reason? Look at what reason is doing! All that means
is more technology.' And there's been this old argument about
technology, even in the nineteenth century—in fact Marxism
grew up in the context of this argument, and the whole early
labor movement was highly colored by an anti-technological point
of view. And one of the things Marxists had to do was establish
that technology wasn't the enemy but certain *uses* of technology.
This argument is now being recapitulated, but on grounds where
the Marxists are at a great disadvantage. In the nineteenth century you could appeal to what was, after all, before your eyes.
'How can you say technology is the enemy when it's every day
creating things which really do make life better? How can you
deny this—that it's better for people to have some minimal
physical comforts and be able to get around more conveniently?'
But in the twentieth century the grounds have shifted, very
radically, and people who now want to make that argument are
very hard-pressed to find anything to appeal to."

Wald is a humanist, but doesn't like the word. He said:
"It has come to represent a rather precious view of things in

American life. In fact the word 'humanities'—I find my back is up. To some people it seems to mean everything excluding science. And when there was a real humanism, when humanism came in during the Renaissance, with people like Erasmus, it included all the science of its day, and went on including all the science of its day, and that's an integral part of the humanist approach. And it's getting to be again. But there was a period in which it was pushed aside, and the thought was: not if you wrote poetry, but if you lectured to people about other people's poetry, then you were a humanist. Whereas if you tried to straighten them out on the nature of the universe and man's place in it you were something else. So I think the word like a great many other words in our language has been degraded. It's like the meaning of a bachelor of arts degree; that didn't necessarily mean you had any connection with arts: it just meant you didn't know any science. And I think one of the things that most needs sorting out in this culture now—and quickly—is science and technology. And I go about, saying whenever I can that science is concerned with knowledge, and in our culture all of it is good. Any other attitude would be a plea for ignorance, and knowledge is always preferable to ignorance. But technology is the application of knowledge to practical ends, and one immediately has to ask—practical to whom? Useful to whom? And there one is in an entirely different situation, and the whole of society must now be taught to get used to the idea that you *never* accept technology: you always question it and ask, is this what we really want to do? And if it isn't, you don't do it. That's the important thing, that all over our society people have been taught to accept any new technology as progress, and as an aspect of fate; but it needs to be constantly judged in terms of what that society wants, and then we should let certain things be done and shut off certain other things, and that's absolutely fundamental. So I recognize that technology can do great things for us and has done great things for us, but it also has done awful things and is doing awful things, and you have to make that distinction and get rid of what you don't want. And you have to get the ordinary citizen to think in those terms—all the time—so he will look around him and ask of everything technological around him: is this raising the quality of my life or just the opposite? And then pick and choose. But what people need to worry about is never science. Science is knowledge. It makes people more at home in their universe. There can't be anything wrong with that. It's technology, and not all technology. The whole point is: know all you can—but do only what it seems right and proper to do. And if one only keeps a simple rule like that, and can only get the whole of society moving on such a rule, I think we'll have it made."

Wald's distinction between science and technology is comparable to the distinction between basic and applied research, and it can be criticized on several grounds. The psychologist Edward L. Walker, for example, has argued that scientists should evaluate even basic research in terms of relevance and social needs; that is, basic research (or science) can be harmful if it has no apparent social value and detracts from research that would have social relevance: thus ultimate human usefulness should be the primary criterion on which the social support of all research should be based. Beyond this debatable point, Wald's distinction seems perilously close to the argument of the National Rifle Association: guns aren't dangerous, people are dangerous. That statement is true, but people with guns are more dangerous than people without guns—and science often has handed society a loaded revolver. If you hand such a weapon to a child and he blows his head off with it, who is at fault? It also is true on the other hand that society has an obligation to grow up now and to demand from its science and technology what actually is relevant to its needs. And surely it is true too, as Wald and Lasch between them have argued, that humanism cannot exclude either science or reason. This means it cannot exclude patriarchal values, in the sense that we have defined them to imply order and rationality. In the sense that they relate to *authority*, however, Fromm in his recent writing has asserted that matriarchy and patriarchy both need to be transcended. Both systems in this context may be seen to arise from man's need to feel at home in the world. To satisfy that need man surrenders his autonomy to one of two authorities: to the mother (who may be nature) or to the father (who may be the state). In either case man remains a child, and Fromm calls instead for a new vision and a new bond: "the harmonious bond of brotherhood in which solidarity and human ties are not vitiated by restriction of freedom, either emotionally or intellectually." This concept would then satisfy the two needs of man: "to be closely related and at the same time to be free, to be part of a whole and to be independent." *I-Thou.*

In the sense that the matriarchal eros is invoked in the form of a moral intuition, it was said earlier that a selfless act can still be immoral. Morality in this context is defined as conduct that looks ahead to consequences—and that would include the consequences of an action that ostensibly is initiated to help other people. Mere strong emotion in this case does not in itself justify an action unless the person involved is willing to examine very carefully not only the consequences of the action but also the source of the emotion. Schwab said: "Certainly there's nothing but moral irresponsibility in the business of simply standing up and beating your breast, or beating somebody else's head in, on the basis of your convictions, without some concern for achieving the goals that you're talking about." This would apply to those so-called revolutionaries of the so-called Resistance for whom the important thing is actually to fail—to live with principles and then to die nobly. As Michael Miles has described them, in the *New Republic,* they represent "less a political action group than a subculture intent on maintaining its identity and developing its cultural style in fashion, language, music and politics." They can be compared to the Communists, who—whatever else they may be—are "serious about success." As for the motivating emotion, the feeling of conviction it provides is not a sufficient test. Bigots, after all, are just as sincere as the radicals in their emotional reactions and convictions of righteousness. Nor can conscience be a guide; you may have internalized a pair of slaphappy parents. Schwab said: "At the heart of all morality is the readiness to suspect that there's some need for a change in yourself. So when you and the uncongenial confront each other, it isn't automatically the case that the un-congenial ought to be dismissed or destroyed. You'd better be very careful about thinking that the strong feeling guarantees the soundness of what you're saying; you may be speaking simply out of a neurotic symptom. I remember years ago when I had a little dog that got a kind of muscular trouble. I passed a divinity student out here on campus. He said, 'Why don't you *destroy* that dog? You have no right to let him live.' And I got mad enough to ask him what he knew about how the dog was feeling, and I demonstrated that the dog was quite unconscious of making a fool of himself and was having a lovely time. And maybe what this guy was worrying about was whatever that sight stimulated in him. So what he wanted to do was get rid of the stimulus, not be moral."

It has been said many times, many ways. Sanity and humanity are a balance of reason and emotion, and in responding to technology a true humanist cannot be a monotheist. He will reverence both Dionysus and Apollo.

But technology also involves at least two other funda-mental tensions. To understand one of them we must in the end look east, to Asia. But before that, in considering the other, we must look first at the black ghetto.

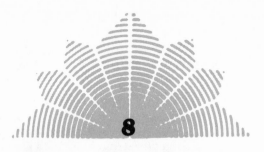

8

Black Identity and Black Panthers

Some years ago I was assigned by my newspaper to cover a national convention of the Nation of Islam. There were only a handful of white reporters in the hall, and we sat together in a special press section that had been roped off near the stage where Elijah Muhammad was speaking. He talked for two and a half hours, and he made effective use of us—jabbing a finger in our direction whenever he wanted to drive home a point about the white devils with the blue eyes of death. He said we were created sixty centuries ago by a mad black scientist called Yakub, apparently the first of the New Biologists. The world had once been populated entirely by black people, the Original Blacks, and all would have been well but for Yakub, a genetic engineer who dwelt on the island of Patmos; in a fiendish series of grafting and cross-breeding experiments he finally managed to produce that loathsome monster the white man. Muhammad told his followers that we were evil incarnate, the cause of all their suffering, and he warned them not to believe what it said in our Poisoned Book. "What fool would love an enemy?" he asked the people of the Lost-Found Nation of the West. Then he turned to us and said: "I most certainly will not teach them to love you. I teach no one to love the devil."

A Fruit of Islam security officer glared at a white photographer and said: "Your grandfather made my grandfather a slave."

"Bullshit," said the photographer. "My grandfather was killed in the Civil War fighting to free your grandfather."

There we were, surrounded by five thousand Black Muslims. But there was reason to believe that this was the safest place for a white man on the whole South Side of Chicago at that moment, and the reason was the expression you saw on the faces of those proud and happy people as they listened to Muhammad: an expression of peace, joy—even ecstasy. He had told them who they were, and they believed him; he had told them they were not inferior to us, and they believed him; he had told them they were superior to us, and they believed him. We had nothing to fear from them, at least for the moment. It was all those people outside the hall, all those yassah-bossing and sorry-bossing people —those were the ones you had to worry about. And the crazy thought came that perhaps Muhammad was an FBI agent: an agent *non*provocateur. Here were these thousands of vital people, and Muhammad had taken every last one of them out of the civil rights movement, where the action was, filling their heads with vague promises of a separatist state that someday would be theirs, a black Israel. This was early in 1964, and we had not yet realized that the civil rights movement already was dead; while death had occurred, we had not yet spoken the obsequies. The Black Muslims were dismissed as a weird cult. Nobody could have known then that their central concern, freshly translated by Malcolm X, would provide the psychological thrust for the post–civil rights movement—that the drive for black liberation would become in a sense a quest for black identity. Nor could anybody have predicted that the Black Panthers would later emerge to contest this development and offer still another alternative to blacks and whites alike.

What happened?

According to the standard psychological argument, blacks and whites in America have always to some extent sought to identify themselves in terms of their racial opposite: a sort of cultural schizophrenia. We have already discussed the concept of negative identity—the idea that we all carry around in our heads a mirror image of ourselves—and we said that an individual who cannot establish a positive identity will sometimes resort to its polar opposite and adopt that instead. But there is another sick way to use one's negative identity, and that is to project it onto somebody else. Thus it is argued that white Americans projected their negative identities onto black Americans, unconsciously attributing to the blacks the evil side of their own nature. This made the whites feel good, knowing they were pure and superior; it also justified the oppression and exploitation of the black people, who deserved what they got for doing and thinking all of those nasty, wicked things. To be black then was to be vile and inferior; blackness was ugly.

This lie would have been bad enough if it only warped the thinking of the white population, or at least one segment of it. But the lie had another still sicker dimension which was examined for example by the black psychiatrists William H. Grier and Price M. Cobbs in their book *Black Rage*. In treating neurotic black patients who in one way or another were failing in life, Grier and Cobbs found confirmation of a sad fact that had long been obvious; they found that black people too believed the lie. Slavery ended with the Emancipation Proclamation, but the stroke of a pen could not end slavery mentality; it lived on in the tormented psyches of black people who had been told for centuries that they were subhumans fit only for menial labor. Technology then reduced the need for such labor, and many of the blacks became economically superfluous. They could go on relief. Or as the white people told them, they could try to "improve" themselves and climb the American ladder of success.

Many of them did try to climb it, and some of them made it; but others fell off just as they were reaching the top—and they fell off because of an inner voice that whispered to them that they were black and worthless, that they could not succeed in the white man's America because they did not deserve to, or that they lacked the ability—maybe they were not even Americans. Who were they really? As Grier and Cobbs put it: "The black man was brought to this country forcibly and completely cut off from his past. He was robbed of language and culture. He was forbidden to be an African and never allowed to become an American."

This sweeping theory has to be modulated. For example, projection in some cases may be partial and of little consequence. As Grier said one afternoon, talking about his book: "Let's suppose that it is the consensus of South Carolina that blacks steal watermelons. Well, blacks may deal with that positively or negatively, but the reaction in either case may represent only a very fractional kind of identification. To say that this is a negative identity is to promote it to a level of importance that it may not deserve. That is, a black may think that yes, I am a watermelon thief, or no, I am not a watermelon thief, or any of the various permutations of that, and it may have only a fractional significance to him, being functional only within certain limitations. And everybody knows there is a selective response to such things. For example, it may be very important to one man that he not have a, quote, 'Jewish nose'—whatever the hell that may mean to his colleagues. Who knows? But for him it may be very important. Well, there's a lot more to America's concept of Jews than a Jewish nose—but that may be the selective kind of response he has. Similarly with blacks. The whole range is very broad, but the chances are that the individual will respond only to some aspect that for some reason or other seems important to him."

Beyond this, we will suggest later that the fall from the ladder may have resulted in many cases not from a fear of failure but a fear of success: that the upward-climbing black may at some point look down and wonder if he is not leaving behind something that is very precious to him. We also will ask if this something might not be the very culture that Grier and Cobbs say the white man took away from him. The fact remains, however, that the black man in the past very often responded to the white man's image of him by pretending that he himself was white. He sought to assimilate himself in the culture and value systems of the compact majority; he cut his hair, treated it with some preparation guaranteed to dekink it, and plastered it down with brilliantine—became what militant blacks now refer to as a "slick-head." An antipathy toward his own blackness can be found in the earlier writings of the novelist James Baldwin, and the concept of ethnic self-hatred has been explored to its depths by Eldridge Cleaver, the Black Panther information minister. Cleaver says that black self-hatred amounted in some cases to a racial death wish, and it also provided "much of the impetus behind the motivations of integration." It resulted in the widespread use of skin-bleaching cosmetics, as well as nose-thinning and lip-cutting operations; it produced a climate in which many Negroes would object to the mating of two very dark-skinned black people. Cleaver says that a Negro who tried to mold his identity in this fashion could become in the end only a self-contradiction: "a white man in a black body." Or as Jesse Jackson once put it, a flesh-and-blood version of the Oreo cookie.

One answer to this has been Black Power, and the declaration that black is beautiful—the affirmation by black people of their black skins and their African heritage. Thus the natural hair styles, the dashikis and African robes, the deep interest in African history and languages, the emphasis on soul food and soul music. Thus the effort to establish and assert a distinctive black identity, whatever that may be. A rejection of many "white" values is necessarily implied in all this, and the implications of the development are hard to assess. We might begin, however, with a distinction that the novelist and social critic Norman Mailer has made between the right wing and left wing of the Black Power movement.

The right wing is the "technological wing," and what it

wants in essence is political and economic power: a larger slice of the pie created by modern technology. The left wing on the other hand is "profoundly anti-technological." It has an "instinctive detestation of science, of the creation-by-machine . . . the hum of electronics . . . the computed moves of the technological society." The black man had been excluded from that society, and yet he had somehow survived in the Africa of the slums. According to Mailer, "he discovered that the culture which had saved him owed more to the wit and telepathy of the jungle than the values and programs of the West." He had a deeper view of creation, and he felt that "he had therefore the potentiality to conceive and create a new culture (perchance a new civilization), richer, wiser, deeper, more beautiful and profound than any he had seen." As the black militant Ron Karenga put it: "The white boy is engaged in the worship of technology; we must not sell our souls for money and machines. *We must free ourselves culturally before we proceed politically*" (italics ours). This is the core philosophy of black cultural nationalism, and as we will see it collides head on with the political strategy of the Black Panthers and others. But the anti-technological mystique is nevertheless shared for example by Cleaver, who writes of a splintered American identity in which the white man came to represent *Mind* (in the sense of a rational, mental, scientific approach to life) while the black man came to represent *Body* (in the sense of an intuitive, emotional, physical approach to life). Mind prevailed, of course, and the black man shook his head sadly at the "Hot-Dog-and-Malted-Milk norm of the bloodless, square, faceless Sunday-Morning atmosphere that was suffocating the nation's soul." America as Cleaver sees it was personified by Pat Boone's antiseptic white shoes and whiter songs; it was strangling on Bing Crosbyism, Perry Comoism, and Dinah Shoreism. But then came Chubby Checker doing the Twist, and before long white Americans were dancing the Watusi and the Frug, the Hully Gully and the Mashed Potato; they had learned from the blacks "how to shake their asses again." In short, Mind was reintroduced to its Body. Meanwhile, as Cleaver expresses it in a chilling metaphor, the white shoes had been splattered with blood. But America in any case had come alive again, "deep down in its raw guts," and Cleaver sees this as a hopeful sign. Man needs to affirm his biology, he writes. "He feels a need for a clear definition of where his body ends and the machine begins, where man ends and the *extensions* of man begin . . . the blacks, personifying the Body and thereby in closer communion with their biological roots than other Americans, provide the saving link, the bridge between man's biology and man's machines."

Many whites are now attracted to this view, and indeed Erikson has proposed that "the question of the Negro American's identity imperceptibly shades into the question of what *the* American wants to make of himself in the technology of the future." In Harlem as in Naples, says Erikson, one finds "an emphasis on artistic self-expression and intense feeling" which "may be close to the core of one's positive identity." The denial of such intense feelings by the white majority "may in turn be part of a negative identity problem which contributes significantly to the prejudiced rejection of the Negro's intensity." Far from rejecting such intensity, however, white America at the moment is making a strenuous effort to emulate it; in fact, the concept of black hyperthyroidism has contributed significantly to the often self-conscious life style of the young white cultural revolutionaries, and (along with the profit motive) it has contributed also to the phenomenon of stage nudity in such plays as *Hair* and *Che, Geese* and *Oh! Calcutta.* Thus we find a drama critic of Eric Bentley's high caliber praising the naked actor as a social savior: ". . . at a time when our urban civilization was most unnatural and unnerving, he asserted the claims of natural man, the claims of the body . . . I don't think our soul is going to be saved until our body is joined to it again." Perhaps Bentley in this case needs to be reintroduced to his Mind, but let's not quibble about that. There are more important matters to quibble about.

It might appear from all this that Dionysus is black and Apollo is white, and that the same color scheme applies also to eros and logos, matriarchy and patriarchy. In connection with the latter dichotomy, much has been made of the fact that the black family in the North at least has tended toward a matriarchal structure in which the dominant figure is the mother—or often the grandmother—a pattern that was encouraged historically by a welfare system that extended its dole for the most part to fatherless homes. The urban affairs specialist Daniel P. Moynihan raised a storm of protest in the black community in 1965 when he issued a report that took quite a negative view of this structure—suggesting that it had emasculated and enraged the black urban male and therefore was a fundamental cause of racial unrest. This presumptuous analysis of human values certainly deserved all the criticism that it received. We have already seen of course that the white family is tending toward the same kind of structure, and it might be asserted that the warmth and compassion of a matriarchal home are responsible in part for those very qualities of emotional vitality that are visualized now as the black man's saving contribution to American society. (A contrary opinion will be offered later, when we talk again to Christopher Lasch.)

One defense of cultural nationalism can be found in the reading that Erich Fromm has given to the biblical injunction to love your neighbor as yourself. To Fromm, this meant among other things that a person can truly love his neighbor only if he has first learned to have love or respect for himself—to have trust in his own integrity as a worthwhile human being. It might be said then that this is precisely what many blacks today are doing—learning to love themselves—and that only in so doing can they eventually rejoin mainstream society as whole men and women. On the other hand, Black Power in this sense often seems to imply and depend upon hatred of the whites (black racism), and in any case a strong argument can be made that cultural nationalism is both bad politics and bad philosophy. Some of its advocates may think they have hit upon something new, but in fact the same route was traveled years ago by Frantz Fanon—and Fanon in the end found it necessary to retrace his steps and seek another way. He had wandered into madness and despair.

A Martinique psychiatrist, Fanon was tormented by his black skin and the zebra striping of his mind; he felt dissected under white eyes: "the only real eyes." At first he tried to be invisible, to hide from those eyes. Then he turned to reason; he would prove rationally that the Negro was a human being. And the white man had to agree with him; the Negro obviously *was* a human being: like the white man, he had his heart on the left side. Which changed nothing, however, and in any case the man to be convinced was not the white man but Fanon. And so at last he leaped head first into the black hole, renouncing the present and the future in the name of a mystical past: the cosmic Negro myth. "From the opposite end of the white world a magical Negro culture was hailing me. . . . Since no agreement was possible on the level of reason, I threw myself back toward unreason." Fanon waded in the irrational, up to his neck in the irrational. "*Eyah!* the tom-tom chatters out the cosmic message. Only the Negro has the capacity to convey it, to decipher its meaning, its import." He told the white man: "Yes, we are—we Negroes— backward, simple, free in our behavior. That is because for us the body is not something opposed to what you call the mind." And he quoted Léopold Senghor: "Emotion is completely Negro as reason is Greek." A friend from the United States told him: "The presence of the Negroes beside the whites is in a way an insurance policy on humanness. When the whites feel that they have become too mechanized, they turn to the men of color and ask them for a little human sustenance." Fanon walked with an air of mystery. Africa! Black Magic! "The white man had the anguished feeling that I was escaping from him and that I was taking something with me. . . . It was obvious that I had a secret." And his cry grew more violent. "I am a Negro, I am a Negro, I am a Negro." Then, one day, he read in Sartre:

In fact, negritude appears as the minor term of a dialectical progression: The theoretical and practical assertion of the su-

premacy of the white man is its thesis; the position of negritude as an antithetical value is the moment of negativity. But this negative moment is insufficient by itself . . . it is intended to prepare the synthesis or realization of the human in a society without races. Thus negritude is the root of its own destruction, it is a transition and not a conclusion, a means and not an ultimate end.

When he read that passage Fanon felt he had been robbed of his last chance, and the black poets had suffered a blow that could never be forgiven; the dialectic had shattered the illusion that his blackness was the synthesis. "Without a Negro past, without a Negro future, it was impossible for me to live my Negrohood. Not yet white, no longer wholly black, I was damned." He suffered; then he decided. "I had tried to flee myself through my kind . . . finding Being in Bantu." But no longer would he exalt the past at the expense of the present and future; the discovery of a Negro civilization in the fifteenth century conferred no patent of humanity on him: "I am a man, and in this sense the Peloponnesian War is as much mine as the invention of the compass. . . . I am a man, and what I have to recapture is the whole past of the world." Fanon proposed the liberation of the black man from himself; the black was no more to be loved than the Czech, "and truly what is to be done is to set man free." The way to do that was to fight. Fanon did fight, and he ended his days opposing the French in the Algerian revolution. In so doing, while he did reject the white values of Western Mediterranean civilization, he did not return to the cosmic Negro myth; he emphasized instead those values that are based on "the concrete conflict" in which colonial people are engaged.

If your bag is dialectics, then, cultural nationalism will not be for you. But Fanon said much more than this; he said in effect that identity is psychosocial, not merely psychological, and massive doses of forced pride are a poor substitute for social justice and social equality. Without such equality the black man will never feel psychologically secure, no matter how much soul he thinks he has, and equality will not be achieved by eating collard greens and sweet-potato pie. What is more, the black man knows it. That is why there is so much anger in his proud talk—the anger of doubt and desperation. Fanon would no doubt ask him whom all that talk is intended to convince.

On television one night a black protester shouted: "We black people need self-respect. *We demand self-respect!*" The example is pathetic but to the point. We suggested earlier that a young person cannot really be a psychological adult and a sociological adolescent, and in the same sense it might be said that black adulthood must also be sociological. For the record again, Erikson for example said he agreed with that analogy. Fanon probably would agree with it too, were he alive here today. Eventually we will enter an objection to this point of view, which needs to be modified, but first it is necessary to examine the impact that Fanon has had on the Black Panthers.

The earlier quotations were from Fanon's book *Black Skin, White Masks,* first published in France in 1952. The Panthers are more likely to quote from a later work, *The Wretched of the Earth,* that was first published in 1961, the year of Fanon's death. Extrapolating from it, they see the black community as an exploited colony which lies within the boundaries of the mother country—America—and their orientation is Marxist-Leninist; disenchanted with Russia, however, they supplement Fanon with readings from Mao's Little Red Book. They speak of revolution (not necessarily violent, but violent if necessary), and they have armed themselves for the stated purpose of defending themselves against the police. Their goal is socialism, and therefore they take a dim view of black capitalism along with other forms of capitalism. All this scares the hell out of the average white citizen; but said citizen also imagines that the Panthers are a gang of black-racist cutthroats who are out for his blood, when in fact they have followed Fanon in rejecting the black synthesis: they seek the white man's support, not his jugular vein. They speak not of Black Power but of People Power, meaning poor people of all shades and hues. In Chicago, for example, the Panthers have formed an alliance with the Puerto Ricans and the Appalachian whites, and Panthers who cannot purge themselves of racism are purged from the party. Most whites probably are not aware that Malcolm X himself had rejected black racism before his death, and the Panthers appear to have been quite successful in overcoming their own racial hostility; if nothing else, their ability to do this is a remarkable example of man's adaptability.

Take the case of Fred Hampton, who was chairman of the Illinois Black Panther party. At Panther headquarters one day he talked about his own "conversion" from racism. "I had to do it," he said. "I did it after the party line was run down, and after we did a lot of intensive studying. We all study together, and we studied the Marx and Lenin theory, and then we put that theory in practice, and we didn't have any trouble doing it." It wasn't hard to do? "It was nothing," said Hampton. "If you've got an open mind and somebody tells you something that's true, and then you find out it's true—you just do it. There ain't no big thing about that." William H. Grier suggests that white racism will end very quickly when whites decide it is to their advantage to end it, and he cites the ease with which this country was able to shift gears psychologically during World War II and after: the good guys became the bad guys, and the bad guys became the good guys, and there was no big thing about that.

Sakharov has written about the plight of the American Negro, and ironically he has told his fellow Russians: "But we must clearly understand that this problem is not primarily a class problem, but a racial problem, involving the racism and egotism of white workers, and that the ruling group in the United States is interested in solving this problem." In America, on the other hand, the Panthers have decided that the problem is more a class problem than a racial problem; they are trying to radicalize the white workers, and they feel that the ruling group has no intention of solving the problem—since the problem when you really come down to it is capitalism. The Kerner Commission report enraged conservative elements by proposing that black unrest was caused by white racism, but a black Marxist perhaps would regard the report as a sinister effort to conceal the problem and protect the capitalist system. After all, it is easy to tell people they should be pure of heart: that provides us with a simple (if impossible) solution. Or so it might seem to a Panther, at least.

This does not mean that Panthers do not recognize white racism as a serious problem, because they do. But the white worker, for example, is considered to be himself a victim of that racism, which blinds him politically. As Hampton put it: "This race question has got people so divided they don't even have a chance to come together and talk. If they did come together they'd understand very clearly that this is a class struggle. We're all in that same class; that makes us all friends. The other people who are oppressing us are all in the same class; that makes them real enemies. Racism is what has put the laboring forces in the situation they're in. But we're saying that as soon as these people come together and unite with real friends, for the purpose of attacking real enemies, that will be the end of all this racism within the labor unions. You have to understand, it's like trying to convince somebody that he's tall and short at the same time, or he's fat and skinny at the same time. But you cannot be in a capitalistic society and have the masses benefit." And that is the Panther message to the white racist.

In rejecting black racism the Panthers also reject black cultural nationalism—what the Panther founder Huey Newton has referred to as "pork-chop nationalism." He said: "It seems to be a reaction instead of a response to political oppression. The cultural nationalists are concerned with returning to the old African culture and thereby regaining their identity and freedom. In other words, they feel that the African culture automatically will bring political freedom. . . . We believe that culture itself will not liberate us. We're going to need some stronger stuff." The conflict between the two viewpoints is extremely bitter, and in fact the Panthers have charged that two of their members were murdered by the "US" organization led by the cultural nationalist Ron Karenga.

Oddly, the Panther position comes close in some ways to that of Eric Hoffer. "What the Negro needs is pride," says Hoffer. "You don't get pride by having the fuzzy-wuzzy hair and a necklace of teeth around you and dressing up like God knows whom in Africa. This is all false pride. There's only one pride, and that's pride of achievement." As for the Kerner Report: "They tell us we are all racists. So we are racists. What kind of a solution is that?" Hoffer of course does not advocate a revolution; his solution is "the building of an effective Negro community . . . a community with vigorous organs for mutual help, self-improvement, and such cooperative efforts as a Negro hospital, a model elementary or trade school, a model Negro suburb, and the like." (For all their talk of revolution, the Panthers have given high priority to self-help activities, organizing free-breakfast programs and medical clinics for ghetto schoolchildren. Some white radicals indeed have branded them mere "reformists," and reform is a deadly sin: if you make life better for people they might not revolt. The question, of course, is what is really "better.") Hoffer thinks it is up to the black middle class to improve the lot of the ghetto blacks and to build the effective Negro community he talks about. Predictably, he has attributed black unrest to rising expectations—the impatience that is generated when conditions begin to improve. There may be some truth to this, but it is hard to tell what Hoffer means by it; he makes it sound like an accusation. It also could mean that blacks for the first time in their history have dared to hope for justice in America.

Christopher Lasch offers a provocative analysis of the black situation in *The Agony of the American Left*. For one thing, he asserts it was a myth that American ethnic groups in the past were able to advance themselves by individual initiative—the old bootstrap theory. According to Lasch, they advanced "not as individuals but as groups conscious of their own special interests and identity." Having first achieved a firm sense of ethnic solidarity, they took over a niche in the economy that earlier groups had not occupied or exploited. The Irish, for example, went in for saloon-keeping and machine politics; the Jews entered the labor movement and created marginal businesses and professions that served a largely Jewish clientele; the Italians also found their thing. These were cases of collective self-help, each new generation building on the advances made by previous generations. It might be argued from this that blacks should exploit the niches they already occupy: sports and show business. Their ascendancy in these fields is regarded of course as tokenism, and there obviously are not enough openings for twenty million first basemen and tap dancers. But that is just the point: the black so far has been limited for the most part to the role of athlete or entertainer. What if blacks made an effort to really take over these industries? As a matter of fact, the black singer and composer Oscar Brown, Jr., had this idea in mind several years ago when he produced a musical revue starring the Blackstone Rangers, a Chicago street organization. Talking about it one night after rehearsal, Brown said: "Negro music has been the basis for many of the innovations in show business. From the Black Bottom to the Charleston, Boogie-Woogie, Jitterbug, and the Twist—all of this came from kids just like these, living in slums. But the people who have produced the music have gotten the least out of it. They've got lots of talent but no professional know-how. Only a few groups and individuals get through at a time, and then everything is set up to exploit their talents. So the idea is to set up organizations the Negroes can run for their own benefit in their own communities, in competition with established show business. And not just the performers. We also want to encourage record manufacturing, costuming, stage design, booking agencies, promotion. It'll be a show business rooted among the people who provide the entertainment. It'll be for us what sugar is for Cuba—a national industry."

Again, a black combine might buy and run a baseball or football team—including the concessions and broadcast rights. Still another suggestion was made recently—possibly tongue in cheek—by the economist Robert Browne of Fairleigh Dickinson University. Complaining about the white monopoly in vice operations, he told the First National Black Economic Conference: "Racketeering, prostitution, and the numbers, if they are to continue, must be put into the hands of the black community."

There might be some opportunities for collective self-help in such areas, excluding the last one. But as Lasch said when the idea was put to him: "Those are very marginal activities, and nobody gets rich that way. Owning a baseball team is a charity, and it's the same thing in entertainment. There isn't any money in it. I think for the most part athletics and all forms of cultural activity have to be more or less subsidized. It's possible for individuals to make a killing in a play or something, but there isn't enough money in those things to support an entire colony, class, or whatever you want to call it." As Lasch sees it, there are no more niches left today for the blacks to occupy. And that is the problem. "What's instructive, I think, are the differences between the situation of Negroes now and the situation of the earlier ethnic groups. Not the similarities. For those earlier groups there were still enough undeveloped areas of the economy to provide a foothold for everybody; now all that has changed." So ethnic solidarity made sense in the past, when it provided a basis for collective self-help; but it makes less sense today, in those terms at least, and that is one reason Lasch and others are basically opposed to its black-ghetto equivalent—cultural nationalism. "From my point of view," said Lasch, "this cultural business is no radicalism at all. It can be so easily absorbed, you know; it's so essentially harmless." For example, a mouthwash company responded to Black Power with television commercials that urged the masses to march for Pucker Power. That is what radicals mean when they talk about cooptation.

The Panthers at the moment represent the principal alternative to cultural nationalism, but in many ways they leave much to be desired. As Leninists they view themselves as an elite vanguard, a small group of enlightened people who consider themselves morally privileged to impose their will on the democratic majority; they also feel privileged to manipulate events in order to "heighten the contradictions" in the society. They are willing to work with whites, but only on their own terms. "The people are educated by the vanguard," said Hampton. "So that makes the vanguard the elite group of the revolutionary struggle. All the people may form an army one day, but the Black Panther party will be the vanguard of that army. So what we're saying is that everybody cannot be in the vanguard—and there's nothing wrong with that. You understand what that means? It means that *we* provide the leadership for all oppressed people. It's up to us what happens. We paid the cost of being the boss. We were the ones in this class that were oppressed the most." Hampton remarked that he had just attended a wake for a young man who had been shot in the head by the police. He added: "And you know, this is bad. But it heightens the contradictions in the community." So of course it also is good.

For anybody who still believes in the values this country is supposed to represent (and to some extent does represent), the idea of a people's dictatorship imposed by revolutionary elitists is just as repugnant as a dictatorship of technetronic elitists. While the latter is possible, however, the former is not—and the best evidence of that is the present distress of the Black Panther party. Not long after I last talked with him, Fred Hampton and another Panther leader, Mark Clark, were shot to death during a pre-dawn police raid on a Panther apartment on the West Side of Chicago. The Cook County state's attorney's police carried a warrant to search for a cache of weapons. Hampton had never made a secret of those weapons—they were there for self-defense, he said—but it is not known at this time if Hampton had an opportunity to return the police fire; he was found dead on a bed where he may have been sleeping when the police broke into the apartment. He had been prepared to die for his beliefs, or his manhood, and probably expected to; during the short time he lived he at least lived as a man, with dignity and purpose, and the way he lived was surely a source of pride for many of his peers in the black community. He did nothing to deserve death, and he should not be dead—those are the simple facts of the matter—but he nevertheless is dead. Many other Panthers also are dead, and still more are in jail.

Unlike many white romantics, the Panthers are not looking for adventure—they are serious about success. But that does not change the political realities in a post-industrial urban state with massive powers of surveillance and law enforcement. It is all very well to study the tactics of peasant guerrillas in some Asian jungle; it might be more instructive, however, to consider the fate of the Jews who rose up against the Germans in the Warsaw ghetto. Blacks must decide for themselves whether their own situation is equally intolerable, and whether a similar uprising is their only option. But one must hope there are better alternatives in America today.

The Panthers can be congratulated for transcending racism, and it is to their credit that they have recognized that the enemy is not the white man. But their colony theory is a fantasy. The black man was exploited in the past, when his muscle was an asset, but for the most part he is not exploited now. As Paul Goodman has said, there may be some exploitation of black people in their own neighborhoods—by slum landlords, for example—but this is trivial compared to the tax cost of welfare payments, social services, special policing and so forth. "Since they are not economically necessary," said Goodman, "blacks cannot get redress by striking and bargaining. Since most whites are not exploiting them, they cannot give them redress by stopping their exploitation." Thus the confusion of the average white man when the black people tell him to "just get off our backs." He may feel guilty enough to think that somehow or other he has been on their backs, but it may not be such a good idea for the blacks to play on such feelings; as Goodman again has said, guilt is repressed resentment and therefore latent dynamite. An extreme example of sick guilt was provided in Chicago by a white schoolteacher who tried to organize a "spit-shine" to atone for the murder of Dr. Martin Luther King, Jr. The teacher distributed handbills that said: "I will present myself at the corner of 63d and Halsted and ask the black community to spit on me as an expression of their contempt for white racism in the United States. . . . I ask you to drown white racism in black spit; I ask you to help me to cleanse my heart." He also offered to shine shoes, and he asked other white citizens to join him. This may explain in part why blacks kicked the white liberals out of their civil rights organizations.

The blacks are oppressed and discriminated against, but in the Northern cities at least they are not exploited; they are excluded and neglected. And if the white man is not the enemy, neither is the rich man. In one sense the enemy is the machine; it has put the black man out of work, and if the Ad Hoc Committee is correct, technology in the end will put almost all of us out of work. Society at some point will be compelled to face this problem and deal with it. It is our failure to do so now that keeps the black people economically depressed. Fundamentally, then, the real enemy is nobody in particular but simply our stubborn refusal to pay the social costs of our technological affluence. It is difficult to see this as a class problem. In the first place, class lines in America are far from clear; beyond this, as we have seen, our present pattern of production and consumption has produced a situation in which everybody suffers—including the rich man. That is the kind of analysis the Panthers hopefully might go on to make, if only they could also transcend their outmoded Marxism. The time is ripe. The system has become so irrational that it no longer pays off very well even in the private sector; the so-called Forgotten American has been required to pay more and more for government undertakings that offer him no tangible benefits, and signs of his restlessness are increasingly abundant. This is no time to antagonize him with prattle about a revolution; as Hampton aptly put it, this is the time to demonstrate to him that he is both fat and skinny—and if present trends continue he will simply be skinny. At worst, radicals who do not care about consequences may drive him to the right and help to consolidate the new conservative majority that some Republican theorists are currently predicting. At best, a liberal government will finally be given a mandate to use its taxing power to provide increased social services: to rebuild the cities, improve the schools, combat pollution, and establish a guaranteed income for every American family. Such a government also will move on the international front to relieve tensions and reduce armaments. Realistically, there is not much chance of any drastic change in the basic structure of the economy and government—and what change there is will probably be gradual. Goodman perhaps was right when he asserted that in complex and highly organized societies "it is only by opening the areas of freedom piecemeal that we will transform our lives." One might hope for something more than this, and work for it too, but it would be foolish to insist on all-or-nothing solutions; it would also be immoral, since the consequence of that would probably be nothing. The contradictions in American society need to be lowered, not heightened.

But let us return now to the cultural nationalists and ask if it really is true that they have nothing to contribute to the necessary analysis of our technological future. Was Fanon right when he said the black man must be liberated from himself?

The late anthropologist Melville J. Herskovits speculated years ago that the culture of American blacks is basically African in origin. That idea was not popular at the time, but the cultural nationalists have now seized upon it to support their own claims. Lasch rejects it and proposes that black culture in this country derived neither from Africa nor slavery but "the experience of the Negro people in the South after the Civil War." The Southern family was patriarchal and stable, and stability was further enhanced by a Negro church that preached an ethic of patience and endurance. But the Southern Negro culture breaks down in the ghettos of the North, where rural values come into conflict with technological values and materialism. The influence of the church is eroded, the family reverts to a "matricentric pattern," and the transplanted black develops a compensatory culture which the anthropologist Oscar Lewis has described as the "culture of poverty." It involves a low level of aspiration and is based essentially on hedonism.

This in essence is Lasch's explanation of Negro intensity: it is nothing more than the short-term hedonism that characteristically is cultivated by people who live on the margins of society. Lasch emphasizes that he does not mean to criticize the inherent values of the Northern black culture—he does not deny, for example, that Negro music may provide us with a "rich record of suffering." He is simply suggesting that such a culture, as a pattern for living, does not offer its members very much in the way of support. He argues that cultural nationalism is not a significant alternative to materialistic technological values, since "most black people have already absorbed those values." And he states that the nationalistic movements that flourish in the Northern ghettos "have little or no appeal in the rural South." He is critical of what he calls "black nonsense," including the idea that "all problems in American society are ultimately traced to white sexual hangups, which presumably black people don't have." For example, the idea that blacks are sexual supermen in comparison to whites. In that connection I once interviewed a black prostitute who over a period of fourteen years had slept with literally thousands of men, black and white, to support a heroin habit. She said she preferred the whites as clients, because the whites come faster and are easier to beat (steal from). She was asked, however, if her experience indicated that blacks actually were superior between the sheets. She laughed and said: "I'd have to say that is the truth. You see, this is all we have had in our lifetime, love and sex. This is all we have had to turn to, and we have taken more time *with* this, whereas the white man has been more sort of studying and going to school and making a dollar."

Lasch in *The Agony of the American Life* was lavish in his praise of Harold Cruse's history of the Negro left, *The Crisis of the Negro Intellectual*, which Lasch described as "a monument of historical analysis." When I last talked to him, however, Lasch said of Cruse: "I just can't follow his recent thought very well. That book of his was confusing enough, but what he's written since is even more confusing. What's really instructive about all this is just the poverty of ideas on the left; you could look at Harold Cruse as a guy who is a living example of the failure of the left. I mean, he's a guy who was a Communist for years and who now is unwilling to discuss socialism or any related question, simply because he spent so many years with people who did discuss those questions and who, it turned out, had absolutely nothing to say. Now he keeps talking about the central importance of cultural front, but I don't know what he has in mind when he says that—or how that distinguishes him from these cultural black nationalists. It's more and more unclear to me what in hell his principal *point* is."

Let us look at Cruse's recent writing, then, and see if we can find the point.

In a discussion of Cleaver and the Black Panthers, Cruse notes that Cleaver has fallen back on Karl Marx, "which is where many of us came in." Cruse says that Marx based his class analysis on social practice in nineteenth-century Europe, and the societies he studied were very different from contemporary American society. For one thing, they did not have to deal with anything comparable to the American race question; more than that, each of these societies had a clearly defined national culture which transcended class lines. In fact, they could all lay claim to "one general cultural communality—the Greco-Christian heritage." This meant they could argue class issues and political issues without first discussing cultural issues; the cultural issues had all been decided, and the various classes were bound together by the concept of nation. This still is true. "What is French is a settled question in France, since every Frenchman knows his place in it, and knows how he and his country came to be what they are in modern times."

America, on the other hand, is a scene of political confusion, and the political confusion in turn simply reflects a more fundamental confusion about the national purpose. "Americans generally have no agreement on who they are, what they are, or how they got to be what they are." They do not respond to a situation out of any real sense of historical determination. "Thus the black search for 'identity' . . . merely underscores the fact that *all* Americans are involved in an identity crisis." The so-called racial conflict therefore is really a cultural conflict, and blacks and whites cannot make a revolution together unless they deal first with cultural questions—and especially the question of black cultural identity. As the Spanish scholar Enrique Tierno Galván has said, America is not and never has been a nation; it has no common culture or common ideals. Instead of common ideals it has common interests rooted in capitalist enterprise—and this has produced what Tierno Galván calls "ideologies which have been mythicized into ideals." The people are helplessly manipulated by these mythicized ideals, Cruse says, and therefore are unable to face political and economic realities. White people, that is. But the blacks were never a part of the political and economic mainstream in America; they are free therefore to seek common ideals of their own, and they have started to do this. "In doing so," Cruse says, "they project what is, in effect, a cultural challenge to the rest of the American people. Either we as a nation create and cultivate . . . common cultural ideals which are expressed in our institutions or our present crisis deepens and we face ultimate social disaster."

If Lasch finds this opaque, the problem may lie in the definition of culture. Culture to Lasch appears to mean either a design for living, as he put it, or—in a different context—a heritage of shared experience that accounts among other things for an individual's taste in music or literature. Either way it is defined, Lasch does not seem to feel it has much relevance in terms of social action. In other words, he seems to regard it essentially as purely "psychological." He also seems to suggest that it is fundamentally a by-product or excrescence of the immediate environment. Thus a Southern black who moves North leaves one culture behind him and develops a new culture that arises from his condition as an impoverished ghetto dweller—a hedonistic "culture of poverty."

But what if we define culture in the terms we used to describe it earlier, as a *mode of perception* and as an *ontology*:

a view of the self in its relationship to the Other, meaning other people and the external environment? Then the question takes on a different dimension, what Edward T. Hall refers to as the "hidden dimension." The black who comes North may leave behind him almost everything but the shirt on his back, but he does bring with him two things that are very important; he brings his spoken language and his mode of perception. And it is the spoken language that in fact determines to a considerable extent the mode of perception, the way a person thinks. Black speech in many ways is radically different from white speech, and it follows that black thought may in some respects be radically different from white thought. It also seems likely that black people do not relate to each other in the same way that white people do.

Hall said: "If you take motion pictures of people in a group and then do a frame-by-frame analysis, you find that people are tied together in ways they don't even realize. A colleague who used an electroencephalograph found that when people are talking to each other their brain waves are in phase, and as I understand it you'll often see this in hospital patients who are in a ward together for a long period of time. Their metabolism gets in phase, and a new patient who's put in the ward tends to throw them out a little bit until he comes in line. So the physiological and behavioral data that we see now tend to indicate that people are locked into very deep synchronization with each other. And the big problem comes from the fact that different cultures synchronize in different ways. Now, in black culture there seems to be a great identity between people—and in fact one of the main differences between black culture and white culture has something to do with this matter of the individual. Because they joke about it. They see our thing going here, and they will say: 'I's an individual.' And this is a joke—because they're so clued in to each other and the way that people interact that the whole concept of the individual as we experience it is a joke. And you talk about the black family. I don't think we really can talk about it with our white metaphors, because we don't have the language to talk about it, but I can tell you an anecdote. One of my married graduate students was living in a neighborhood that was part black and part white, and she had a baby. The little black children, as soon as they heard about the baby—well, of course they wanted to see it, which is normal—but then whenever she came out of the house they would run over and they would want to know about the baby. How was the baby? They were identified with that baby; they asked detailed questions. So this is a group thing where the person is automatically important, and there is a deep interest on the part of everybody who's involved in that baby. And the white kids couldn't care less."

Hall does not buy the idea of a culture of poverty based on short-term hedonism. Discussing the prostitute mentioned earlier, he said: "I'd like to add a little more depth to what the prostitute said. These people, black people, are very gentle people, and they are very feeling people. But you have to be very fast to catch it. And they're extraordinarily subtle. For example, we were working with some black subjects, and we found they're ever so more precise than we are. The way they'll align their chair with a desk, for instance. One of my assistants who was a German and who happened to notice that kind of thing pointed out to me that when black people came in they would take the desk chair and would line it up, without even knowing that they had done it. He started moving the chair maybe half an inch, and they would align it. Then he kept reducing the amount that he moved it, and they finally ended up moving it back about a tenth of an inch. And they didn't know they were doing it. So these are subtle people. They are so subtle they make us look like Mack trucks going through a kindergarten. And sex is just a part of life, and it's like everything else; if you are tender and subtle it's going to come out one way, and if you have trouble confusing yourself with a machine it's going to come out another way. And if you experience yourself as very much a part of everybody else it's going to come out one way, and if you experience yourself as separate from everybody else, to the point that you begin to think of the male orgasm and the female orgasm as separate things, then it's going to produce an entirely different set of consequences. So it isn't that this was all that they had, as the prostitute put it. This is just one of the things that we were not able to take away from them, or that white culture was not able to suppress in them. Because they have this rather incredible capacity for relating to people in a very intense and real way. I'm not saying that all whites don't have this, but in general we tend to see ourselves as separate, and we fail to see the incredibly subtle ways in which people can relate to each other."

Consider again the black man who hesitates as he is climbing the ladder of white success. "The blacks have this kind of group identity," said Hall. "But there is this one person who is different, and that's the Man, and wherever the Man happens to be a whole new set of rules are established, and the Man sets his own rules. So you have two sets of values. But when *you* become the Man, then this automatically sets you apart, and I think that in this situation there is a separation anxiety—a genuine separation anxiety. 'What happens to me if I suddenly move from this position to this other position?' All of a sudden you're faced with the fact that you're going to have to take on a new identity—and give up probably the one thing in your life which is real." As Erikson heard a black woman student exclaim one day: "My God, what am I supposed to be integrated *out of*? I laugh like my grandmother, and I would rather die than not laugh like her."

"There's this fantasy of going back to the jungle," said Hall. "I think it's a literary thing. Our black people aren't going back to the jungle, and they wouldn't want to go back. What they do want is something they don't know that they want. They want to be able to experience themselves for what it is that they are, and to come to some kind of peace with themselves in this regard. The whole point is that people have things to give to each other, and we're never going to solve the problems of this world until we accept the fact that we have things to gain from each other and that we can really learn from each other. Each culture has developed its thing. But until we find out what these things are, we're going to continue to make a hash of things, because they're always going to be in conflict. I would say this to the blacks as well as to the whites."

This may explain why Cruse insists that we cannot decide on our social goals until we reach some agreement on our cultural values; the values indeed will determine the goals. Tierno Galván said that white America at best has certain common interests that are rooted in capitalist enterprise. In a more fundamental sense, however, those interests are rooted in technological enterprise. If technology in fact tends to produce the kind of superculture that Kenneth Boulding described in an earlier chapter, it is understandable that many blacks may instinctively feel threatened by it. For it would ultimately destroy their own culture. On the other hand, we said that we may have a choice of different technological futures; the choice—if we have one—will depend on our values, and the black man cannot share in that choice unless his own values are taken into consideration. His values cannot be considered until they are defined, and to begin with *he* must define them himself. Then he will have to explain them to the whites. This will be very difficult, for a culture, as we have seen, is something that people normally have without knowing that they have it—and in translating it the black man may be at a loss for the necessary white metaphors. Before he can move into the future with any confidence, however, it is absolutely essential that he has some idea of what he will have to give up. It also is essential for whites to understand what the black man may have to contribute. In the meantime his presence in the society may act as a brake on the kind of by-the-numbers superculture that will almost certainly develop unless we move to prevent it. Unless their cultural values are integrated into our technological institutions, it is possible that some blacks may choose to remain behind, as it were, in separatist enclaves comparable to the Amish. But it would be infinitely preferable if they were permitted instead to enrich our institutions. As Wald said: "They feel they have a special contribution to make to American life. It's the black thing. It's the black contribution. And I think that's right. They seem to have accumulated that precious quality that is in such short supply right now—humanity, soul. They're warm, vital, responsive, emotional people, and gee, we need those things. And they can bring them to us. There is a second thing— and that is, I think, that black Christianity is a very different thing from white Christianity, and it's ever so much closer to what Jesus represented. It seems to me it may be the only Christianity in America today that's obviously something like what Jesus talked about. And the whole symbolism of the Negro in America is an Old Testament symbolism. 'Go down, Moses, way down in Egypt land; tell old Pharaoh to let my people go.' They have a lot to teach us. That black thing is a precious thing, and they want to keep it intact and bring it into American life as it is. And that's a fine idea. I don't think we want to lose the integrity of the black thing in American life." Cleaver has written that America's destiny will not be fulfilled "until Paul Bunyan and John Henry can look upon themselves and each other as men, the strength in the image of the one not being at the expense of the other," and Erikson has proposed that blacks and whites may "join their identities in such a way that new potentials are activated in both." Baldwin wrote years ago that "we, the black and the white, deeply need each other here if we are really to become a nation—if we are really, that is, to achieve our identity, our maturity, as men and women . . . to end the racial nightmare, and achieve our country, and change the history of the world."

That is what Cruse talks about, the necessity now for America to become a nation—to achieve its identity. If identity indeed is sociological, as Fanon indicated, it also is psychological, and the black man will never feel socially secure unless there also is psychological or cultural equality. If this is so there is very little logic in the antagonism between the cultural nationalists and groups such as the Panthers; they should be working together —on the one hand to define their values and on the other hand to implement them. The nationalists perhaps have tended to over-emphasize African origins; as far as black culture goes it is not so much the source that counts as the content, and there should be a serious effort not only to live that content but also to articulate it—for blacks and whites alike. But as for the source, it must be more than poverty; as for the content, it must be more than hedonism.

The culture-of-poverty concept, as we have seen, comes from Oscar Lewis, but there are excellent grounds on which to dispute that concept—or in any case to modify it—and they can be found oddly enough in the foreword to Lewis's study *Five Families*. The book contains case histories of five Mexican families whose lives are dreary, loveless, and hateful. But as Oliver La Farge points out in the foreword, only four of these families are poor, and in fact "the most dreary, the most utterly loveless, the most hateful, are the *nouveaux riches* Castros . . . a family to dismay Chekhov, to stand Zola's hair on end." The Castros indeed are hedonists. "They have achieved a North American material culture. They have a two-toned car and plumbing, they even eat a North American breakfast. At the end of the day, Señora Castro curls up with a translation of a North American best-seller." But in effect they really have no culture at all: "they are merely uprooted, divorced from the enrichments of their own sources without having received any substitutes other than objects; they are sounding brass and tinkling cymbals, being without love, being true to nothing." La Farge attributes all this to "the onslaught of the Age of Technology . . . a new material culture that shatters the nonmaterial cultures of the people it reaches, and that today is reaching them all." This shattering of a former culture can result, to be sure, in an unsatisfactory impoverished existence, but it can also result in an unsatisfactory affluent existence. The malaise, then, is not a product of the poverty: it is a product of the technological superculture (or technological *non*-culture). If we are interested only in social justice—meaning in essence a larger slice of the pie—the ghetto dwellers in the end will simply be transformed into black Castros. In so far as they have managed to retain their culture, it can hardly be true as Lasch said that they have already absorbed the materialistic technological values—and to argue against the social worth of that culture is to attack the one source of strength and humanity the black people have left. It also would be a mistake to confuse hedonism with the capacity to respond to life with passion and emotion; the hedonist cannot *respond* to anything, he can only be stimulated.

White America should respond now to the cultural challenge that Cruse has described—although in fact it is not even necessary in this connection to talk about culture; the black contribution may also be found simply in black experience. As Cruse points out, the black man has been excluded from the political and economic mainstream in this country, and the positive aspect of that has been noted by Baldwin: "The American Negro has the great advantage of having never believed that collection of myths to which white Americans cling." His advantage is our advantage, since he can help us now to identify those ideologies that have been mythicized into ideals—among them perhaps the ideology of maximum production and maximum consumption: the idea that more technological affluence will automatically solve all of the problems that have been accumulating in the public sector. The black man is one of those problems, and it is obvious to him that we have not yet found the solution. He has been telling us about this.

As for production, black culture as a value system tells us that a man's humanity does not depend on what he produces; it is conferred on him by the fact of birth. This might help us face some problems of a leisure society. As an ontology and mode of perception, however, black culture may help us also to confront not only the problems that perplex us but the mysteries as well: such as who we are and why.

> My mother bore me in the southern wild,
> And I am black, but O! my soul is white;
> White as an angel is the English child,
> But I am black, as if bereav'd of light.
>
> My mother taught me underneath a tree,
> And sitting down before the heat of day,

She took me on her lap and kissed me,
And pointing to the east, began to say:

"Look on the rising sun: there God does live,
And gives his light, and gives his heat away;
And flowers and trees and beasts and man receive
Comfort in morning, joy in the noonday.

"And we are put on earth a little space,
That we may learn to bear the beams of love;
And these black bodies and this sunburnt face
Is but a cloud, and like a shady grove.

"For when our souls have learn'd that heat to bear,
The cloud will vanish; we shall hear his voice,
Saying: 'Come out from the grove, my love & care,
And round my golden tent like lambs rejoice.' "

Thus did my mother say, and kissed me;
And thus I say to little English boy:
When I from black and he from white cloud free,
And round the tent of God like lambs we joy,

I'll shade him from the heat, till he can bear
To lean in joy upon our father's knee;
And then I'll stand and stroke his silver hair,
And be like him, and he will then love me.

—William Blake

the Age of Aquarius
228

Hippies, Heretics, and History

To understand the youth rebellion it is necessary to distinguish between hippies and radicals. There was a time when it was easy to do so. But now it is not so easy, and the implications of this development are ominous—in fact alarming—not only in terms of the youth population itself but also in terms of our technological future.

The problem simply stated is that radicals are becoming more like hippies; the latter, for all their charm, are ideal patsies for the technetronic managers, and the danger involved is that the cultural revolution will ultimately result in social autism: a kind of hedonistic quietism that will represent less a Great Refusal than a Great Cop-Out. The public has always tended to confuse the alienated flower child and the activist protester, applying the term "hippie" to both of them in a loose definition based essentially on hair length and drug use. But long hair does not a hippie make, and contrary to popular opinion the political activist until recently was basically opposed to the use even of "soft" drugs such as marijuana; he felt that drugs and politics did not mix very well, and the Maoist-oriented Progressive Labor wing of the New Left, for example, still holds to that position. Pragmatically, drug possession exposes the radical to the possibility of arrest and increases the opportunities for police harassment of political groups; beyond this, as we will see, there are complex philosophical objections to the use of drugs by the members of such activist organizations. But the pattern of drug use has changed considerably in recent years. We will trace those changes and examine their consequences.

There emerged in the early 1960's a drug movement that made sensational claims for such psychedelic drugs as mescaline, psilocybin, and—especially—LSD. Its leaders and practitioners for the most part were introspective adults, and the movement at first attracted the interest mainly of psychologists, philosophers, and theologians. This development was paralleled by the so-called Leap to the East—a widespread interest in such philosophies as Hinduism and Japanese Zen Buddhism—and indeed the gurus of the drug movement began to interpret the psychedelic experience in terms of those philosophies. At one level the claims were fairly modest. It was said, for example, that a mild psychedelic such as marijuana would often help a person to see himself in a more honest light: that it revealed the extent to which much of his conduct was sham and pretense, artificial role-playing, a big act, his response to life largely a conditioned reflex, just one cliché after another, a mindless performance, a meaningless display; that it jarred the person out of his mental rut—his usual way of looking at the world—allowing him to be more open to experience, more sensitive to other people, more realistic in the goals he might seek. But marijuana is to LSD as a sip of beer to a fifth of bourbon, and it was said of LSD that it unlocked all the secrets of the universe; it permitted a mystical experience which answered the identity question on a grand scale: it told the person who he was—who he *really* was—and it told him who

God was as well.* Three aspects of the psychedelic experience interest us here in so far as they relate to technology and to the cultural revolution; these involve: (1) the relationship of the self to the external environment, (2) the relationship of the self to other people, and (3) the concept of time or history.

The psychedelic experience, like the religious experience, almost always includes an altered sense of identity or self. The drug mystic no longer identifies himself with the little self he thought he was—with the "I" he was always talking about, or the name on his driver's license, or even the reflection he sees in a mirror. William James once wrote: "Religion is the belief that there is an unseen order—and that our supreme good lies in harmoniously adjusting ourselves thereto." The drug mystic feels that he has somehow come into direct contact with that unseen order (which he may call God, or ultimate reality). But he does more than adjust to it; he melts into it and becomes in fact a part of it. He no longer ends at the tips of his fingers. Indeed there is no place where he ends and the rest of the world begins; he is at one with the universe; he is life itself, which ever was and ever will be; he is pure Being; he is immortal, and full of joy.

The Freudian has a ready explanation for all this: the subject's ego has ceased to function, at least temporarily. No longer able to test reality, he is dominated now by his infantile id: he has regressed to the primary stage of undifferentiation. And that is all there is to it. Freud himself offered that analysis of the religious mystic's experience in *Civilization and Its Discontents,* and it also has been pointed out that a confusion of inner and outer reality is one characteristic of schizophrenia. But the drug mystics take a dim view of Freud; if there is an id, they argue, then the id perhaps represents the awareness of a primal truth— the unity of all life—and the ego in its development obscures the memory of that truth. There is an old saying of the Jews, quoted by Martin Buber, that "in the mother's body man knows the universe, in birth he forgets it." Or to quote from *Matthew*:

* A comparison of psychedelic mysticism and religious mysticism can be found in *The Private Sea.*

"Except ye be converted, and become as little children, ye shall not enter into the kingdom of heaven." As for schizophrenia, there is a school of opinion—endorsed by the Nobel laureate Linus Pauling—that the disorder may result from a biochemical imbalance; this in turn suggests the possibility that a schizophrenic may be locked into a chemically induced mystical experience from which he cannot escape. It is not our intention here to explore the validity of these views; the point is simply that the psychedelic drug experience has made many young people in this country especially sensitive to technology's tendency to regard man and nature as antagonists—and it also has made them more receptive to Asian philosophies that reject this attitude as both alien and alienating.

Eastern wisdom has opposed the technological impulse that inspires man to take the world apart and—hopefully—put it together again in I-It relationship, like a thoughtless child who takes apart a toy. Preferred instead is the I-Thou relationship of the Chinese Tao. As the philosopher Huston Smith has said, it is typical of Western man to speak of "conquering" Everest; the Taoist would speak instead of "befriending" Everest. Eric Hoffer actually talks about "the war with nature." Marcuse in this connection quotes C. F. von Weizsacker: "And what is matter? In atomic physics, matter is defined by its possible reactions to human experiments, and by the mathematical—that is, intellectual—laws it obeys. We are *defining* matter as a possible object of man's manipulation." If this is so, says Marcuse, "then science has become in itself technological." This in turn contributes to a scientific or technological rationality—a way of thinking—in which men themselves are regarded as matter: "as units of abstract labor power, calculable in units of time." Technology thus becomes in itself a form of social control and domination. "The scientific method which led to the ever-more-effective domination of nature thus came to provide the pure concepts as well as the instrumentalities for the ever-more-effective domination of man by man *through* the domination of nature. . . . Today, domination perpetuates and extends itself not only through technology but *as* technology, and the latter provides the great legitimation of the expanding political power, which absorbs all spheres of culture." In debasing nature, man ultimately debases himself as well. The instrumentalization of things leads inexorably to the instrumentalization of man. If this seems farfetched, let us not forget B. F. Skinner and the technological rationality of behavioral psychology—which defines man, in effect, as a possible object of man's manipulation.

In short, Western man appears to be engaged in a kind of rape of Mother Nature. And we all know what that makes Western man, in the common parlance. One price he pays for this is alienation and isolation, the loss of the cosmic connection: the feeling that he is at home in his own universe, not a cat burglar who has crept through a window to steal the silverware. He also pays another price: the loss of wonder. This too appears to be inexorable, and a very good example was provided by a former colleague, the science editor Richard Lewis, who covered the flights of Apollo 8 and Apollo 10, the two lunar-orbit missions that preceded the actual moon landing. Lewis remarked on the sense of awe that was evident in the astronauts' reports that were radioed back from the first mission. The crew read from *Genesis*, "viewing a scene that imbued them with the marvel of the creation." They described the lunar landscape as a surrealistic frozen hell; it was "forbidding" and "foreboding." Which reminded Lewis of the Polar Sea chants of the ancient mariner: "The ice was here; the ice was there; the ice was all around . . ." By contrast, the reports from the second flight were casual and scientifically objective: "Hey, Charlie, the best I can figure out we're passing now out of the Ocean of Storms into some more rugged country. . . . There's no doubt there's been some volcanism there. . . . Boy, this planet is really something." Asked how he felt, one of the astronauts informed Earth he felt "horny." Lewis attributed the change of mood primarily to the fact that Apollo 8 had blazed the trail. The first flight had conquered the moon, and the second flight in consequence was almost routine. "Both crews are similar in outlook, background, education, and training," said

Lewis. "At a cocktail party they are so homogeneous in appearance and behavior that they all seem to have come out of the same mold."

F. S. C. Northrop proposed that the West and East independently discovered (or came to emphasize) two different aspects of reality. The West developed a kind of abstract knowledge that enables it to manipulate matter and to predict that a given cause will produce a given effect; it discovered what Northrop called the *theoretical component in things*: a causal order which cannot be seen or directly experienced but which must be there —because it works. Thus physicists could postulate the existence of electrons or protons without ever seeing one. The scientific method, which is based on the theoretical component, is concerned for the most part with particles of matter (seen or unseen); it is forever chopping the universe into little pieces, as the day is chopped into twenty-four hours. There is reason to doubt that such a method can ever offer an adequate explanation of life as a whole, or the meaning of life; one might as well try to understand or appreciate a symphony by studying the individual notes. But the theoretical component has nevertheless allowed Western man to reconstruct his environment; it has created technology and all the fruits of that technology, both bitter and sweet —including such labor-saving devices as the vacuum cleaner, the electric dishwasher, and the hydrogen bomb.

But what of the East? A puzzled Eric Hoffer once wrote:

It is strange that in Asia, where civilization had its birth, the separation from nature and the ability to hold it at bay should be much less pronounced than in the younger civilization of the Occident. In Asia, Africa, and Latin America the man-made world seems precariously stretched over the writhing body of nature. . . . Once the Occident withdrew its hand, the dragon of Asia would move in and sink its yellowed teeth of time into all that the Occident had built and wrought, and gnaw away till naught was left but a skeleton of ruins.

The explanation is that the East had discovered another kind of knowledge: a knowledge that is based on the visible world —the world of immediate experience; the world as a man sees it *now*, at any given moment (if he has the eyes to see). And not a world chopped up in pieces, nor indeed a world chopped up into hours and minutes, but a *whole* world in which time flows unnoticed. Not a world to be used or taken apart, but a world to be lived in and related to in serene or joyful response. The East discovered what Northrop called the *aesthetic component in things*, and the world from this point of view can be seen as an *undifferentiated aesthetic continuum*. There is a lot of helium in the vocabulary here, as Maslow likes to put it, but the concept itself is elementary. As the Zen master said: "It is too clear and so it is hard to see. A dunce once searched for a fire with a lighted lantern." Or again: "In one blink of your eye you have missed seeing." Eastern philosophy often is thought of as other-worldly, and often enough it is, but at this common level it is just the opposite; its only concern is what you see right before you: "the immediately experienced, emotionally moving, all-embracing aesthetic continuum common to all things and all persons."

While the West has been examining the score, the East was listening to the symphony. But the West once listened too. Evidence of that can be found among other places in the 1556 edition of *Le Grand Propriétaire de toutes choses*, a thirteenth-century encyclopedia that contains the compiled writings of the Byzantine Empire. As Philippe Ariès has demonstrated, this source indicates an antiquo-medieval science that emphasized in all categories the fundamental unity of nature. "I am inclined to think," writes Ariès, "that this rigorous concept of the unity of Nature must be held responsible for the delay in scientific development, much more than the authority of tradition, the ancients or the Scriptures." Modern science cannot influence any aspect of nature unless it has isolated that aspect from nature as a whole. But the science of *Le Grand Propriétaire* holds that it is impossible to do this without upsetting the cosmic order.

Knowledge of Nature is limited to the study of relations governing phenomena by means of a single causality—a knowledge which can foresee but cannot modify. There is no escape from this causality except through magic or miracles. A single rigorous law governs at one and the same time the movement of the planets, the vegetative cycle of the seasons, the connections between the elements, the human body and its humours, and the destiny of a man . . .

It is sometimes argued that Western technology has its roots in the Judeo-Christian concept of a Creator: a technician god who manufactured the universe and strung it with twinkling lights. Or sometimes it is argued that our concept of God is a product of our technological mentality: if something exists, somebody must have made it. But on this point the Bible is ambiguous. We are told in *Genesis* that the Creator made man in his own image, and that he instructed Adam and Eve to "subdue" the earth and to have "dominion" over all that moved upon it. On the other hand, Adam and Eve were expelled from Eden for eating from the tree that would make them like gods. God also punished the first would-be astronauts, the Mesopotamians, for their attempt to build a tower that would reach to the heavens. He said: "Now nothing will be restrained from them, which they have imagined to do." So he confounded their language, and he scattered them over the face of the earth. Obviously, he did not approve. (There is nevertheless a possible explanation in Western religious tradition for the technological impulse, and this will be discussed in the next chapter.)

It is possible that the origin of technology in the West may be related in some way to cultural patterns that are based in turn on elements of language; for example, the verb. But the fact remains that the all-out war on nature was not declared until fairly recent times, and there has been consistent opposition to the concept of an inherent conflict between man and his environment. That opposition has been strengthened by the impact of drug mysticism, Eastern philosophy, and of course the abuses of technology itself—which now threaten to create an environment in which man perhaps can no longer exist. *Le Grand Propriétaire* suggests that medieval science may have recognized intuitively what we now call ecology or the balance of nature, the often subtle relationship that exists between organisms and their environment. We are dependent upon vegetation for the air we breathe; but we are covering the planet with a blanket of concrete and polluting the atmosphere with industrial wastes. Sakharov points out that over a period of one hundred years a 10 per cent annual increase in wastes will be multiplied twenty thousand times. The undeveloped nations are rushing to industrialize, and it is conceivable that the planet could be made uninhabitable in a comparatively short period of time. Indeed, the need for international arms control may soon be less urgent than the need for international cooperation on the problems of pollution—what Sakharov has referred to as geohygiene, or earth hygiene. Our smokestacks are more dangerous to life than all the volcanos that ever erupted, and in this sense the war on nature is not a war at all; it is suicide. Once again, it seems, we have met the enemy and he is us. It is encouraging, therefore, that young protesters appear now to be turning their attention increasingly to the problems of ecology and environmental control.

Let us turn now to the second aspect of psychedelic mysticism and the cultural revolution—the relationship of the self to other people.

We proposed earlier that American attitudes on this subject may have been influenced to a considerable degree by the ontology and political philosophy of the English philosopher John Locke (1632–1704). Locke stated that the human soul is a conscious mental substance, as distinct from all material substances including the human body; it may inhabit a body, but it will survive the death of the body: it is immortal. As such it is completely independent and self-sufficient; there is no organic relationship whatever between one soul and another. Locke's political philosophy is based on this ontology. If the individual is free and independent in his essence, he also should be as free and independent as possible in his earthly existence—and it follows from Locke's ontology that there is no natural law on which to base a form of government to regulate his relationships with other individuals. Whatever government is established will derive its authority from one source only: the majority consent of the individuals who enter into a social contract and agree to surrender a part of their freedom in order to protect their self-interest—their self-interest being the material substances that constitute their property. And their property of course includes their bodies. The only purpose of government is to prevent one person from taking another person's property, including that person's body (or life). Beyond this there should be as much freedom as possible, and therefore the best government is the one that governs least.

In terms of ideological influence, John Locke was to the American Revolution what Karl Marx was to the Russian Revolution. His ideas dominated the thinking of Thomas Jefferson and the other American patriots; they thus found expression in the Declaration of Independence and later the Constitution of the United States.* Jeffersonian democracy emphasizes liberty and laissez-faire individualism, but it does so by placing property rights above human rights—the welfare of the individual above the welfare of the society. It was opposed by the Federalists, who based their theory of government on the Aristotelian concept of an organic society, and for Lincoln at least this was the fundamental issue involved in the Civil War. Businessmen have often resorted to the federal principle, but for Jeffersonian ends: to protect their property by creation of protective tariffs, for example; but liberal politicians have also resorted to it whenever they have sought to redress social injustice. Unfortunately, there is inherent in federalism the problem of

* For a contrary view which seriously disputes Locke's historical influence, see John Dunn's *The Political Thought of John Locke* (Cambridge, England, 1969).

bureaucratic remoteness from the flesh-and-blood society, and it is rather ironic that some radicals in reacting to this remoteness have called for a return to Jeffersonian ideals of individual liberty and self-determination. If those ideals were carried all the way back to their philosophical foundation, the radicals would have something they hadn't bargained for.

Locke's atomistic ontology was rejected of course by Marx and by Engels. They wrote, in *The Holy Family* (1844):

The members of civil society are not atoms. The specific property of the atom is that it has no properties and is therefore not connected with beings outside it by any relations determined by its own natural necessity. . . . The egotistic individual in civil society may in his non-senuous imagination and lifeless abstraction inflate himself to the size of an atom, i.e., to an unrelated, self-sufficient, wantless, absolutely full, blessed being . . . [but] each of his senses compels him to believe in the existence of the world and the individuals outside him, and even his profane stomach reminds him every day that the world outside him is not empty, but is what really fills. Every activity and property of his being, every one of his vital urges becomes a need, a necessity, which his self-seeking transforms into seeking for other things and human beings outside him. But as the need of one individual has no self-understood sense for the other egotistic individual capable of satisfying that need and therefore no direct connection with its satisfaction, each individual has to create that connection; it thus becomes the intermediary between the need of another and the object of that need. Therefore, it is natural necessity, essential human properties, however alienated they may seem to be, and interest that hold the members of civil society together; civil, not political life is their real tie. It is therefore not the state that holds the atoms of civil society together, but the fact that they are atoms only in imagination, in the heaven of their fancy, but in reality beings tremendously different from atoms, in other words, not divine egoists, but egotistic human being. Only political superstition today imagines that social life must be held together by the state whereas in reality the state is held together by civil life.

Let us assume for the moment that America's fundamental attitudes and institutions actually *are* rooted in Locke's ontology. This might explain in part our ingrained reluctance to deal with social needs in the public sector. Northrop wrote, a quarter-century ago: "Consciously or unconsciously, the Lockean doctrine of the self-sufficient, independent moral, religious, and political person has become so much a common-sense assumption of the vast majority that in a political showdown, when emotions are raised and traditional, instinctive reactions are released, the laissez-faire, individualistic response triumphs over the organic, social principle." In America this is reinforced by the Protestant emphasis upon individual conscience, which tends to blame social evils on the failure of individuals rather than the failures of society. It will be argued of course that most Americans have never heard of John Locke, and that few have read him; but it also is true that most Germans have not read Hegel and most Russians have not read Marx: their basic attitudes must nevertheless be influenced by those philosophers to the extent that the concepts of Hegel and Marx are reflected in the very structure of German and Russian society. Most Americans have not read the Bible, but psychologically or otherwise almost every American must be influenced in some way by the fundamental assumptions in that book.

A more subtle objection to Locke's influence is raised by Edward T. Hall. "Philosophy," he said, "is an expression of something which is already there—in the people." In other words, their culture (as we have defined culture). Hall added: "The educated Germans used to go through a sort of identity crisis when they would go to college to decide which of the philosophies they were going to live by. And they would take them and compare them. This wasn't so difficult for a German, because most of the philosophers they were concerned with were German philosophers. So basically what they were doing was comparing different German life styles, and these philosophers had sort of crystallized out basic elements of these life styles. The students were saying: 'What kind of a German do I want to be?' Only they didn't realize that this is what they were doing, or that this was not being a Chinese or anything else like that. The process was similar in some ways to what we go through when we buy an automobile—and the differences were about that great too, as far as the choices they had."

Hall's objection obviously is valid, in the sense that all effects have causes. Something already in existence must have caused Locke to formulate the ontology he did, and we know in fact that his philosophy was inspired in part not only by the social practice of his period but also by Newtonian physics. But let us go deeper than this, by going back in time. According to Fromm and others, as we have already seen, medieval society was organic in structure; the individual as we know him did not yet exist, and people clearly did not think of themselves as isolated atoms: they were part of a unified social order, and they found their identity in social solidarity. The emerging concept of the individual has been attributed to the Protestant Reformation and the rise of capitalism. As we also have seen, however, Ariès has suggested that the idea of the individual is more basically rooted in the concept of the family.

The modern family began to develop only in the seventeenth century—which was Locke's period—and was firmly established in the century that followed, which of course was the period of Jefferson and the American Revolution. Ariès wrote: "In the eighteenth century, the family began to hold society at a distance, to push it back beyond a steadily extending zone of private life. . . . The old code of manners was an art of living in public and together. The new code of manners emphasized the need to respect the privacy of others." The iconography of the sixteenth century is seldom devoted to family scenes; its most frequent representation is the crowd: "not the massive, anonymous crowd of our overpopulated cities, but the assembly of neighbours, women and children, numerous but not unknown to one another." Life until the seventeenth century was lived in public, and houses were open to callers at all hours of the day or night; indeed the concept of the private home did not exist either, and houses were designed for communal living. People lived on top of each other in all-purpose rooms, and there was no such thing even as a separate bedroom. That was the reason beds were curtained, to provide just a small bit of privacy—beyond that, privacy scarcely existed at all. The concept of the family arose with the concept of the child, and our history since that time can be seen as a long effort "to break away from others, to escape from a society whose pressure had become unbearable." Ariès was tempted to conclude that "sociability and the concept of the family were incompatible, and could develop only at each other's expense."

Further evidence of this may be found in the fact that the group identity of the kibbutz was achieved only by breaking up the traditional Jewish family and rearing children together in isolation from their parents. Similarly, the Communists found it necessary to eradicate family ancestor worship to create the organic anthill that is Red China today. And it is possible that the interpersonal relatedness of black Americans may derive in part from the precarious status of the black family during slavery, when a capacity for communal identification may have provided some psychological protection against the sudden rupture of family ties. Whatever the case, it must be conceded that John Locke's influence on the mentality of white American society may have been less direct than it appears on the surface; he may simply have confirmed an atomistic ontology that already existed, consciously or unconsciously. Be that as it may, we are less concerned with the origin of that ontology than we are with the fact that it seems to be eroding—that something else may be taking its place.

The evidence for this change can be adduced with the aid of proxemics.

Proxemics is a term coined by Hall to describe theories

relating to man's use of his environmental space as a specialized function of culture. One such theory is based on observations which indicate that there exists in the animal world a curious dichotomy between "contact" species and "noncontact" species. Contact animals huddle together and apparently require physical contact with each other; noncontact animals completely avoid touching. Among the former are the walrus, hippopotamus, pig, brown bat, parakeet, and hedgehog; among the latter are the horse, dog, cat, rat, muskrat, and hawk. It has been suggested that the noncontact animals are surrounded in effect by private zones, or invisible bubbles of space which in normal situations they find necessary or desirable to maintain between themselves and their fellow animals. According to Hall, men too have their invisible bubbles of private space. "Everybody has a line drawn around him somewhere," said Hall. But where the line is drawn will vary from one individual to another, from one country to another, or from one cultural or ethnic group to another. People who live in areas bordering the Mediterranean seem to pack together much more closely than do northern Europeans, the English, and Americans. Arabs often appear to have no private zone at all; they flock together in crowds, touch each other freely, and breathe in each other's faces while conversing; indeed they have no word to connote privacy, but they do have a saying: "Paradise without people should not be entered because it is Hell." Americans in contrast have been for the most part a noncontact species, and Hall has an interesting collection of candid snapshots that reveal their spacing habits. Waiting for a bus, for example, Americans will space themselves on the curb at precise intervals, like sparrows on a telephone wire; pressed together inside the bus, with their rigid postures and blank expressions they appear to deny the existence of their fellow passengers.

But such behavior is changing. The hippies are clearly a contact species. They huddle together, like walruses, and the typical hippie crash pad is comparable in many ways to the crowded, all-purpose communal room of the Middle Ages. Something like 400,000 young people attended the now-famous Woodstock Music and Art Fair at Bethel, in the Catskill Mountains of New York. They were packed together for three days and nights, in a sea of mud, and the policemen who were assigned to the event were utterly astonished. Said one: "I've never seen that many people in so small an area who acted so peacefully." Said another: "This was the nicest bunch of kids I've ever dealt with." Apparently there was not so much as a single fight; the young people shared their food and their shelter and related to each other in what appeared to be perfect harmony. They even shared their drugs—including LSD—and according to one estimate at least 90 per cent of them were smoking marijuana.

There may be a connection between the drugs and the harmony.

By the mid-1960's the psychedelic drug movement had spread to the youth population, and in general—at first—the young people seemed to accept the Eastern mystique that had been imposed upon the psychedelic experience by such people as Aldous Huxley, Alan Watts, and Timothy Leary. Trips were commonly described as mystical religious experiences, and they were assessed in terms of Hindu and Buddhist metaphysical concepts. In a mystical experience—as in Asian ontology—the relationship of the self to other people is in essence the same as the relationship of the self to the physical environment; there is for the mystic no distinct point where he ends and other people begin. This is particularly true in the case of Eastern mysticism, which tends to be pantheistic and monistic. In so far as it is pantheistic, it rejects the idea that God or pure Being in any way transcends man, and the Eastern mystic solves his identity crisis in a rather dramatic fashion by concluding: *"I'm God."* In so far as Eastern mysticism is monistic, it rejects the idea that there is more than one Self. In denying that his little self is his true identity—that it has any lasting reality—the Eastern mystic also denies the reality of all the other little selves (you, for example). They and he are the same thing . . . and one thing . . . and that one and the same thing is God, the eternal One. All people are really the same Person.

Western mysticism in its orthodox form also tends to emphasize the immanence or indwelling nature of God. The Western mystic will feel in many cases that he is a part of God, that he in some way shares in God's nature or essence. *But* there is always some element of otherness. Thus St. Augustine wrote in his *Confessions*, of his own vision: "I am both a-shudder and a-glow. A-shudder in so far as I am unlike it, a-glow in so far as I am like it." The Western mystic also retains a sense of otherness in connection with people, although he does experience himself as somehow connected to them by ineffable bonds of love and relatedness. Judeo-Christian belief rejects monism along with pantheism; it is pluralistic and insists that the individual self or soul is both real and everlasting, surviving death itself. In fact the concepts of pantheism and monism are repugnant even to some Hindus. Thus the bhakti yogi says: "I want to taste sugar. I don't want to *be* sugar."

Serious drug users today are less likely to evaluate their experience in mystical terms—either Eastern or Western. Attitudes have changed, and so has the drug vocabulary. For example, listen to our young friend Molly as she raps about acid now:

"Everything about it has changed. Two, three years ago acid was a totally new kind of thing, and the only context it could be related to was this mystical Indian thing. You know, nirvana and all that. But now it's kind of an entity in itself. I mean it's not nirvana, and it's not mystical—it's *acid.* And acid is a chemical that goes to your brain and keeps your synapses open, you know, and that's what it is. And I think that's a lot more honest. It's got its own thing now—it's been translated into Now terms. It's like taking the Bible—some kind of institutionalized religion —and making it workable. Throwing all that garbage out, so to speak, and making it work. So you take what it was supposed to be, and the way it was used, and you give it its own thing—you bring it up to date. Like now I take this mystical nirvana thing— this feeling, this cohesive *thing*—and now I translate it into terms that are acid terms, that sound like what I feel. I mean, I would rather say, '*Oh, wow!*' than say, '*Holy Krishna!*' Because when I say that, I know what it means—depending, you know, on how I say it."

But what does it mean, Molly?

"I don't know, exactly. But it's always there. It's this thing, you know—this unity thing. I mean, I went through this period when I was merging into tree trunks and hearing sitars in my head and all that, and it was all very interesting. But that's not *it*. Or we'd sit around and rap about some sort of universal whole, you know. But that's not it either. All it really is—you're just simply acknowledging that there is something that binds people together, and I don't pretend to know what it is, but it's there, and that's what's important. Now I find myself in this unity thing whether I'm tripping or not, and I believe in a brotherhood and a fellowship. It's like going and just being calmly aware that there is a bond, and it can be anything from a cohesive intelligence or God to just the spaces in between that hold everything together. And you get into the fact that there are spaces in between everything. But I look at those spaces in between not as chasms but as—I don't know. What do you call it when you've got a space that's holding two things together? Okay, they're all part of a whole maybe. But it's more like a lot of separate little things tied together, you know, on strings, like a big circle or something. And there's a connection. But each of those things has a mind of its own. I mean, it doesn't go all to one place—and then go down to somebody else. It has to go across, between people. You have to establish these lines. And that's where it's at."

This obviously is not Lockean ontology—whatever else it may be—and it may explain in part the phenomenon of Bethel. If ontologies are culturally determined, as Hall believes they are, then the cultural revolution may be in the process now of creating a new ontology—or returning, perhaps, to an earlier one: the organic ontology of medieval society. If the rise of the family contributed to the decline of that society, it is possible that a change in family patterns may be contributing now to a different trend. Studies indicate that the conventional hippie—the alienated drug user—tends to come from a home in which the father fails to offer a positive role model or coherent set of values; the family is dominated by an intrusive and basically frustrated mother. Unlike the radical, the hippie is almost always in open rebellion against those values the father does express or represent. The radical, on the other hand, tends to share his family's values, while seeking to extend them. But as we have seen, the structure of this family may tend to be matriarchal and socially nurturant; it might be described in fact as *extroverted*. (By way of contrast, Daniel Offer's "normal" families appear at least to be more traditionally introverted.) Beyond this, the prolongation of the psychosocial moratorium means that a young person in most cases must wait longer now to start his own family—which may inspire him to identify more intimately with his peer group. In this sense—in so far as it may represent simply a youth subculture—the cultural revolution may be viewed as creating merely an enlarged family that falls somewhat short of the family of man. Even at Bethel, according to some reports, there seemed to be a mood of *us* (the young) as opposed to *them* (the adults). In medieval society, it will be remembered, there was no sharp distinction between the young and the old, and this may have allowed that society to be more truly organic than ours by its nature can ever hope to be. The fact remains, however, that many young people today are making a conscious effort to change their spacing habits—and this effort in fact is not limited to the young or to drug use. The sensitivity training pioneered by the Esalen Institute in California is also a part of it. Hall, for example, agrees that such a movement is taking place, and his only objection would be that it is a very conscious phenomenon.

"Oh, they've been trying," he said. "And not just the hippies. All kinds of people now are trying to overcome the distance between them and other people. But this is still a deliberate thing, and what's interesting is, if you watch a young couple just walking around holding hands, the distance that they use from each other, in nine cases out of ten, is no different than the distance they would use ordinarily. In other words, they have to consciously push themselves. The way a boy walks with a girl is still an American way, as contrasted, say, with the way a Frenchman walks. The Frenchman pulls the girl in so far that she becomes part of his body practically. And it's natural for them, because this is the way they are. But some of this sensitivity stuff we've been working on—it's like a foreigner who comes to this country and insists on using our slang when he doesn't know how to use it. Or a mother who tries to talk baseball with her kid. You know, people are very sensitive to the rules of a.system even though they don't know it has rules. So when I see a bunch of characters out at Esalen who are strangers, quote, 'feeling' each other, this makes my hair stand on end. Because there are rules for feeling each other, and you only feel each other for very specific reasons. But you don't feel each other for the reasons that they are feeling each other—and if you did, you wouldn't do it that way. So these are made-up systems, and what we're seeing now on our home front are very good examples of what we look like when we go overseas and try to go native. It makes the local nationals terribly uncomfortable, because the whole thing is an awful joke. So I think there's this self-conscious quality which is different from the kind of packing together you see of people who are what I call contact people, who are brought up this way. But this doesn't mean that eventually we won't develop a new vernacular. We very well may. Because I think that these kids are responding to something—and something which is very real."

Exactly what they are responding to is difficult to say. But it may be that Robert Frost touched upon it in his poem *Mending Wall.* "Good fences make good neighbors," said the poet's neighbor. To which the poet replied:

> Before I built a wall I'd ask to know
> What I was walling in or walling out,
> And to whom I was like to give offense.
> Something there is that doesn't love a wall,
> That wants it down.

Who can say? If Molly and her friends can retain that unity thing into their adulthood, the instinctive reactions released in a political showdown may not be the ones that Northrop talked about; some day in the future, it may be the organic, social principle that triumphs over the atomistic, laissez-faire response. In fact, the kind of economic conversion experience we spoke of earlier may very well depend upon this—a complete reversal of the "common-sense assumption of the vast majority," a change not only in our thinking but in the way that we think. Then perhaps this country will be willing at last to meet its social obligations. In so far as it contributes to this kind of reversal, the drug experience must be regarded as a positive aspect of the cultural revolution.

But there is another aspect that is not so encouraging, and this relates to the drug mystic's concept of time or history.

Traditionally, the religious mystic has sought to break out of time, and consequently to break out of history. In seeking the unseen order that underlies the phenomenal world, he seeks the eternal—and eternal here is not to be conceived as endless time: it is outside of time altogether. The mystic in a sense denies the reality of time, and in so doing he necessarily dismisses the importance of history in human affairs. He asserts that eternity —or nirvana—is to be found in the here-now present moment; he therefore ridicules the empirical Western mind that seeks to explain the meaning of existence through cause-and-effect relationships, living constantly in the past and in the future, using the past to predict and indeed to explain the future.* This is one reason the empirical Westerner finds the mystical experience so hard to understand—a difficulty that Plotinus touched upon when he wrote:

* The simplistic cause-and-effect explanations of classical science and technology do not apply in the case of the advanced pure sciences, such as quantum mechanics, which are concerned instead with functional relationships between variables. For an excellent discussion of causality from this point of view, see Victor Guillemin's *The Story of Quantum Mechanics* (New York, 1968).

Every search moves to a first principle and stops when it has reached it . . . every inquiry is either about what a thing essentially is, or its quality, or its cause, or the fact of its existence. But the existence of That, in the sense in which we say that It exists, is known from the things that come after It; inquiry into Its cause is looking for another principle beyond It, and there is no principle of the Universal Principle.

If you explain everything in terms of some other thing that caused it, how can you possibly explain the First Cause? The mystic believes that he has arrived at this First Cause or Universal Principle—at *that which is*, or the godhead itself, the *I Am That I Am*—and that is why he says that the rational, verbal, cause-and-effect mind will never understand it. He has arrived at the Cause of All Effects. And since this is outside our mundane cause-effect sequence, it also is outside of time. St. Augustine, for example, spoke of the Light Unchangeable: "It made me. . . . He that knows the Truth, knows what that Light is; and he that knows it, knows eternity." Tauler, a fourteenth-century German mystic, spoke from his vision:

There is no past nor present here, and no created light can reach unto or shine into this divine ground; for here only is the dwelling-place of God. . . . This ground is so desert and bare that no thought can ever enter here. . . . It is so close and yet so far off, and so far beyond all things, that it has neither time nor place. It is a simple and unchanging condition. A man who really and truly enters, feels as though he had been here throughout eternity.

And finally this quotation from Richard Jefferies, a nineteenth-century English mystic:

I cannot understand time. It is eternity now. I am in the midst of it. It is about me in the sunshine; I am in it, as the butterfly floats in the light-laden air. Nothing has to come; it is now. Now is eternity; now is the immortal life.

Albert Schweitzer criticized Hinduism precisely because it does deny time, and therefore the significance of human history. But as the quotations indicate, this point of view has not been restricted to the East; in fact, all forms of mysticism have tended in this direction, and that is one reason the Western church has never felt at ease about its own mystics. Indeed, the church in its time has condemned those mystics who fell into the error of quietism—"idle basking in the divine presence," or the eighteenth-century version of dropping out. It is the old dispute of Martha and Mary, the activist and the contemplative. But it is one thing to say that the mystic denies time in the sense of past and future significance; why on the other hand is he so very often unconcerned about the evils which exist in the here-now present moment? This may be traced to another, related characteristic of mysticism. Just as it rejects the dualism of past and future, mysticism tends also to reject *all* dualisms—including the dualism of right and wrong, good and evil. For the mystic there is an eternal "rightness" to things, and the world is just as it should be. The original sin of Eden was man's presumptuous decision to judge the world, knowing good and evil; the mystic does not judge, and therefore he is beyond anxiety. The perception of right and wrong arises from the error of perceiving the world in a fragmentary fashion, looking at the parts instead of the Whole. Seen as a Whole, life is perfect and complete. As the orientalist Alan Watts expresses this viewpoint, it is proper and rational to speak of "up" and "down" when you are referring to activities here on the Earth; out in space, however, or in the universe as a whole, there is no up and there is no down: nor is there good and evil.

But Western religious tradition is rooted in the concept of time expressed as history. History is not an illusion, nor is it unimportant. God moves in it. And this idea, along with monotheism, was Judaism's most significant contribution to the ancient world. As Huston Smith has pointed out, Judaism begins with an historical event—the Exodus—the very wonder of which impressed upon the Jews the conviction that God had chosen them to lead mankind toward a Kingdom of God in the world. History therefore was vitally important to the Jews, who believed among other things that it called for *collective* social action. Moses did not think it was enough for an individual Hebrew slave to attain his inner freedom, to find some personal Canaan in Egypt. The Hebrew people as a whole had to band together to end the Egyptian bondage, achieving outer freedom as well; they were called to find a Promised Land for all. They also felt that history must be closely studied, for there come ripe moments—tides in the affairs of men and nations—when God expresses his will to those he has chosen. And so it was that Judaism provided the very basis for social activism and social protest.

There has always been a fundamental tension between the activist and the mystic, and this tension in turn can be related to a fundamental question: *Where do you locate the Kingdom of God?* Do you locate it in the future or the present—in Canaan or in Egypt? Does it already exist—is it truly within you, waiting to be recognized—or does it have to be created? The mystic is content to live in the here-now present moment, and that is where he locates the Kingdom of God: for him *now* is the Kingdom of God, and now *is* the Kingdom of God. The world this instant is a perfect paradise for those with the eyes to see it. The activist of course says otherwise, and for this reason there was in the beginning a very distinct and often hostile division between the political radicals and the original hippies or flower children. The hippies felt that the radicals were themselves the prisoners and dupes of the irrationally rational system—materialistic Babbitts, preoccupied with the problem of economic inequities within the technological society. Indeed the radicals were overly concerned with problems as such—problems that were largely man's own creation—while the hippies were concerned with the more ultimate mysteries of life (the meaning of human existence and the final answer to the identity question). Suppose for example that the day arrives when all of the problems have been solved: no more war, no more prejudice, no more hunger or want. We are all sitting out there on our suburban patios, in the bright sunlight, blacks and whites together, sipping cooling drinks while the steaks sizzle on charcoal fires. Then we look at each other, vaguely disturbed, and somebody finally says it: "Well . . . *now what?*" The hippies had already addressed themselves to that question. They suggested that the radicals lacked either the wisdom or the courage just to sit down somewhere, in a chair maybe, and just *be*. As Paul Tillich had said, it takes courage to be.

Or acid.

The radicals for their part viewed the hippies as romantic Doctor Zhivagos who were trying to lead wholly personal lives in a period of social upheaval—and as Strelnikov told the good doctor, history will not allow that; history has killed that possibility. So the tension here can also be expressed in terms of Hamlet's question: is it better to *be,* or better not to be but rather to take arms against a sea of troubles, and by opposing end them? Drop out or resist? Which shall it be, if either?

The sharp distinction between the hippies and radicals was still apparent in 1967, when the sociologist James T. Carey studied the Berkeley drug colony and found that the hard-core acidheads there had rejected altogether the possibility of changing the social order through political action; they had developed instead "a distinctive life style which celebrates political disengagement." Many of the heads in fact were former student activists, New Left dropouts who had been deeply discouraged by their efforts to reform the university and had decided that the larger society as well was impervious to any qualitative change. There seemed to be a progression from activism to political alienation. The activists frowned on drug use, regarding it as incompatible with serious political activity, and few of them indulged even in the occasional use of marijuana, let alone LSD. The heads for their part distrusted the somber New Left, which they felt was just as hostile to their life style as any other element of the straight society. They believed that "the only change for which one can work is change within oneself, and that massive change can come only from individual transformation." In this sense they were optimistic, for the psychedelic drugs were able to produce such transformations; ultimately, acid would transform the world: there would be a cultural revolution, if not a political one. Meanwhile, the heads demonstrated to the world by their own lives that there were other ways to live—that a "slave" could free himself.

The following year, in 1968, the Yippies appeared upon the scene.

The Yippies basically were three people—Abbie Hoffman, Jerry Rubin, and Paul Krassner. They announced the formation of YIP, the Youth International Party, which had as a main objective the "blending of pot and politics into a political grass leaves movement—a cross-fertilization of the hippie and New Left philosophies." Krassner later said the YIP "never really existed" and was "merely a slogan to bring together the New Left and the psychedelic dropouts." But Hoffman in particular had a genius for manipulating the news media, and the Yippie philosophy received widespread publicity. Let us look at that philosophy, as Hoffman has described it in *Revolution for the Hell of It.*

Hoffman says the New Left was too up tight and lacked a sense of humor, a zest for fun. "People who take themselves too seriously are power-crazy. If they win it will be haircuts for all. Beware of power freaks." The goal is total freedom, and freedom is a state of mind. "One learns reality is a subjective experience. It exists in my head." Hoffman calls for a Politics of Ecstasy or a Politics of Being that will combine the life styles of Fidel Castro and Andy Warhol: not so much guerrilla warfare as "monkey warfare." He tells the radicals to stop trying to organize everybody but themselves; he tells them to live their vision. In short, do your thing. "Be your thing." And that will be the Revolution. "Revolution is in my head. I am the Revolution. Do your thing. Do your thing. Do your thing." The idea is to create new living styles and thereby to develop "a model for an alternative society." Hoffman asks for the legalization of marijuana and other psychedelic drugs; he also wants to separate the concept of productivity from the concept of work. "Work is money. Work is postponement of pleasure. . . . We must abolish work and all the drudgery it represents." Cybernation eventually will result in freedom for the whole society. "A good many people will have to change their ideas on competition vs. cooperation, work vs. play, postponement of pleasure vs. instant gratification. . . . But above all this, more people have to begin to live the revolution and live it now." Why wait for cybernation? Hoffman tells the radicals: "Look, you want to have more fun, you want to get laid more, you want to turn on with friends, you want an outlet for your creativity, then get out of school, quit your job. Come on out and help build and defend the society you want." And he described his own vision of that future society:

We will fly the flag of nothingness over the Pentagon and a mighty cheer of liberation will echo through the land. "We are Free, Great God Almighty, Free at last." Schoolchildren will rip out their desks and throw ink at stunned instructors, office secretaries will disrobe and run into the streets, newsboys will rip up their newspapers and sit on the curbstones masturbating, storekeepers will throw open their doors making everything free, accountants will all collapse in one mighty heart attack, soldiers will throw down their guns. "The War is over. Let's get some ass." No permits, no N.Y. Times ads, no mailing lists, no meetings. . . . Extend all boundaries, blow your mind.

Hoffman of course is a master of the put-on; he is a showman and a con artist. But it would be a mistake to suppose that he is not essentially serious about that vision of his, because he is, and that vision in turn is now in many ways the essence of the cultural revolution. The Yippies should not be given too much credit for this—they were probably less a cause than an effect— but there has in fact occurred a fusion of New Left protest and hippie life styles. It has become increasingly difficult to determine where protest ends and life style begins: to a considerable degree, life style at the moment appears to be in itself the principal form of protest for some of the young white dissenters (as it also is for the black cultural nationalists). To be sure, this includes a good deal of rhetoric about a political revolution—the cultural revolution ultimately will lay the basis for a political revolution, by creating a new consciousness that undermines the basic assumptions of the one-dimensional society. It also includes at the moment an increased emphasis on "action" and the forcing of confrontations. But one cannot help feeling that the rhetoric and the confrontations are simply a part of the life style or modes of expression; that they are ends in themselves—a way of life—and that, consciously or unconsciously, they have no transcendent purpose.

One symptom or aspect of all this has been increased acceptance of drug use within the New Left. And the drug scene as a whole has become ugly and promiscuous. Where dangerous drugs once were used with reverence or respect, in the name of a noble cause, drugs far more dangerous are now used in a wholly frivolous manner. The innocent flower child has given way to the plastic hippie and the speed freak, who often enough may use heroin to ease himself down from a methedrine high, and little pretense is made of seeking mystical insights: the object is pleasure. There remain today very few of the original hippie types—those barefoot Quakers whose thing was love—and by and large the few who are left no longer seem to think that acid will save the world; they have only to look around them to disabuse themselves of that happy notion. New Left drug use so far has been limited for the most part to marijuana, which is smoked mainly for relaxation and a mild euphoria, and hopefully the politically oriented young people will continue to exercise caution about the harder psychedelics (though there is not much basis for that hope). Meanwhile, much of their energy and enthusiasm is absorbed in efforts to legalize marijuana—and this represents one of the disappointing aspects of the cultural revolution. Keniston could say only a few years ago that the young people hardly ever demonstrated on their own behalf; they were concerned almost exclusively with the welfare of the underprivileged and the oppressed, the outcasts of the society. This is no longer true,

except in the sense that they now view themselves as the oppressed—following the line laid down by Hoffman and Marcuse,
whose idealism in practice may strike some observers as being
curiously like selfishness.

As for marijuana, it is possible that one of the first acts of
a technetronic dictatorship would be to legalize the drug. Brzezinski has written:

*Mechanization of labor and the introduction of robots will
reduce the chores that keep millions busy with doing things that
they dislike doing. The increasing GNP (which could reach approximately $10,000 per capita per year), linked with educational
advance, could prompt among those less involved in social management and less interested in scientific development a wave of
interest in cultural and humanistic aspects of life, in addition to
purely hedonistic preoccupations. But even the latter would serve
as a social valve, reducing tensions and political frustration.*

Keniston has been accused of romanticizing the young
radicals; it is safe to say in any case that he has not been a stern
critic of their activities. When I last talked to him, however, he
seemed to have developed some doubts.

"I'm very much of two minds on this," he said. "I mean, I
think cultural revolution is kind of deceptive perhaps, in that
what one ends up with is basically a kind of culture of leisure
which is not too different fundamentally from, you know, doing
your thing in the suburbs—with the barbecue pit and everything
else. I do think that some of the most attractive things in some of
these humanist young people have to do with a new life style—
that side of it—and their kind of ease and search for contact and
community and so forth. I mean, this is very appealing. On the
other hand it's not very political. And it seems to me rather a
luxury in some ways."

Christopher Lasch was of one mind on the subject.

"This whole cultural revolution has come to absolutely
nothing," he said. "Politically or socially. I mean, it's just what

Brzezinski said. It's hedonism. And hedonism is a terrific thing for American capitalism at this point—because if you're looking around for new markets, that's a pretty good one. What really was needed was consumers of culture, consumers of popular culture, consumers of sex, consumers of enjoyment. Marcuse is really dumb on this issue. He doesn't see this at all. Because he's so committed to the psychoanalytic framework, which sees all this as deeply liberating. Whereas it seems to me that it just creates more possibilities of infinitely more efficient control. I mean, hedonists are above all the easiest people in the world to control, to manipulate. There'll always be guys who'll be glad to run the country, who aren't interested in anything else, who are very smart and adept at working the machinery and don't have time for that other kind of life, who have all these hangups and therefore presumably are not liberated—like Herman Kahn, I suppose, although he's a little hedonistic himself, I imagine."

The cultural revolutionaries then can be criticized on strategic grounds; in stressing inner freedom they fail to appreciate the important connection between inner freedom and outer freedom, or they fail to recognize that the former does not in itself provide the means for achieving the latter—that on the contrary, a preoccupation with self-liberation lends itself too easily to domination by others. A case has been made that Zen quietism contributed significantly to the rise of militarism in Japan—not all the Japanese were intent on *satori*—and the Tibetans were doing their thing when the Red Chinese marched into their country. People whose minds have been liberated cannot escape the polluted atmosphere; they can refuse to fight in a war, but they cannot refuse to die in a nuclear holocaust that might result from a miscalculation on the part of the managers. The cultural revolutionaries will insist of course that they are engaged in active protest, trying to prevent all this. As noted, however, there is reason to suspect that this is merely a part of their cultural style, and it might be argued that the increased violence of that protest may have something to do with the fact that they have decided at last to take advantage of their affluent status. Having repressed in the past what may be natural urges, they now atone for their hedonism by mounting savage attacks on the evils of society. If so, it is fortunate for them that there is so much real injustice out there for them to protest against. Whether they are doing anything to improve the situation is another question, and their method of attack suggests that they may be more interested in expiation than they are in results and consequences. As Hoffman has said in connection with guerrilla theater tactics, "the play's the thing." The real victims of injustice appear to sense this, and the Panthers for example seem inclined to regard the cultural revolutionaries as "nonrevolutionary clowns." The technetronic society can easily tolerate a court jester such as Abbie Hoffman, with belled cap and slapstick. His antics raise grave doubts about our inherent capacity to control the managers in that era of leisure predicted by the Ad Hoc Committee. But like the Fool in *Lear*, the cultural clowns are not quite as foolish as they seem; if their method is mad—and bad—we will see later on that there may also be some wisdom concealed in their madness as such.

Meanwhile, the cultural revolution can also be criticized on philosophical as well as strategic grounds. While they are too loud to be classified as quietists, the young people involved have something in common with the orthodox mystics—and that is their fascination with the present; if the mystic lives *in* the moment, the hedonist lives *for* the moment. Their experiences are different—the mystic is serenely content, while the hedonist at best probably enjoys what Marcuse has referred to as "euphoria in unhappiness"—but their temporal attitudes may have similar consequences in terms of their orientation to the future. The mystic and the hedonist alike are more concerned with being than becoming, and hedonism might be described in fact as a state of frenetic stasis. This may be traced in part to the drug experience, since the effect of most popular drugs is to enhance the pleasures of the here and now. This is certainly true of LSD, and its widespread use would undoubtedly tend to pacify the non-managerial population. The effects of marijuana are far less dramatic, and its advocates argue with considerable logic that this drug is far more benign than alcohol in its short-term effects: it is not physically addictive; it is not known to cause any organic disease such as liver cirrhosis; it tends to promote introspective behavior rather than the aggressive, acting-out behavior that is often stimulated by alcohol; rather than numb the senses to the point of mental oblivion as alcohol does, it tends to heighten sensitivity to the external environment.

But the alcohol analogy can also be turned around, and it is necessary to consider the problem of drug management. Some people can manage alcohol, and others cannot; we know we have as many as eight million people in this country who cannot. Some people can manage marijuana, and others cannot; if marijuana were legalized we would probably in time have more than eight million people disabled in some way or another by the two drugs together. There would probably be fewer alcoholics, since some of them would no doubt switch to marijuana and become dependent on that, but other people who can manage alcohol might not be able to manage marijuana. In any case, we would probably have more drug-dependent people than we already do. In addition, the behavioral effects that marijuana presently produces may have something to do with the user's expectations, and marijuana might well promote altogether different behavior if it were consumed in a different legal and social context. All the arguments for and against legalization are too complex to examine here; the point is simply that marijuana like other drugs tends to orient the individual to the present moment, at least temporarily, and there is some contestable evidence that marijuana in its long-term effects may tend to promote amotivational attitudes and behavior—that the user in some cases may lose interest in future-oriented activity. If so, as we have already suggested, the legalization of marijuana would be a logical move on the part of a technetronic dictatorship.

But criticism of the cultural revolution is not limited to this factor—to the possibility that it might lend itself to elitist manipulation. Even if democratic institutions were somehow preserved, the society envisaged is nevertheless utopian in nature and therefore tends to end history within history. Tillich in his *Systematic Theology* wrote that utopianism is "progressivism with a definite aim: arrival at that stage of history in which the ambiguities of life are conquered." He added:

Clearly, the power and truth of the utopian impetus has become manifest in the immensity of success in all those realms in which the law of progress is valid, as foreseen in the Renaissance utopias; but at the same time, there has appeared a complete ambiguity between progress and relapse in those realms in which human freedom is involved. Realms involving human freedom were also envisaged in a state of unambiguous fulfilment by the utopianists of the Renaissance and all their successors in the revolutionary movements of the last three hundred years. But these expectations were disappointed with that profound disappointment which follows every idolatrous reliance on something finite. A history of such "existential disappointments" in modern times would be a history of cynicism, mass indifference, a split consciousness in leading groups, fanaticism, and tyranny. Existential disappointments produce individual and social diseases and catastrophes: the price for idolatrous ecstasy must be paid. For utopianism, taken literally, is idolatrous. It gives the quality of ultimacy to something preliminary. *It makes unconditional what is conditioned (a future historical situation) and at the same time disregards the always present existential estrangement and the ambiguities of life and history. This makes the utopian interpretation of history inadequate and dangerous* [roman ours].

We are back to the question of where one locates the Kingdom of God. The mystic says it is located in the present moment, and he condemns the inability of most of us to live in that moment; the implication is that we are existential neurotics who cannot bear to face something: namely, ourselves. Involved in this is the concept of growth and progress, including economic growth and our obsession with the GNP. Involved more fundamentally is the question raised by Teilhard: should our goal be to make the world a comfortable dwelling place, or is the world indeed to be regarded as a machine for progress? The mystic believes that the world already is comfortable, and he is content to live in it as it is; the hedonist believes that it should be made as comfortable as possible—and many humanists agree that this should be our principal objective. But the futurist on the other hand believes that our real objective lies ahead of us in time, and that something in our nature attracts us to the future in the same sense that something in iron attracts it to a magnet. The future is the Kingdom of God, and we are evolving toward it: the kingdom then is not to be located in any given moment or situation—nor is it to be located in any *anticipated* moment or situation, for the future is the future and it remains open. We will not rest in the Kingdom of God until history has ended and we are outside of time—until the Last Times or the End of the Days.

The Kingdom of God is used here simply as a shorthand symbol for an ideal state of mankind—with or without God. But the tension that exists between growth-oriented futurism and here-now humanism is not a subject of interest to most academic philosophers, who are still preoccupied with linguistic analysis. Theologians, on the other hand, are now giving serious attention to the philosophical problems involved in this tension. The futuristic view in fact is an essential aspect of the radical Theology of Hope which superseded the short-lived Death of God theology. Political radicals so far have not paid much attention to radical theology, but the theologians nevertheless are speaking directly to the issues we have discussed in this book—including the cultural revolution—and the Theology of Hope provides us with a conceptual framework within which it may be possible to evaluate these issues. So let us turn now to this "new" theology, examine its origin, and consider its consequences.

the Star Gate

The idea that God moves in history—which we owe to Judaism—represents in essence an evolutionary view of the cosmic process, or at any rate a future-oriented view, and this outlook was shared in the beginning by early Christianity. If we look back two thousand years we find the Jews awaiting the coming of their Messiah, who would bring history to an end and who would usher in the Kingdom of God—a secular kingdom according to some Jews or a divine one according to others. Jesus appeared in Galilee and said that the Kingdom of God was at hand, which implied of course that it lay in the future. He died on the cross, and his followers awaited his second coming, which would herald the coming of the kingdom. It was supposed that this event would occur very shortly, and the early Christians in consequence were preoccupied with the future and the promise it held for them: their viewpoint was primarily *eschatological*, or concerned in other words with the doctrine of "last things" and the day of judgment.

But Jesus did not return as expected, and there gradually occurred what Martin Werner has called the "de-eschatologization" of the Christian faith. The idea grew that the Kingdom of God had arrived with the birth of Jesus and that it was present in the institution of the visible Catholic Church—a concept that can be traced in particular to the influence of St. Augustine. Thus the early expectation of the second coming gave way to the idea of salvation within the church, and there was for the faithful a shift of emphasis from the future to the present. The theologians for their part turned their attention from the future to the past; as Werner put it, they sought to understand the problems of present existence by exploring their origin. They studied the creation, evil, and original sin. In doing so they were considerably influenced by Greek metaphysics, and one result of this was a body of dogma that virtually precluded an evolutionary or futuristic understanding of mankind or the universe—a development which the historian of philosophy Arthur O. Lovejoy has assessed in his classic *The Great Chain of Being*.

Among the neo-Platonic ideas that found their way into Christian thinking was a concept Lovejoy has called the *principle of plenitude*. This idea equates God's goodness with fecundity. It would be jealous of God to deny existence to anything which potentially might exist; since God is perfect, and therefore not jealous, it is in the nature of God to create everything it is possible for God to conceive. This of course implies a kind of divine determinism: God does not will the creation of all things—he is compelled to create them by the goodness of his nature. Furthermore, since he is perfect, he must create all things at the same time. We therefore live in a static universe in which all possibilities have been fulfilled from the beginning. And since this universe as God created it must contain all things, it must of necessity contain all possible evils—a theodicy which can be traced to Plotinus, who said it is better that an animal should be eaten by another animal than not exist at all, it being in the nature of certain animals to be eaten.

Thomas Aquinas could not accept the idea that God is

not free to do as he pleases—to create or not create—but St. Thomas was enough taken with the principle of plenitude to suggest that an angel and a stone were better than two angels. This sort of thinking led logically to the kind of "optimism" that Voltaire was spoofing in *Candide*. It meant we should accept the existing order. Far from denying there was evil in the world, as Lovejoy has pointed out, eighteenth-century optimism was absorbed in demonstrating the necessity of evil (all evils are necessary evils). But the idea of a static and complete Chain of Being started to break down in the eighteenth century, and it did so according to Lovejoy because "it left no room for hope, at least for the world in general or for mankind as a whole." Voltaire and Dr. Johnson both attacked it, and gradually the concept of nothing new under the sun gave way to evolutionary concepts: the principle of plenitude was reinterpreted to represent not the inventory of nature but its program.

This development began in science and philosophy, but in the nineteenth century—with the impact of Darwin—it spread to Protestant theology in America and England. By the end of that century liberal Protestantism had incorporated evolutionary thought into an optimistic theology of never-ending progress. A similar trend appeared for a brief period in Catholicism—the movement referred to as modernism—but this was snuffed out in 1907 when Pope Pius X condemned it as a "synthesis of all heresies," and Pope Pius XII as late as 1950 still objected to "the monistic and pantheistic interpretation that the whole world is subject to continual evolution." The Protestant progressivists in turn were humbled by the horrors of World War I and the anguish of the Great Depression, from which there emerged the dark pessimism of existentialism and the neo-orthodoxy of the Swiss theologian Karl Barth. Prideful man once again had been brought to his knees. His scientific and cultural achievements counted for nothing in Barth's magisterial theology, which emphasized a starkly transcendent God, wholly other than man, and the primacy of divine revelation: the Word of God as revealed to us in Jesus the Christ and known to us only by faith. But man's faith in his own works had merely been eclipsed; it gradually reasserted itself, and in the mid-1960's it surfaced in America as the Death of God.*

While God's supposed demise meant something different to almost every theologian who proclaimed it, we might define it very broadly as optimistic secularism. With the possible exception of Thomas J. J. Altizer, who believed that a once-transcendent God had become wholly immanent in the world through his incarnation in Jesus, nobody really meant that a supernatural deity had suffered cardiac arrest. The movement derived much of its impetus from the German theologian Dietrich Bonhoeffer, who had been murdered by the Nazis in 1945, and it took from Bonhoeffer the concept of a "religionless" Christianity in "a world come of age." This called among other things for a moratorium on God talk. It served no purpose to talk about him, after all—he was by his nature beyond our powers of comprehension—and therefore the proper study of mankind was man (or God in this world, "the beyond in our midst"). We had to stop running to God with all of our problems, like frightened children; we had to grow up and accept our responsibilities. And this was good. Contrary to popular opinion, the Death of God was not a pessimistic theology; it was in fact a joyful celebration of the rational, problem-solving secular man who lived and thrived in the worldly technopolis that the theologian Harvey Cox described with such enthusiasm in his influential book *The Secular City* (1965).

Cox declared that "the era of metaphysics is dead" and that "politics replaces metaphysics as the language of theology." This meant an end to speculation about the ultimate nature of God or the ultimate nature of Being, and it meant we should no longer concern ourselves with the transcendent aspect of God. "God wants man to be interested not in Him but in his fellow man," said Cox. The British Anglican John A. T. Robinson wrote in his *Honest to God* (1963) that men in the past had mentally located God "up there" in a place called heaven; with the coming of the rocket age, they tended to think of God as "out there" in

* This movement in theology has also been described in *The Private Sea.*

some remote corner of space; the idea now was to think of him as here in our midst, as revealed to us in our relationships with other people. Robinson did attempt to rescue the concept of transcendence by defining it as an unconditional aspect of our nature— something within us, not ours to command, that compels us to love one another if we are to be whole men. Since we cannot command this part of our nature but can only respond to it, it transcends us, and this something we must respond to, this unconditional demand, is God—or God at work. But Robinson was something of a loner in the secular crowd (he never identified himself with the Death of God people); while his book was widely read in this country, the American theologians for their part were ready to abandon transcendence altogether. They would act "as if" the transcendent God were dead, and in so doing they would affirm the holiness of the secular. Above all else, the Death of God meant an affirmation of the profane world; it meant saying *yes* to this world. And in this sense we were told that it was "liberating" to think of God as dead or absent.

The death of the Death of God was officially pronounced by *Time* magazine in May of 1969—some two to three years after the actual event. The movement had already begun to expire in 1966, when it was discovered and temporarily resuscitated by the popular press. By 1967 it was obvious that theology was in a period of transition; while a new synthesis had not as yet been clearly defined, the Death of God thesis had given rise to an atmosphere of antithesis in which theologians of many persuasions could be heard speaking of the need to go *"beyond the secular."* This mini-movement was in part at least a result of the pessimism produced by urban rioting, political assassinations, and the escalation of the Vietnam War. But it also had other sources, and it went at first in two directions.

On the one hand, it represented a return to ritual and mysticism. The hippies had demonstrated that some people at least are not content with the busy, secular world of our immediate experience; they crave some form of contact with the unseen order that James talked about, and if they cannot find it in church they will turn to psychedelic drugs, witchcraft, astrology, spiritualism, Eastern meditation, ESP, tarot cards, and Ouija boards. Andrew Greeley, for example, saw in psychedelia a rebellion against hyper-rationalism and "the resurgence of man's need for the sacred in the face of secularized society." He described the hippies as neo-sacralists who were reasserting those elements of religious practice that the church had been downgrading in its hot pursuit of relevance: the ecstatic, the ceremonial, the ritualistic, and the communitarian. Cox began to talk about the need for inner religious experience and a "theology of celebration." Browne Barr, minister of the First Congregational Church in Berkeley, concluded that sensitive and idealistic young people have a natural capacity for emotionally stimulating religious experience; that hippie gnosticism was a clear indication of their appetite for spiritual ecstasy and rapture. The churches had decided that their mission in the modern, post-metaphysical world called for social relevance and social activism, but their congregations did not appear to appreciate their efforts along those lines. Consider the results of a national Gallup poll consisting of six surveys conducted over a twelve-year period. Americans of all faiths were asked: "At the present time, do you think religion as a whole is increasing its influence on American life or losing its influence?" The responses, omitting the "no difference" and "no opinion" answers, were as follows:

	Increasing	Losing
1957	69%	14%
1962	45	31
1965	33	45
1967	23	57
1968	18	67
1969	14	70*

* As Martin E. Marty points out, the respondents in this case were probably referring to the influence of the institutionalized churches and not to religion as such. There is every reason to believe that religion during this period, outside the churches, became increasingly important as a force in American life.

These statistics no doubt reflect in part the Roman Catholic dissension on birth control and other matters, as well as backlash from political conservatives. But the liberal churchmen also found themselves waiting in vain for the pews to fill up with all those concerned young people who had rejected religion as too other-worldly, and some of them began to wonder if the real mission of the church perhaps was not so much to be active itself but rather to sustain people in their personal and social encounters with the world—to offer them a transcendent source of strength that could heal and comfort as well as inspire them. A young medical student who is both a Buddhist and a socialist was telling me recently why he left the Protestant faith. "I quit," he said, "when my church became relevant." Similarly, Barr suggests that social concerns "are the consequence of Christian faith, not its substance." And the Socialist party leader Michael Harrington wrote in 1967: "The Church must fight for the earthly implication of the heavenly values it affirms; it can never again divorce God from the Negroes, the poor, those dying in war, and the rest of humanity. But over and above that witness to the temporal meetings of the eternal there must be the assertion of the eternal itself." The eternal of course is the province of the mystic, and in its early stages there was some reason to think that the beyond-the-secular phenomenon was in essence a conservative reaction to secular liberalism and progressivism— that theology was preparing to withdraw again to an other-worldly metaphysics, outside of history, that would not address itself directly to the problems of man in his society; that it would seek instead to reestablish the timeless and absolute "truths" of the Greek logos.

But—for a time at least—a second trend prevailed.

The mainstream of *post-secular theology* in this country was moving in another direction, responding to a dramatic development that had occurred in European theology. This development in turn could be traced—ironically—to the influence of a Marxist-atheist, the German philosopher Ernst Bloch, who had laid the foundation for a return to the pre-Greek metaphysics of primitive Christianity.

Bloch had been a professor of philosophy in East Germany until 1961, when he accepted a post at the University of Tübingen in West Germany. Orthodox Marxists had condemned him as a revisionist, and small wonder. His major work, *Das Prinzip Hoffnung,* or *The Hope Principle,* asserted that the fundamental truth of human existence was expressed in the future-oriented view of biblical eschatology. Bloch did not accept the biblical concept of a personal and transcendent living God. But he did believe that the Bible provided the basis for a truly eschatological human consciousness that drives man toward a future that is unknown and undetermined: a *not-yet* consciousness that responds to the possibility of a new life, and therefore allows man to hope and obliges man to act. In this sense biblical eschatology is superior to the narrow dialectic of dogmatic Marxism, which tends to suggest that a given thesis must lead inevitably to a given antithesis and synthesis—and which therefore fails to provide for novelty and the possibility of a wholly new creation. On the other hand, it is necessary for Christianity to reassert its original message and to rescue itself from the equally deterministic and history-denying concepts of Hellenistic ontology. Bloch thus opened the way for a continuing dialogue between Marxists and Christians and did much to shape the thinking of the two principal architects of the Theology of Hope, the German theologians Jürgen Moltmann and Wolfhart Pannenberg. Both have acknowledged their debt, and Pannenberg has written: "Perhaps Christian theology will have Ernst Bloch's philosophy of hope to thank if it regains the courage to return to its central category . . . He has recovered the eschatological thought-pattern of the biblical traditions as a theme of philosophical reflection, and also for Christian theology."

The Theology of Hope represented a radical departure from European neo-orthodoxy, and theologians in America wasted little time in importing it to fill the vacuum left by the Death of God. Moltmann's book *The Theology of Hope* was published here late in 1967, and by April of the following year the *Los Angeles Times,* for example, could report to its no doubt startled readers that hope was "now the hottest theological issue in this country." If any further proof were needed, our most dependable weathervane had suddenly stopped spinning in the theological breezes—and its arrow pointed directly toward hope. Said Harvey Cox: "I think that if we can affirm anything real which also transcends history, it will be the future as it lives in man's imagination. . . . If theology can leave behind the God who 'is' and begin its work with the God who 'will be' . . . an exciting new epoch in theology could begin . . ."

An epoch in contemporary theology would appear to be about three years. But there is reason to believe that the Theology of Hope has something more substantial to offer than its evanescent predecessors—which the church historian Martin E. Marty has described with some justice as "nervous" theologies—and it seemed at first that its significance might be lasting and profound.

For one thing, God talk was in again. So was metaphysics. And the metaphysics of hope does indeed go far "beyond the secular" and the world of our immediate experience. Yet it is not otherworldly: its concern is with this world. It does not accept reality; yet it is not unrealistic: it seeks a better reality. It does not locate the Kingdom of God in the here-now present moment; yet it does not seek to escape from that moment: it seeks to transform it. Its God is not present among us; yet he is not a dead God or an absent God: he awaits us in the future, and calls for us to come to him. He is not the Ground of Being, as Tillich would have it, nor is he Being itself, as the Greeks would have it. He is Not Yet. He is Becoming. He does not exist outside of time in some eternal realm from which he breaks into history to influence human events. He moves *in* history, and he too has a future; he is a God with "future as his essential nature." For Bloch he *is* the future; but for Christians he is something more: he also is the promises that have been given to them in the past. Above all, he is the promise of Easter.

Secular theology had erred in supposing it could ignore

the question of the future, which ultimately means the question of death. The relevant theologians thought that they had come to grips with the real problems of secular man; but they told him nothing of his future, and nothing of his death. And his death is relevant to him. For any man—even secular man—the one question that theology must answer is the question of his death. Otherwise, theology itself is irrelevant to him. He need not depend upon it if it provides him merely with an ethics to live by; ethical standards are available from other sources, and they are as stated: something to live by. They do not deal with the question of death.

Moltmann asserted that a noneschatological, bourgeois Christian faith had "banished from its life the future hope by which it is upheld, and relegated the future to a beyond, or to eternity, whereas the biblical testimonies which it handed on are yet full to the brim with future hope of a messianic kind for the world." Because of this, "hope emigrated as it were from the Church and turned in one distorted form or another against the Church." The relegating of man's hopes to the "last day" or the end of history "robbed them of their directive, uplifting, and critical significance for all the days which are spent here, this side of the end, in history." Christianity is hope, and its mission is to transform the present; it therefore causes not rest but unrest, not patience but impatience. "It does not calm the unquiet heart, but is itself this unquiet heart in man. Those who hope in Christ can no longer put up with reality as it is, but begin to suffer under it, to contradict it. Peace with God means conflict with the world, for the goad of the promised future stabs inexorably into the flesh of every unfulfilled present."

Bloch's hope is based on the irresistible attraction of the future, and its only faith is a faith in that future and the strength of its attraction. But Christian hope is the expectation of those things which faith believes have been promised by God, and some theologians indeed would prefer to speak of a Theology of Promise. Altizer's theology was founded on the Incarnation— when God entered the world to become the world. But for Moltmann and Pannenberg, the promise made to man is symbolized by the Resurrection. The risen Christ gives man the faith to hope that for him too there will in some sense be a future that contradicts death; and not for him alone but for mankind as a whole, collectively: for all who now suffer there awaits a "transcendental homeland" where they will find their true identity. Moltmann and Pannenberg differ somewhat on the implications of the Resurrection, but as Moltmann puts it: "Christianity stands or falls with the reality of the raising of Jesus from the dead by God. . . . A Christian faith that is not resurrection faith can therefore be called neither Christian nor faith."

This is no doubt true. It is not our purpose here to defend that faith, as the theologians of hope have interpreted it, but simply to describe it—and also to suggest how it may apply to some of the problems we have discussed in this book. To some extent it might be described as a synthesis of neo-orthodoxy and secular theology. In so far as it acknowledges the question of death, it rejects the shallow optimism of secular theology; but it remains involved with the secular world. Like neo-orthodoxy, it is based on revelational faith in a transcendent God; but unlike neo-orthodoxy, it does not belittle man's efforts to transform his world nor deny him a role in the process of history. Its God is transcendent not in spatial terms but in temporal terms; he is not "up there," and he is not "out there," nor is he even present to us "in our midst." He is *ahead* of us in time. Like the God of *Exodus*, he precedes us in the cloud by day and the pillar of fire by night, urging us to follow; he stands on the road ahead and beckons man to his ultimate but undetermined destiny. He leads us out of Egypt.

Egypt too is temporal. It is the present moment. And the present moment is "the worst of all utopias—the utopia of the status quo."

Moltmann addresses himself directly to the question raised by the mystics, acidheads, cultural revolutionaries, and many humanists who rebel against the concept of futuristic, never-ending progress: *"Does hope cheat man of the happiness of the present?"* In answering the question, Moltmann makes it clear to us that he understands the point of view which answers in the affirmative; he says of man: "He remembers having lived, but he does not live. . . . He hopes to live, but he does not live. He expects to be happy one day, and this expectation causes him to pass over the happiness of the present. He is never, in memory and hope, wholly himself and wholly in his present." It is not merely the happiness of the present but *the God of the present* that the Christian hope appears to cheat us of. But Moltmann cannot accept the God of the present, who is represented by the timeless Greek logos. (Beware of Greeks bearing Gods.) This is the god of Parmenides: eternal, immortal, and absolute Being, the logos referring to a reality which is there, now and always; but there can be no logos of the future, unless the future is the eternal recurrence of the present, and this is not the future of Christian hope. "The Christian hope is directed toward a *novum ultimum,* toward a new creation of all things by the God of the resurrection of Jesus Christ." In rejecting the God of the present, the Christian therefore must also reject all "epiphanies of the eternal present." Which brings Moltmann back to the question, does the Christian hope cheat man of the happiness of the present? Moltmann answers:

How could it do so! For it is itself the happiness of the present. It pronounces the poor blessed, receives the weary and heavy laden, the humbled and wronged, the hungry and the dying, because it perceives the parousia of the kingdom for them. Expectation makes life good, for in expectation man can accept his whole present and find joy not only in its joy but also in its sorrow, happiness not only in its happiness but also in its pain . . . because in the promises of God it can see a future also for the transient, the dying and the dead. . . . It can approve of movement and be glad of history.

Moltmann proposes that German idealism and European romanticism were "the first reactions to the new conditions created by the industrial revolution." He adds: "From that age and that way of thinking comes the idea that man must become identical with himself because primarily and originally he was and is so. . . . [He must] turn from his distractions to reflect upon himself and his true, eternal Ego." Which may explain some of the identity-crisis reactions to the conditions of post-industrial society in America.

On the subject of identity, Moltmann writes:

. . . the decisive question for Christian experience is not whether and how man in the fluctuating variety of his social commitments, or at the point of intersection of all these roles in which he is always only partially involved, can be "himself" and can maintain his own identity and continuity with himself. The point of reference of his expressions and renunciations, his activities and sufferings, is not a transcendental Ego upon which he could and must repeatedly reflect in the midst of all his distractions. But the point of reference is his call. It is to this, and not to himself, that he seeks to live. It is this that gives him identity and continuity—even, and indeed precisely, where he expends himself in non-identity. He does not preserve himself by himself, in constant unity with himself, but in surrendering himself to the work of mission he is preserved by the hope inherent in that mission. . . . In Western social philosophy today . . . we repeatedly find attempts to retain the idea of estrangement and regain the human nature of man by means of transcendental reflection. "I no longer coincide with my social 'I,' even if at every moment I am together with it. I can now in my social existence be conscious of the role, so to speak, which I take upon me or put up with. I see myself and my roles falling apart" [Karl Jaspers]. By means of such reflections, the self-consciousness of man withdraws itself from the compromising, confusing, social reality. In constant reflection, in irony and in criticism of the corruptness of conditions, it regains that detachment in which it thinks to find its infinite possibilities, its freedom and superiority. Yet this subjectivity reflecting upon itself, which does not expend itself

in any social task, but soars above a reality that has been de-
graded into an "interplay of roles"—this faith that feels bound to
no reality, not even its own—turn man into a "man without at-
tributes" in a "world of attributes without man" (R. Musil). They
rescue the humanity of man in an inner emigration in which
man now only "accompanies" his outward life, and in so doing
they abandon conditions to final corruption [*roman ours*].

There is a connection here to the mind-blowing "liberation" of the cultural revolution. Consider for example an article
which recently appeared in one of the underground newspapers,
the *Los Angeles Free Press,* charging that Abbie Hoffman (of all
people) is too politically oriented. The acid-oriented writer reported that Hoffman had tried to take over the stage at the Bethel
rock festival for a political forum and was repulsed by a per-
former who struck him with a guitar. The article described Hoffman as a "mini-politico" and called on young people to develop an
"alternative culture" within our "sick society." It added: "The
age of politics is finished. It served its purpose and it's irrelevant
now. . . . The only way to get freedom is by deciding that you're
free. If you fight authority, you acknowledge it, you give it power.
If authority is ignored, it doesn't exist any more."

So goes the cultural revolution, in a logical extrapolation
from the works of A. Hoffman himself. Moltmann has this sort
of thinking in mind when he quotes Theodor Litt: "Whoever
attempts to get rid of the antinomy by proscribing the world of
organized labour as being the result of a mistake, and by recom-
mending a withdrawal into the inward life as being the only
possible way of salvation from the consequences of this mistake,
abandons that world to a disorder that will sooner or later also lay
hold of his artificially defined spiritual world." Moltmann himself
observes: "An acceptance of the present which cannot and will
not see the dying of the present is an illusion and a frivolity."

The Theology of Hope, then, would appear to reject the
direction in which one element of the youth rebellion seems to be
headed at the moment. The ontology of that theology will explain

in turn why we have in this book referred so frequently to the subject of "identity" without offering a precise definition. "The world is not yet finished," wrote Moltmann, "but is understood as engaged in a history." Man too is not finished, but engaged in a history; his identity awaits him. And according to some of the theologians of hope, this also is true of God. The *I Am Who I Am*, they say, is more properly translated: *I Am Who I Will Be*.

This brief account of futuristic theology has not yet mentioned the contribution of the Roman Catholic scientist and theologian Teilhard de Chardin. Teilhard in fact was years ahead of the Protestants in constructing a theology of the future: a magnificent construction that sought to reconcile the facts of science and the tenets of Christian belief. Teilhard proposed that life is evolving inexorably in the direction of increasing complexity and also, in consequence, of increasing consciousness; that evolution is leading toward a final state of super-complexity and super-awareness in which mankind will leave the earth behind to become pure spirit, rejoining the godhead. Much of Teilhard's work was suppressed during his lifetime, but his ideas have had an enormous influence on theological thought since his death in 1955 (and while their theologies are not the same, it is curious that Moltmann's *Theology of Hope* does not contain a single reference to Teilhard). Catholic theology in general remained tame and conservative from the modernist period until Vatican II (1962–1965), but Catholicism since then has been anything but tame. Today, outside of Rome, it often appears more radical than radical Protestantism, and it has produced a number of prominent scholars and theologians who are closely associated with future-oriented or hope theology—among them Johannes Metz, Leslie Dewart, Karl Rahner, Walter J. Ong, and Edward Schillebeeckx.

The Theology of Hope potentially is far more radical than the Death of God ever was, and it is interesting, as noted, that the secular theologians failed to stir the interest of political radicals including the New Left activists they no doubt thought they would appeal to. Some of the reasons for this were made very clear in a talk that New Leftist Steve Weissman was invited to give at a Conference on Radical Theology late in 1966 (reprinted in *New Theology No. 5*). Weissman told the Death of God theologians that he did not care very much for their bright-eyed secular optimism, which struck him as little more than a churchy variation on Daniel Bell's end of ideology. It was the same kind of pragmatic optimism that imbued the new breed of problem-solving managers who were going to take over the technetronic society, and indeed the so-called radical theologians seemed ideally suited to serve the "religious needs" of that managerial class. Weissman was not impressed by the fact that they had said *yes* to the world. They had said *yes* to technology and to the irrational, one-dimensional mentality of the technological society. Weissman told them about Marcuse and the need for qualitative changes in the uses of technology, and he was particularly hard on Cox and William Hamilton: they were technetronic theologians who criticized only the superficialities of the system, not its structure, and their kind of radicalism could produce only those quantitative changes that simply strengthen the irrational and repressive character of the structure. The problem was not one of manpower planning, "which promises to keep unemployment low while providing workers for the degrading assembly-line production of immediately absolescent automobiles." The problem, as Marcuse had put it, was to calculate the minimum of labor that is necessary to satisfy the vital needs of all members of the society. The problem was not how to say *yes*, which the theologians were very good at, but how to say *no*. Jesus was no inspiration to revolutionaries, for revolution is political and must aim at the sources of power. "Like LSD, Christ might have offered important pre-revolutionary insights. But opposition, political opposition, is what must be rendered unto Caesar." Weissman said he had "lost faith that dialogue with the radical theologians is important." And he summed up: "The point is that neither Jesus nor the Christian sources can provide much of a guide to questions of political strategy."

But now we have the Theology of Hope, and, as we have

seen, an essential element of that theology is its capacity—indeed its necessity—to say *no* to the given and *yes* to the new: to challenge the status quo and create the future, accepting nothing that is. It is hardly surprising, therefore, that hope theology has been seized upon to justify a politics of revolution. This has not yet produced a systematic Theology of Revolution, but it has certainly resulted in a good deal of revolutionary theologizing—which can be ascertained very easily by flipping the pages of *New Theology No. 6*. Richard Shaull, for example, has emerged as one of the leading spokesmen for a revolutionary commitment as a Christian imperative, and his essay on this subject is instructive.

Shaull begins by talking about technology and technological rationality, which of course is actually irrational: "what it really offers is a new form of enslavement." It creates "extraordinarily well organized and effective pressures for conformity which make real independence and opposition almost impossible." What is needed from the Christian community is "a clear *No*" (read "Great Refusal"). "Modern technology has made it possible for us to be no longer obsessed with the production and distribution of goods. We can now cut the economic realm down to size, put this particular form of human activity in its allotted place . . . and free ourselves from obsession with it and its rewards." There must be *"new spheres of freedom . . . a movement toward ultimate freedom . . . new dimensions of freedom . . . men liberated for creativity . . . the formation of personal and group self-identity over against the system . . . 'the poetry of guerrilla action' . . . the creation of a style of life that breaks the power of the old order over us, challenges its values . . . "* All this will be made possible by a God of hope "who is bringing a new future into being" and whose word of promise "upsets old stabilities, arouses dissatisfaction with the old order, and frees us to expect and serve the things that are to come." But the actual job will be done by "a vanguard that is free to see what is happening, discern the shape of the future, and accept a new vocation over against the system . . . cadres of men and women who are as seriously concerned as the Marxists in China . . . the sect." We are told that "a small minority of the Western middle class is to become a vanguard" and that bureaucratic institutions will be systematically subverted from within by "small groups of people committed to constantly upsetting their stability."

We can agree with Shaull that the present system of production and consumption is not rational at all, and that a first order of business must be for society at large to "establish proper political controls over the economic order." Aside from this fundamental verity, his analysis can be faulted on several grounds— not the least of which is its undemocratic and arrogant suggestion that the fate of the society should be determined by elitists (including himself, presumably) who are "free to see what is happening." Also, his belief that bureaucracies are vulnerable to internal sabotage comes close to Galbraith's unfortunately naive faith that those institutions will be reformed by the new breed of enlightened and educated managers. Weissman himself sees the futility of this idea, observing: "One has a vision of the masses of junior executives, bolstered by their third martini, all on a given day placing chewing gum in the office postage machine. But most of the spiritually dispossessed aren't even that close to the levers of the machine . . ." Shaull's comments on life style and personal liberation are less vivid than Abbie Hoffman's but otherwise comparable. One has to wonder if he is serious about success, and in fact the historian James Hitchcock has taken Shaull to task on this point in the *Christian Century.*

Hitchcock, commenting on Shaull's theories, writes that "it is precisely this concern for 'revolution' which casts doubt on the genuine worldliness of the modern Christian. . . . The present Christian preoccupation with revolution implicitly calls for a stance of separation from the world for purposes of judging, condemning, and transforming it." Having flirted with secularism, theologians are now trying to recover a fundamentally religious and other-worldly posture—while deluding themselves that they are being "relevant" in a worldly way. Historically, revolutions have failed to produce the dramatic cultural transformations envisaged by Shaull—and Third World revolutions in particular will probably emphasize economic growthmanship, resulting in materialistic societies very much like our own. "To hope for revolution in a total sense is therefore to hope for the absurd. . . . For the Christian radical, revolution is therefore the moral equivalent of heaven." And since the underclass in this country is primarily interested in improving its own materialistic status, not in mental liberation, the revolutionary Christian in America is "doubly committed to things unseen." But not at all aware of it perhaps.

There is another, more fundamental objection. Shaull's theology is pure Marcuse cloaked in Christian symbolism and brought up to date with fashionable hope rhetoric. It says absolutely nothing that *One-Dimensional Man* does not say, and it does not acknowledge its source. Weissman at least told us the name of his guru, and paid his respects.

Shaull invokes the name of God and offers us the program of the affluent and alienated youth subculture, the new wretched of the earth; he offers us the cultural revolution, whose Marx is Marcuse and whose Lenin is Hoffman. And if God is the future, or has the future as his essence, then Shaull's deity is a false god: not *the* future but *a* future; not the Kingdom of God but utopia; not liberation from death but liberation from the economy. Shaull here has nothing to say about death, which is the question of the future, because his theology is not open to the future; it gives "the quality of ultimacy to something preliminary," and therefore is idolatrous. Moltmann no less than Tillich recognizes the danger of theological utopianism that ends history within history, and he realizes that the Theology of Hope can be easily perverted. He says of this theology that it "opens a future outlook that embraces all things, including also death, and into this it can and must also take the limited hopes of a renewal of life, stimulating them, revitalizing them, giving them direction." But he adds:

It will destroy the presumption *in those hopes of better human freedom, of successful life, of justice and dignity for our fellow men, of control of the possibilities of nature, because it does not find in these movements the salvation it awaits, because it refuses to let the entertaining and realizing of utopian ideas of this kind reconcile it with existence. It will thus outstrip these future visions of a better, more humane, more peaceable world —because of its own "better promises" (Heb. 8.6), because it knows that nothing can be "very good" until "all things are become new." . . .*

It might be said that the function of theology is to formulate statements about the human condition which, in so far as they are true at all, are universally true—valid for all men at all times and not conditioned by the peculiarities of an historical situation. Such statements may apply to a given situation and inspire men to action; they may in some cases provide a justification for armed rebellion against an established order; but they will transcend the rebellion itself, and they will apply with equal force to whatever new order may arise in the wake of the rebellion. They will say something that has meaning for a victim of injustice and an old woman who lives dying in a nursing home, an urban guerrilla and a Fiji Islander: all people at all times.

Shaull's statements in this sense are not theological; it remains to be asked if they are conditional statements that have some basis in an unconditional theology that transcends them but does not contradict them. If they do, the theology in question cannot be the Theology of Hope. Shaull's revolution is the cultural revolution, and the freedom sought by this revolution must ultimately be recognized as freedom from the future: an epiphany of the eternal present. The cultural revolutionary wants to live for the moment, if not in it, and to do this he must be liberated from time and the tug of the future. He is, as was said, a hedonist. Even the humanist who wants to make the earth a comfortable dwelling place is a hedonist—if this is all he wants. This is why the Theology of Hope potentially is far more radical than the secular Death of God theology. In its dissatisfaction with the given, it cannot tolerate an unjust world; it charges us now to transform this world—to put an end to prejudice, war, hunger, and all forms of oppression. But it does not stop there. It does not find in these things "the salvation it awaits." Such a world will one day be achieved, and that will be not the end but a beginning. On that day theology may well join forces with science and technology to say *no* to the unknown, *no* to the unattempted, and *no* to reality as we presently experience it. It will share with them the "passion for the possible." The Theology of Hope, then, provides a potential basis for the reconciliation of theology and science; more than that, it suggests that science is the true and fitting handmaiden of biblical eschatology—that it alone can lead us to the *novum ultimum*: to the Star Gate of our transcendental homeland.

Exodus II.

A reconciliation of science and theology by no means implies that science need accept all the tenets of *Christianity*— a genre of eschatology that includes the resurrection as a symbol of promise and an article of faith. Biblical eschatology is Judaic as well as Christian, and we are simply suggesting that the essence of the primitive biblical consciousness in no way conflicts with science, but rather that it may in fact find its ultimate expression in the scientific enterprise—an enterprise that is dedicated to exploration and discovery, growth and progress, a new man and a new creation.

Some people no doubt will find this an attractive prospect, and others will not. Teilhard, as noted earlier, predicted a "total and final split in humanity, not on the level of wealth but on the basis of their faith in progress." And there is ample cause to be wary of the futuristic, eschatological enthusiasm displayed by the sort of person Teilhard called *Homo progressivus*: "a man for whom the future of this earth counts more than its present." Teilhard was such a man himself, and his cosmic view caused him to dismiss much of the pain and suffering he saw all around him in the present moment. He wrote: "Evil, in all its forms— injustice, inequality, suffering, death itself—ceases theoretically to be outrageous from the moment when, *Evolution becoming a*

Genesis, the immense travail of the world displays itself as the inevitable reverse side . . . or better still, the price of an immense triumph." As he reflected on the first atomic explosion in Arizona (and neglected to mention the one in Hiroshima), his thoughts went only to the "new sense of power" created by "that famous sunrise." A door had been forced open, and man had become a new being. "In the glow of this triumph how can he feel otherwise than exalted . . . the very worth of science itself was on trial. . . . To fly, to beget, to kill for the first time—these, as we know, suffice to transform a life." Teilhard, as a priest, served as a medical orderly in World War I, but not because he preferred it that way. He viewed the war as "a crisis of birth," an epochal moment in our evolutionary progress, and he wrote in a letter from Verdun: "At the sight of this place of bitter affliction, I was deeply moved that I had the honor to be present at one of the two or three points at which, in this hour, all life of the universe converges and recedes. These are painful points but—I believe it more and more—a great future will emerge from here." And in a later letter: "Believe me, I would prefer it a hundred times to throw hand grenades or handle a machine gun, rather than to be so useless."

Similar thoughts have been expressed by other technophiles. Buckminster Fuller celebrates World War I as "the first industrial war," and Marshall McLuhan has written: "War is accelerated social change, as an explosion is an accelerated chemical reaction and movement of matter." The same kind of thinking is invited by the Theology of Hope and already is expressed by some of its advocates. Religion professor Vernard Eller, discussing the ethic of promise, wrote in the *Christian Century*: "That it operates out of a different context . . . (the future Kingdom of God rather than the present kingdom of this world) is bound to put it in rather severe tension with the world. To have one segment of society, the Christian minority, pushing ahead toward its absolutist, perfectionist goal will not set too well with the majority whose only interest is to accommodate to the world as it is." Eller then applied the ethic of promise to one of the theoretical cases used by Joseph Fletcher to illustrate the situation ethics of the New Morality. A woman prisoner in a concentration camp is desperate to escape and go to the aid of her hungry and homeless children. A guard offers to permit her escape if, as Eller put it, "she will submit to his lecherous advances." Fletcher's sensible advice was: "Submit." But Eller called for a "heroic refusal" on the ground that "in the Kingdom women will not have to submit to adultery, sacrificial or otherwise." He added: "It may be that the mother is called to sacrifice her own freedom and perhaps the very lives of her children. . . . But some people are going to have to volunteer to pay the price— as God already has paid and is paying the price—if the Kingdom ever is to become reality. . . . In any case the woman's act is predicated not on how it will pay off in the present but on whether it points towards God's future."

In the light of such statements, the attitudes they reflect, and the terrible price we already pay to maintain our scientific and technological base, it must be asked if our eschatological consciousness is not in fact a form of brain disease and *Homo progressivus* a madman who will destroy this planet in his efforts to transform it. It must be asked if scientific rationalism is rational at all, and it must be asked if our obsession with growth is not in itself a symptom of mental imbalance. As René Dubos has written: "All societies influenced by Western civilization are at present committed to the gospel of growth—the whirling-dervish doctrine which teaches: produce more so that you can consume more so that you can produce more still. One need not be a sociologist to know that such a philosophy is insane." And yet, what are the alternatives? It is certain that there are no easy answers, if there are indeed any answers at all, but I believe myself that the wisest words I have seen on this subject were written by a scientist, the biologist C. H. Waddington.

Waddington, replying to Dubos, acknowledged that there is now occurring a series of revolts, especially among the young, which challenges not only the existing technology but rational thought as such. What is more, these movements go deeper than mere politics and economics; they are concerned with the very character and quality of human life. But Waddington suggests that the kinds of rationality and technology under attack are largely those based on physics and the study of inanimate matter. When the concepts of physics are applied to the living world, the results are a rationality that views human life on the whole in terms of Newtonian determinism (behavioral psychology), and a technology that emphasizes maximum output with no regard for social consequences. Waddington expresses his own distaste for this kind of rationalism—which indeed is irrational—and he recommends that we put in its place a rationalism based on the biological sciences. This kind of rationalism would include a concept of "growth" as the biologist observes it. Waddington writes:

There is very little in the biological world—except cancer!— which grows in the unrestrained way which has characterized, for example, the automobile industry. Normal biological growth is a well-regulated and harmonious process; the legs and arms and head and belly keep pace with one another. The trouble with the modern technological world is not "growth" of the kind which characterizes biological organisms, but uncontrolled growth in which each aspect of the society increases as fast as it can with only minimal cross-reference to the situation of other parts. . . . In the biological world almost nothing is "maximized"—except some variable which no one has yet satisfactorily defined but which is important for evolution. And this variable is related not to the organism under immediate consideration, but to the number of its offspring, and even that is maximized only over the long term of many generations, not just from one generation to the next. And, more importantly, there are apparently no timeless, eternal, or universal biological laws, as in physics; every biological unit has a history, indeed one might say, is a history—a circumstance which physicists find unnerving.

In place of a maximization of entities whose essence is independent of time, biology deals mainly with balancing, or "optimization" of things which are very complex, and which have histories, and whose stability and balance are going to be tested over a long period—a number of generations. In a developing embryo, for example, there are all sorts of control mechanisms which adjust the sizes of the organs to one another to produce a harmonious whole; or in an ecological system, the numbers of animals and plants in the mutually dependent species are usually controlled—not always effectively—so that they stay in balance.

The kind of understanding of its most general subject matter—such as evolution—which biology attempts to achieve is much more akin to the kind of understanding of human history we aim at than that which physics gives of the interactions of any nameless hydrogen atoms. Biologists don't attempt to say of living things in general (it may be different of a few matters of detail) that so-and-so must *happen*, but rather, this seems to have *happened*, and it is after all quite easy to see how it might have done so. . . .

Another characteristic of biology is the thoroughgoing way in which it transcends the physicist's simple-minded distinction between the subject and the object. An evolving population, by the behavior of its members, chooses—or creates—the environment which exerts natural selective pressures on it. There is no preordained unavoidable rat-race; the biologist is studying situations in which the possibility of "dropping out"—migrating elsewhere—is always available. Again, biologists who study perception, or the acquisition of knowledge and understanding of the external world by the developing child, find themselves forced to recognize that in neither of these processes is the subject a merely passive recipient of whatever the "objective" imposes on to it. On the contrary, both in learning how the world works, and even in apprehending it in perception, an active and indeed creative participation of the "subject" is essential. A drop-out who objects to being treated as a "thing" might think differently if we were in a world dominated by a biologically oriented outlook which denied that there are any "things" quite independent of the subjects who observe them.

the Star Gate
287

Unfortunately there are still rather few biologists, and therefore an even smaller proportion of the general public, who have realized the true nature either of the fundamental insights of modern biology or their implications for a culture concerned with how to live as a truly human organism.

After the first wave of enthusiasm there occurred in this country a negative reaction to the European brand of hope theology—and, with this, at least a partial return to the mystical emphasis of the initial beyond-the-secular movement. "I get the impression that things have quieted considerably," says Marty. "There's no single theologian that everybody's turning to with a lot of attention right now. There's no movement. I think everybody was marched up and down the hill too often in the 1960's to respond too quickly now, in the 1970's. I think there'll be a lot of serious, quiet work done now, at least for a while." But there is nevertheless a good deal of attention being paid now to "play" theology, which stresses a kind of Zen clownishness, and Marty tells me that *New Theology No. 7* will reflect a preoccupation with the concept of transcendence—including the ecstatic self-transcendence of the comical mystic. Coupled with this is a deep interest in nature and ecology, and in this connection some theologians have abandoned eschatology to reconsider the ecological implications of the creation. They have turned their attention from the future to the present and the past, and in so doing they often appear to be gravitating toward the concepts of the cultural revolution.

The social ethics scholar Gibson Winter believes this development represents in part a rejection of the "project-oriented" Theology of Hope and a technological culture that proposes "unlimited growth as a principle of reality." In so far as European hope theology is radically future-oriented, he suggests, "what it simply does is endorse the kind of unlimited technology that we now see destroying us."

It is easy to see how the Theology of Hope might appear to endorse that kind of technology, and it is easy to see why there might be second thoughts about this theology in a country that is suffering so terribly from the abuses of an unrestrained technology. And, needless to say, the new emphasis on nature and ecology is a welcome phenomenon. But there also is a danger. Teilhard warned that evolution one day might go on strike, once it became aware of itself, and once it finally recognized the painful nature of the long road ahead. And the danger is that the retreat into mysticism may represent not so much a compensatory reaction as a failure of nerve. As Waddington has indicated, the problem is not growth as such but growth that is not balanced and organic. The solution to this problem is not an evolutionary boycott.

We are not required to choose between rationalism and anti-rationalism, technology and nature, the present and the future, continued growth and hedonistic stagnation. Everything that lives grows, and when it stops growing it begins to die. Inherent in the growth of individuals and societies, as in the evolutionary process itself, is an ever-increasing complexity of organizational structure which, while it creates new problems of its own, also serves to liberate man from the deterministic laws that prevail in the domain of unorganized (and therefore nonliving) matter. The growth of man in consequence is not to be viewed as a conquest over nature but rather as a triumph of nature, of which man is the conscious apex. We must grow, and will. And this being so, any would-be revolution opposed to growth as such is not a revolution at all but rather—as Brzezinski has argued—a counterrevolution. Successful revolutions have always been historically relevant, in the sense that they related themselves to the *future* and thus ushered in new historical eras. Examples, says Brzezinski, were the French Revolution, the Bolshevik Revolution, and the 1848 Spring of Nations. A counterrevolution, on the other hand, is essentially nonprogrammatic and based on the *past;* it fails to provide a program for the future and therefore is certain to fail itself. Examples of this are the Luddites and Chartists in England, "who reflected the traumas of an agrarian society entering the Industrial Era; their response was spasmodic and irrelevant to the future." It may be said in general of counterrevolutions that "they do not provide meaningful programs and leadership for the coming age on the basis of an integrative analysis which makes meaningful the new era. Rather, they reflect concern that the past may be fading, and a belated attempt to impose the values of the past on the present and on the future." Some of the recent upheavals have been led by "people who increasingly will have no role to play in the new technetronic society." They find themselves becoming historically obsolete, and their violent reaction is not a revolution but "merely —and sadly—the death rattle of the historical irrelevants."

Brzezinski's criticisms are clearly appropriate in so far as they relate to the protesters' lack of a strategy and their temporal orientation. But one cannot share his apparent optimism that the future can safely be left in the hands of the technetronic managers, nor his assumption that the protest is irrelevant. It is not irrelevant but simply ineffective. The problem is to make it effective. The cultural revolution in particular is not only ineffective but also contra-effective; it recommends that we rush to establish the kind of "liberated" society that automation already is producing—an essentially hedonistic society that will have neither the power nor the will to control the managers, who must be controlled. Emmanuel Mesthene warned in his Harvard report that such control will become increasingly difficult as the technology becomes increasingly complex and specialized; he proposed in fact that "elaboration of a new democratic ethos and of new democratic processes more adequate to the realities of modern society will emerge as perhaps the major intellectual and political challenge of our time." If he hopes to participate in those processes the average man will find it necessary to devote increased attention to his public role as a citizen, and possibly also less attention to his private goals and satisfactions. Mesthene said: "The citizens of ancient Athens seem to have been largely public beings in this sense, while certain segments of today's hippie population seem to pursue mainly private gratifications."

That of course is one of the social dangers inherent in affluent leisure; on the other hand, citizens may need more freedom from the economy in order to exercise their public responsibilities—a largely work-free society may be a prerequisite to democratic control of a complex technology. The cultural revolutionaries should understand in any case that their "think free" approach is not a solution to the problem of an advanced technology but rather an aspect of the problem.

But their protest is relevant. They recognize quite clearly that our present concepts of growth are demented, and that is why we suggested earlier that a certain wisdom is concealed in their madness. More militant revolutionaries may regard them as clowns, but the militants have failed to challenge any of our fundamental assumptions about technology. They would offer us at best a change of managers, and possibly they would slice the pie somewhat differently, but there is no reason to think that a technology they controlled would preserve any of the cultural and emotional values that are expressed for example by the black nationalists and by other racial and ethnic groups in this country. If indeed we can decide what kind of technology we want in the future—if we can pick and choose, as de Jouvenel proposes —then those values must be considered.

But Henry Adams' law of acceleration indicates that we cannot wait too long to decide, else we are carried past the point where a choice is still possible. In this sense the black nationalists, the protesting young people, and the humanistic assertion of matriarchal principles may now provide us with some braking action on the technological Juggernaut. You cannot steer with brakes, but neither can you steer without them. As for the extension of the psychosocial moratorium, we have said that it can be regarded as socially beneficial in that it represents a potential source of objective social criticism; but that criticism must be effective criticism, and the young people from a personal standpoint might feel less frustrated today if they would make a greater effort to be effective rather than merely to be right. What comes out of the moratorium is especially significant because it gives us some idea what we can expect from the Ad Hoc society of which it may be only the precursor.

As it is, some of our young critics are now overreacting to the abuses of the present technology, and what some of them seem to offer us essentially is a choice between humanism on the one hand and technology on the other. What we need is a humanized technology. A model for such a technology is provided by the growth process as it occurs in any healthy biological organism, just as Waddington has indicated. This means an acceptance of technology, an acceptance of science, an acceptance of growth, and therefore also an acceptance of futurism or eschatology. It means that the earth is intended to be neither a comfortable dwelling place nor a machine for progress but rather—as Teilhard himself suggested as an afterthought—"an organism that is progressing." And who can say to what it is progressing? Can an acorn imagine the oak? Only one thing is certain, that Abbie Hoffman's masturbating newsboy is not the Star-Child.

But as Waddington also has pointed out, there is a difference between normal growth and abnormal growth, and our society at present is an example of the latter. Our space program, for example, at this point in time is cancerous, and much of our private production is cancerous. The problem is not so much capitalism but simply unbalanced development, and Russia has demonstrated that such imbalance is not peculiar to capitalist economies. In this country, the thalidomide responsible for our atrophied public sector is the atomistic ontology which, as we have seen, is in part at least a by-product of the Newtonian physics that influenced Locke—a fact that adds weight to Waddington's analysis. The best hope for a cure is that unity thing that Molly and her friends have going for them now—or, more elegantly, the Aristotelian concept of an organic society. It is one thing to state that concept and something else to translate it into "the commonsense assumption of the vast majority." But this is what must be done. If such an assumption prevailed, there is no reason we could not meet our social needs within the basic context of our present economic structure; without this assumption, it is wasted breath to talk about alternative structures. They will not be accepted.

Lockean ontology has already been eroded by the waves of immigration that established in America a number of ethnic enclaves that are actually organic subcultures within the greater society. We are now witnessing in America a reassertion of ethnic identity, and—while it no doubt conceals a certain degree of white backlash—the overall development is probably a healthy one. But as Harold Cruse has pointed out, such enclaves are not bound together by a common American culture which effectively transcends them. The problem is not to assimilate these enclaves or subcultures into the emerging technological superculture, which is not really a culture at all but rather a mechanical and inhuman nonculture. The problem is to integrate them into a viable American culture. They would enrich it by their very diversity; at the same time they would be preserved as functioning parts of an organic whole. What is wanted is harmony, not homogeneity. As we have seen, the youth population itself now constitutes one of these organic subcultures, comparable in many ways to an ethnic enclave. And for all of their faults, and all of their nonsense, our young people in the end are the ones who may create in America a truly organic society—when they themselves are the vast majority and a part of the system they seek to transform.

They will not do it if they continue to insist on revolution in a total sense, or by rejecting technology, when so much could be accomplished by a more rational use of our existing technology. As Fanon said to the Third World: "No, there is no question of a return to Nature. It is simply a very concrete question of not dragging men toward mutilation." One might settle for that, for the moment at least, and it is a hopeful sign that many young people appear to be developing a pragmatic, political approach to the problems of our technological society. Meanwhile, even as Waddington talks of applying to society the concepts of biology rather than the concepts of physics, other scientists are talking of applying to biology the concepts of physics—"genetic engineering." On the whole, one is not encouraged.

Maybe it will turn out well. Maybe someday we will accomplish a technology without technologism, a synthesis of take-apart science and put-together humanism. But maybe it will not turn out well, and there is no guarantee that it will—there can only be the hope that it will, although it is necessary to hope. Nature is profligate with her seeds and her planets, scattering them in countless number so that here and there a few might flourish. We are one world circling a star in a galaxy of a hundred billion stars in a universe in which the galaxies themselves are counted in the billions, and we are at the moment not doing very well on this world of ours. We should try harder. Aquarius is possible. So is Armageddon.

Index

Index

Homosexuals, 73
Honest to God (Robinson), 266
The Hope Principle (Bloch), 270.
    See also Bloch, Ernest.
Hopi Indian, 35, 155
Hull, Clark, 184
Humanism, 5–6, 9, 13–14, 17, 19, 37,
    41–42, 78, 262, 292; and the
    family, 166; humanistic revolt,
    171–172; international approach,
    126; matriarchal, 160–161, 182;
    quarrel with academic behavior-
    ism, 184–188; revolt against, 192–
    197; pedagogues, 45–46; youth,
    167
Humanist, 113, 124, 138, 146, 148,
    159, 262, 282
"Human nature," 42. *See also* Freud,
    Sigmund.
Human transplantation, 11
Huxley, Aldous, 244

I Ain't Marchin' Anymore! (Rader),
    99
I Am That I Am, 250
I Am Who I Will Be, 277
Id, 20–22, 36, 40, 63, 192, 231. *See
    also* Freud, Sigmund.
Identity, 51, 211–212, 277; Ameri-
    can, 203; black, 199, 204, 220–
    223; collective, 8; conflicts, 63;
    diffusion, 54; ethnic, 293; femi-
    nine, 191; foreclosure of, 54; for-
    mation, 52–54; group, 242; inner,
    57; negative, 54–55, 69, 200, 204;
    personal, 182; positive, 55, 200,
    204; psychosocial, 57, 207–208;
    question, 230–231; search for, 60;
    social solidarity, 241; universal, 9;
    youth, 6. *See also* Adolescence;
    Erikson, Erik H.
Identity crisis, 49, 53, 56, 61–62, 240;
    all American, 220, 275; normative,
    68; psychosocial, 8
Ideology, 6, 10, 17, 38, 83, 191, 220;
    end of, 278; common (science),
    156–157; conservative academic,
    101; maximum production and
    consumption, 227
I-It relationship, 232
Illinois Black Panther party, 209
Immortality, 11
Income, guaranteed, 217
Income-through-jobs distribution sys-
    tem, 136
Individualism, 27, 100; initiative,
    211; laissez-faire, 238; liberal, 46
Individuation and personal complex-
    ity, 100–102
Industrial era, 6, 14, 50–51, 77, 136,
    289

Industrial revolution, 6, 137
Infant mortality, 44–45
Institute for Policy Studies, 121
Intellectuals, 6, 10, 52, 101, 105,
    148–149
Intercollegiate Socialist Society, 37
Interracialism, 167
Israel, 62, 101–102
I-Thou, 196, 232

Jacobs, Jane, 180–181
Jackson, Barbard Ward, 123
Jackson, Jesse, 202
James, William, 30–36, 42, 158, 231,
    267
Japan, 156–157, 258
Jaspers, Karl, 275
Jefferies, Richard, 250
Jefferson, Thomas, 8, 147, 238, 239,
    241
Jerusalem, 22
Jesus, 44, 225, 263–266, 278
Jews, 178, 212, 215, 231, 251–252,
    263; families, 165–166; in ghetto,
    101
Johnson, Samuel, 265
Johnson, Mrs. Virginia E., 191
Johnson, Lyndon B., 119; adminis-
    tration, 128
Jupiter, 6
Judaism, 251–252, 263
Judeo-Christian concept of Creator,
    236; pluralistic belief, 245
Jung, Carl, 38, 174–175

Kahn, Herman, 258
Karenga, Ron, 203, 211
Keller, Helen, 23–25
Keniston, Kenneth, 51, 57–60, 101–
    104, 166–172, 256–257; elite, 65;
    youth theory, 94–95, 99
Kennedy administration, 118, 128,
    143
Kerner Commission report, 210–211
Keynesian system, 117
Keyserling, Leon H., 127–129, 141
Kibbutzim, Israeli, 45, 62, 101–102;
    and group identity, 242. *See also*
    Bettelheim, Bruno.
King, Dr. Martin Luther, Jr., 85, 215–
    216
Kingdom of God, 103–104, 252, 261–
    264, 271, 281, 284–285. *See also*
    God.
Koestler, Arthur, 182, 184
Korea, North, 37; war, 117
Krassner, Paul, 254
Kremlin, 125

Labor, 138, 147; abolition of, 16;
    child, 50; movement, 193, 212;
    repressive, 16; unions, 210

Index

305

A Note on the Author

William Braden was born in Evanston, Illinois, and studied at the Medill School of Journalism at Northwestern University, where he received a master's degree in 1953. Since 1956 he has been a reporter for the *Chicago Sun-Times,* writing on a wide variety of subjects. His first book, *The Private Sea: LSD and the Search for God,* was published in 1967 and widely praised as a synthesis of theological concerns. Mr. Braden's many prizes include the Marshall Field Award for Distinguished Reporting. He lives in Dundee, Illinois, with his wife, Beatrice, and their two daughters, Anne and Jennifer.